BATTLE IN THE ROCKS

When the first Mexican soldiers were less than a hundred yards away, Bent said, "Let's commence this *fandango.*"

Walsh fired, and a Mexican in the front rank fell. The sound of the shot slapped off the mountain wall and then back.

The mountain men opened up. Firing evenly spaced volleys, they decimated the first several ranks of foot soldiers, until an officer reared his horse and shouted at his men. The soldiers turned and fled, leaving more than a dozen dead men behind.

Then Bent's men waited. Almost an hour passed before the troops came at them again. This time, a dozen riders roared around the curve and jammed their horses to a stop, pulling them down as they did. Each man had a pistol in hand, and as their horses fell, they shot the animals and hunkered down. Moments later, foot soldiers raced around the curve.

Bent's men got off two volleys before the tide began to sweep over them. . . .

*The Forts of Freedom Series by John Legg
from St. Martin's Paperbacks*

WAR AT BENT'S FORT

JOHN LEGG

ST. MARTIN'S PAPERBACKS

WAR AT BENT'S FORT

Copyright © 1993 by Siegel and Siegel Ltd.

The Forts of Freedom series is a creation of Siegel and Siegel Ltd.

ISBN: 0-312-95053-5

Printed in the United States of America

St. Martin's Paperbacks edition/March 1994

10 9 8 7 6 5 4 3 2 1

In memory of
Zelda "Sis" Beamer Murray,
my mother-in-law.
Without you,
there would've been no Karen,
and therefore,
life would not be nearly so sweet.
I'll never forget you.

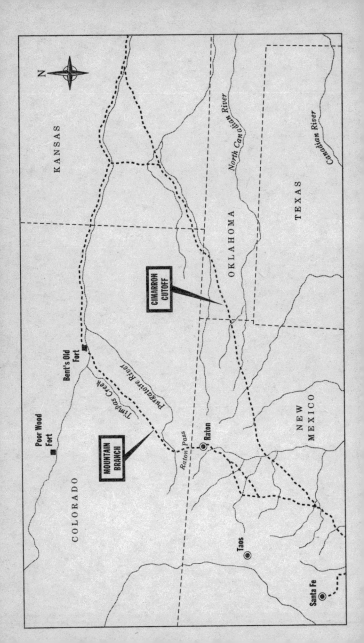

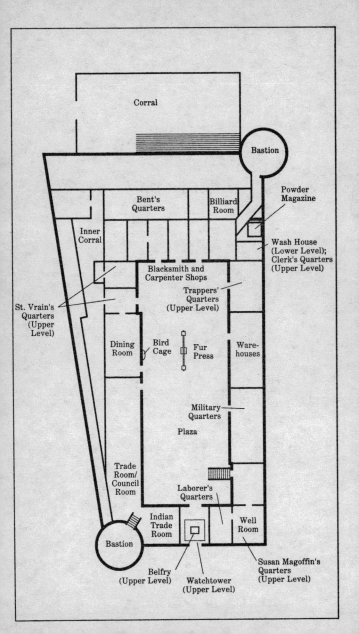

Corral

Bastion

Powder
Magazine

Bent's
Quarters

Billiard
Room

Inner
Corral

Wash House
(Lower Level);
Clerk's Quarters
(Upper Level)

Blacksmith and
Carpenter Shops

Trappers'
Quarters
(Upper Level)

St. Vrain's
Quarters
(Upper
Level)

Dining
Room

Bird
Cage

Fur
Press

Ware-
houses

Military
Quarters

Plaza

Trade
Room/
Council
Room

Laborer's
Quarters

Bastion

Indian
Trade
Room

Well
Room

Belfry
(Upper Level)

Watchtower
(Upper Level)

Susan Magoffin's
Quarters
(Upper Level)

【1】

Art Honnicker peered through the wind-whipped snow, not quite sure he believed what he thought he saw. Finally, though, he had to acknowledge it. He turned, wind almost knocking him off the roof of one of the three wood buildings inside the small, shabby stockade.

"Damn wind and snow anyhow," Honnicker muttered as a fresh gust of wind whirled up from Fountain Creek, bringing with it stinging particles of snow. Honnicker turned and placed his musket across the two-foot gap between the building and the stockade wall.

Shivering, he cursed again at the ice that had formed on his scraggly mustache and beard. Then, cupping his mittened hands around his mouth, he bellowed, "Couple men comin', Cap'n."

Moments later a short, wiry man pushed open the door of the cabin across from the one on which Honnicker stood guard. He stepped out into the maw of the storm and glanced around the small stockade he and his men had built not long ago. He pulled his capote tightly around his slim, muscular shoulders and strode across the small compound.

"You say someone's comin', Art?" William Bent asked as he climbed the shaky wooden ladder to the roof of the cabin. Though he was barely twenty-two years old, he was used to commanding men. He was small of stature, but strong and fearless. There was no one in all the Stony Mountains could say William Bent was a slacker, or was undeserving of the trust his older brother, Charles, had saddled him with. He had been in the mountains more than six years now, and had done all that these other men had done, and then some.

"Yessir, Cap'n," Honnicker said, using the honorific Bent received with being given command of this ragtag band of mountain men.

"Can you tell who they are?"

"Not yet. Only that they're Injuns."

Bent and Honnicker watched intently for a minute. Neither could see anything in the whirling maelstrom, but both were patient. Two figures suddenly appeared out of the storm, just in front of the gate.

Bent half slid, half climbed down the ladder as the two young, bedraggled Indians moved warily into the log stockade. He made a hand gesture signifying they were welcome. It was returned tentatively.

"Come," Bent said magnanimously, "sit at my fire and warm yourselves. There's coffee and fresh meat."

The two Indians looked blankly at Bent, and he repeated the invitation in halting Spanish and then in sign. The Indians nodded.

Bent turned and walked away, never worrying that the two might attack him. He had more faith in some Indians than many men did.

Within moments a group of men, American, French, Spanish, and Indian, were sitting in a semicircle around the small fireplace in Bent's cabin. Mugs of coffee were passed around, quickly followed by bowls of stew from the three-legged caldron sitting in the flames. No one said anything for a while. Finally Bent took the initiative. "You boys from around here?" he asked. He figured they could all converse readily enough by using a combination of Spanish and sign.

The slightly older-looking Indian nodded. Using the two languages, plus a few mangled words of English, he got across the point that they lived farther east, out on the prairies along the Arkansas River.

"You are Cheyenne?" Bent asked, making the sign for those people—a slight chopping motion with the right index finger on the left hand.

Again the finely chiseled bronze face bounced in affirmation.

"How'd you come to be in so poor a state?" Bent had never dealt with the Cheyenne, but he had heard others talk about those Indians. One of the things he had learned was that Cheyennes, whether from the southern branch, as these were, or the northern ones, were a proud people, tall, straight, and good warriors.

The two sitting before him now certainly were taller than many of the Indians Bent had encountered, and they were handsome of face. They also looked like they had had a string of bad luck lately.

The older Cheyenne shrugged, not wanting to answer.

"What's your name?" Bent asked the same one, letting the other question drop for now.

"Winter Hawk," the warrior said in sign, making the translation of his real name as easy as possible for the whites.

"And you?" Bent asked, pointing to the other.

"Black Feather."

Silence spread among the men as they sipped their coffee, slurped their stew, and chewed bits of meat found in the broth.

Bent figured he would try again to find out what had left Winter Hawk and Black Feather in such sorry condition. But just as he was about to question them, Seth Walsh stuck his snow-covered head inside the cabin door. "More men's comin', Cap'n," Walsh said flatly.

"Who?"

"A bunch of goddamn Comanches, by the look of them. Hard to tell for certain under all them robes and blankets and such."

"They at the gate?"

"Yep," Walsh offered quietly. He was a big, burly redhead, who spoke so softly that more often than not the men had trouble hearing him. But he was pure hell in a brawl. "Art's tryin' to chew the fat with 'em, keep 'em occupied till we figure out what the hell we're gonna do."

Bent nodded. "They say what they want here?"

"Them two, as best as I can figure from all their damned jabberin'," Walsh said, pointing at the two Cheyennes.

Bent nodded again, brain already working over the problem.

"I say we give them two red devils over to the Comanches," Wilbur Spivey declared. "They don't mean shit to us."

Bent glared at Spivey. He had never taken a shine to the tall, broad-shouldered man. Though they had been neighbors in Missouri, Bent had had some reservations about hiring Spivey. He had known the dark-eyed, bearded man would bring trouble, but he'd let himself be talked into it by his older brother, Charles. And, he had to admit, Spivey was a good man to have on your side in a scrap.

Bent spit tobacco into the fire. His razor-thin face twisted into a scowl. He hadn't spent the past six years or so wading in the damnedest cold streams a man could think of, risking pleurisy and rheumatiz and Blackfoot arrows just to ruin everything by being hasty and giving in to the demands of a cretin like Wilbur Spivey.

Bent thought of several reactions, but it all came down to the fact that the Cheyennes seemed a lot friendlier than the Comanches. Hell, everybody on the plains knew the Comanches were the nastiest bastards they would face on the Southern Plains. The Cheyennes might outnumber the Comanches, but they still seemed like the underdog.

Bent suddenly shoved himself up, his wiry frame uncoiling smoothly. "Luis," he said urgently, mind made up, "you and Seth keep these two boys"—he pointed at Black Feather and Winter Hawk—"here under your watch."

"What're ye gonna be up to, Cap'n?" Walsh asked.

"Foilin' them damned Comanches." He glared around the circle of men, finally stopping his gaze on Spivey. "Any of you boys give this away, and I'll have your hides made into *parfleche*." With that, he spun and headed out of the cabin.

Bent strode up to where an angry Honnicker and a few of the other men were trying to keep a band of eight Comanches from coming into the fort. "Somethin' I can do for you boys?" Bent asked calmly.

The war leader ran off a long spate of talk in his own language. His plump moon-face was twisted up in a fierce scowl, a look that was heightened by the dabs of black paint spattered on the face under a hat made of wolf skin, the head still on it.

Bent stood there patiently for a little while, hands clasped behind his back. Then he began to whistle a nameless ditty of his own making. He looked for all the world as if he had not a care in the world.

The Comanche war leader sputtered to a halt and looked at Bent partly in fear, partly in anger. He was more than half certain this short, bandy-legged whiteeyes was crazy.

Bent stopped his whistling. "Now," he said quietly, "there somethin' I can do for you boys?"

The war leader started off again on another spiel of Comanche, and Bent began his whistling again. Several of the mountain men standing warily behind their leader began to snigger. The Indian ground to a stop again. Then, in halting Spanish—and more fluently in sign—he told Bent: "We want the Cheyenne dogs who came here." The hand language even managed to convey the Comanche's anger.

"Ain't no Cheyennes here," Bent said blandly, never taking his eyes off the dark, glittering orbs of the Comanche's.

"You lie!" Singing Buffalo signed furiously.

Bent spit some tobacco juice to the ground. He didn't hit the Comanche's moccasins, but he hadn't really been aiming for them either. "You know, boy," Bent said harshly, "I've kilt better men than you for a lot less in the way of insults."

"But—" Singing Buffalo signed.

Bent cut off the talk with a chopping motion. "I won't suffer such insults inside my own fort, damn you," he said in Spanish and signs.

"We followed the tracks of those two Cheyenne dogs to here," Singing Buffalo said, face etched in irritation.

Bent shrugged. "Was a couple of Cheyenne warriors come through here a little while ago, but they never stopped. Just traded for some jerky and such and moseyed on."

"We will look here!" Singing Buffalo said, arms and hands working frantically in signs.

"Listen to me, you walleyed festering pile of buffler shit," Bent snapped in English, neither knowing nor caring whether the Comanche understood him, "I said there ain't no Cheyennes here, and that's all there is to it. You bastards want to come against us, there's gonna be one hell of a pile of dead goddamn Comanches when it's all done."

The light of recognition came on in Singing Buffalo's eyes, and Bent felt a rush of satisfaction in having learned that the Comanche knew enough English to understand pretty well what he had just said. That would make it easier, Bent figured.

Bent spit again, being careful this time not to let the foul brown residue get too close to the Comanche leader. He was unafraid of these Indians, but at the same time, he could see no reason for insulting the warriors unnecessarily.

"I suggest you all haul yourselves out of here and go on back where the hell you belong."

"No!" Singing Buffalo said it in English, and the single word came out thick and harsh. He folded his arms across his robe-covered chest.

Bent did not have to say anything. Most of his men were standing in a semicircle behind him. Half drew back the hammers of their rifles. The rest moved hands toward hatchets or butcher knives.

Singing Buffalo and Bent continued to stare at each other for some moments. Finally the Indian nodded once. Then he said something in Comanche. Bent could not understand the words, but he understood the derisive laughter from the other Comanches.

Bent let fly another gob of tobacco liquid. This time he hit the Indian's buffalo robe.

Singing Buffalo glared, eyes wide in disbelief. Never had he, Buffalo-Who-Sings-in-the-Night, been insulted so grievously. His hand flew reflexively toward the tomahawk under the robe.

"You pull that 'hawk on me, boy," Bent drawled, "and you're gonna be some sorry son of a bitch." He smiled, but there was no humor in the thin lips. "You're gonna look funnier'n hell tryin' to squat to shit with that 'hawk stickin' out your fat ass."

The mountain men chuckled, though none relaxed his vigilance.

"I'll remember you," Singing Buffalo said with choppy hand signs.

Bent shrugged. "Don't reckon I'll lose any robe time over such." He paused. "Now, go on, git."

Singing Buffalo's face was a distorted mask of hatred as he spun and stalked out of the fort. A few moments later the men inside the small fort could hear horses galloping away.

"You've made yourself an enemy there, Cap'n," Walsh said quietly, stepping up alongside Bent.

The smaller man grinned a little. "I suppose I did at that." He smiled more. "But we got us two friends back there." He chucked his thumb over his shoulder, toward the cabin.

The two Cheyennes stayed the night in the fort, grateful for the warmth, food, and protection the log walls provided. They talked with Bent as the other men who were not on guard duty sat and listened. Before long the small room was filled with a pall of tobacco smoke.

In the morning, Winter Hawk and Black Feather ate hungrily at Bent's fire. Bent went outside, leaving them alone. He was checking the supply of fodder when Winter Hawk and Black Feather found him.

"Do you have horses we could use?" Winter Hawk asked, embarrassed that he and Black Feather had been reduced to begging.

Bent stood there in the cold light of the new day and thought for a moment. He could see no reason not to give the two Cheyennes a horse each. They had nothing to trade, of course, which was very evident. Still, Bent figured he should help them. The two might not make it back to their village on foot, seeing as how it was the dead of winter and they were a far piece from home. It would not hurt to give them a couple of horses from the small herd Bent had with them.

Besides, Bent figured, helping these two warriors might lead to a development of trade with the Cheyennes. That, in and of itself, would not be a bad thing. More importantly, in just the one night of talking with the two warriors, Bent had come to admire the Cheyenne people, at least enough to want to get to know them better.

Bent turned. "Mr. Spivey!" he bellowed. "Cut two horses out for the Cheyennes here."

"You just gonna give them goddamn red-skinned bastards a couple horses?" Spivey asked. He was almost incredulous.

"Not only that," Bent said, voice as cold as the weak sunlight, "we will escort them at least partway toward their homeland." He paused. "So, Mr. Spivey, saddle my horse, yours, and Mister Walsh's."

"You sure that's wise, Cap'n?" Seth Walsh asked as he moved up to stand beside his boss.

Bent shrugged. "I got me a suspicion that them damn Comanches are just waitin' out there for our two new friends. I figure that between those two"—he pointed at Winter Hawk and Black Feather—"and the three of us, eight stinkin' Comanches won't present a problem."

"Agreed, Cap'n," Walsh said with a small grin. The thought of counting coup on some Comanches invigorated him.

Bent looked at the Cheyennes. "You boys understand any of that?"

Both shook their heads.

Bent explained it with signs and Spanish. When he finished, the two Cheyennes looked a little relieved. They were not afraid of the Comanches, but their medicine had gone bad of late, and they were happy to have some protection along.

Winter Hawk nodded and turned to Black Feather. The two warriors chatted in their own language. Both were mighty impressed with the bandy little white man.

Minutes later the small troop was riding out into the snow fields, heading toward the upper reaches of the Arkansas River not far away. The worst of the snow had ended sometime after midnight, but the temperature had fallen more. It was a frigid, gray day, with the sun straining mightily to show its pale, chill face.

"How long you aim to ride with these boys, Cap'n?" Walsh asked.

Bent shrugged. "Till I figure they can make it back to their village on their own." Bent was glad to have the big, quiet man along. He and his brother Charles had hired Walsh only two years ago, but already William Bent considered him a good friend and a trusted lieutenant.

They were riding along, skirting the brush and trees along the Arkansas River, when suddenly Spivey yelped and then fell off his horse, three arrows sticking out of him, two in the chest, one in the throat. He lay there bleeding into the snow and ice.

By that time, though, Bent and his other companions were off their horses. The animal Winter Hawk had been riding kicked and snorted in pain from the two arrows that had driven deep into the animal's flesh several inches below the withers.

Winter Hawk ripped out his knife, slashed the pony's throat, and leaned on the horse until it had quit struggling.

The other men tugged and jerked on their horses, getting them to lay down. Winter Hawk jumped up and ran the few feet to Spivey's horse and did the same with it as the others had done. Then Winter Hawk and Black Feather unlimbered their bows and arrows. Bent and Walsh slid their rifles up over their horses.

"You see 'em, Cap'n?" Walsh asked.

"No," Bent said flatly. He was annoyed at having been ambushed so easily. And, despite his dislike for Wilbur Spivey, he did not like losing any of his men.

"There," Winter Hawk grunted in Spanish, pointing.

Bent and Walsh looked at the Cheyenne and tried to follow where he was pointing. "Keep yourself ready, Cap'n," Walsh said. He thought he had seen something amid the brush that did not look right. He fired. A moment later came the sound of someone or something falling in the mostly leafless brush. Walsh hurriedly reloaded.

They waited, lying on the ice and the snow, under a feeble sun. Their body heat began to melt the snow and ice, and before long they were wet through on the front. The horses also did not like lying this way, and frequently moved to get up on all four legs, forcing the men to exert a considerable amount of strength to keep them in place.

"Damn, Cap'n, how long we gonna stay here?" Walsh asked after nearly half an hour. "Christ, I'm freezin' my nuts off." He and Bent were wearing thick wool capotes, with leather belts around the outside. In or on the belts were their knives, tomahawks, and pistols. The Cheyennes had heavy blankets wrapped around them. Despite the thick garments, the cold from the ground continued to seep into them from below.

"What do you suggest?" Bent asked flatly. He was annoyed at the situation, too, and suspected what Walsh had in mind.

"Charge 'em."

Bent had been right in his suspicions. He didn't like the idea, but he could think of no better plan. He nodded, though Walsh could not see him do so. He explained to the Cheyennes what they wanted to do.

"We'll fight with you," Winter Hawk said firmly.

Bent looked around, making sure everyone was as ready as he could be. Then he roared, "Now!"

The four men swept onto their horses as the animals were rising. Bent slapped his horse's rump with the barrel of his rifle, and the animal burst into a run. He took a quick glance around. He and his three companions were riding full out, flattened against the horses' necks.

Suddenly it was raining arrows. Bent ignored them

as best he could, and moments later pounded into the brush. A Comanche came flying out of a thicket to Bent's right. The Indian hit Bent, knocking him off the horse.

Bent said a silent prayer of thanks that the Comanche had not come down atop him. As it was, the Comanche landed oddly on one of his own knees, and he grunted softly.

"Son of a bitch," Bent breathed. As he jerked himself up to his feet, he pulled out his butcher knife. He threw himself toward the Comanche, managing to land with one knee on the Indian's stomach. As he drew his knife hand back, set to plunge the blade into the Comanche's heart, he heard something behind him. He jerked his head around and saw a lance-wielding Comanche about to put him under.

Bent was frozen, seemingly unable to move. Then an arrowhead suddenly appeared out of the middle of the Comanche's chest, a piece of heart flesh hanging very distinctly from the pointed tip. Bent managed to roll out of the way as the Comanche toppled.

Winter Hawk stood there, bow in hand, a cruel grin across his face. "You save me; I save you," he said in thickly accented English.

Bent nodded. Then Winter Hawk disappeared. The five or six seconds it took for that to transpire allowed the Comanche who had jumped Bent to recover some of his wind, and he rather rudely brought Bent's attention back to him by kicking him in the side.

"Son of a bitch," Bent muttered as he finally stabbed the Comanche. But the blow was not a fatal one. The Comanche swung a short, sharp punch to Bent's head, knocking the white man sideways.

As the Comanche awkwardly and unsteadily got to his feet, Bent swore again and jerked out one of his pistols. He snapped the hammer to full cock with his left hand, stuck the pistol out and fired. The .50-caliber ball, pushed by a hefty charge of powder, slammed the warrior back several feet. The Indian hung loosely for a moment, then fell.

Bent knew as soon as he fired that the Comanche was dead. He didn't need to sit there and watch, but he sort of kept an eye on the Comanche as he hastily reloaded his pistol.

Several shots rang out, and Bent could see lingering clouds of powder smoke caught in bare tree branches. War whoops and curses burst out from behind brush.

With reloaded pistol in hand, Bent grabbed his rifle and slipped through the brush, heading for where he had heard most of the sound coming from. He moved cautiously, wary about what might pop up all of a sudden. Finally he spotted a patch of brown different from that of the stunted tree trunks and bare brush. He set his rifle down against a hackberry bush, then raised his pistol, cocking it at the same time.

He was about ready to fire when something big and powerful hit him in the side. He fell, his shot going harmlessly into the air. He looked up at Walsh, who was offering him a hand up.

Bent took the offered assistance and stood. "What'n hell'd you go and do that for?" Bent asked, half in irritation, half in surprise.

"Hell, it didn't shine with this ol' chil' to have ye go'n kill one of our new friends." He laughed a little. "That there's Black Feather."

"Shit," Bent muttered. He hurriedly reloaded again, but an eerie silence seemed to have swept over them in just the past few moments. He looked, and could not see Black Feather.

Both white men whirled, pistols pointed and ready at the sound of rustling branches. Then they spotted Black Feather and Winter Hawk, who moved smoothly up to them.

"Fixed them sons a bitches good," Winter Hawk said, proud of his fine—though rather limited and new —command of English.

"Reckon we did that," Walsh said with a hearty laugh.

"How many'd each of you get?" Bent asked. He wasn't aiming to keep score, such as it was. He was concerned there might still be some Comanches lurking about, and did not want to be surprised by them. "I got one, and Winter Hawk there helped out on another'n."

"I got three," Walsh said, "includin' the one I shot afore."

"I kill two others," Black Feather said, pulling himself up straight.

"I only kill one," Winter Hawk said. He looked crestfallen.

"Well, you did help me with that other one there, Winter Hawk," Bent offered in soothing tones. "That counts for a heap."

Winter Hawk did not look appeased, but he seemed a little more upbeat than he had been moments ago.

"Eight come to the post," Bent said, somewhat relieved, "and eight're gonna be feedin' the worms soon."

They heard a galloping horse and a fading war cry.

"You boys checked all them you supposedly put under?"

Winter Hawk and Black Feather nodded. So did Walsh. He paused. "All but that first one I plinked behind the bush," he said quietly. He turned and stalked off.

Walsh returned in a few minutes. "Ain't no one behind that bush," he said, self-anger in his voice. "I checked all the others. They're all gone under. The one I didn't see, though, is their war leader—that obnoxious bastard, whatever his name was."

"Singing Buffalo," Bent said.

"Yep, that's it." Walsh shook his head, still irked at himself for not being more thorough. Then he sighed.

"Well, I expect we ain't gonna see ol' Singing Buffalo for a spell. Not when his medicine's gone this bad."

Bent nodded. He stuck his pistol back into his belt. He looked at the two Cheyennes. "You two got the Comanche ponies?" he asked.

Both grinned and nodded.

"*Bueno.*" Bent pointed to Walsh and then himself. "We'll take our own horses back now."

Winter Hawk and Black Feather nodded. They did not need the white men's horses, not when they had seven Comanche ponies to take to the village with them. Their excursion had not been in vain after all.

"Mr. Walsh," Bent said, "would you see that Spivey's carcass is across a horse? I'll see about gettin' a fire goin' so's we can eat."

"What about them two?" Walsh asked, pointing to the Cheyennes.

"I expect they're gonna be busy the next few minutes," Bent said flatly. He wanted no part of such doin's. "I reckon there's a reason they call 'em the Cut Arms."

Walsh nodded, then left, hoping the horses hadn't run off too far.

Bent began gathering wood, trying to keep away from where the dead Comanches were. He had no desire to watch Black Feather and Winter Hawk going about their grisly work. He had seen it before, and did not think he needed to see it again. Not unless forced into it.

The small stockade looked even worse with the spring's greenery and wildflowers spreading over the high plains leading to the massive edifice of the San Juan Mountains.

Despite the small fort's shabby appearance, neither Charles Bent nor business partner Ceran St. Vrain looked askance. They had spent their time in the mountains and were used to such makeshift places.

"Hell of a fort you got here, little brother," Charles said with a low chuckle as he dismounted. He handed the reins of his horse to one of the hired men he had brought along.

Charles was slightly taller than William, and a bit more stout. Being ten years older than William also left him with a touch of gray in his hair. The years hadn't slowed him appreciably—the past year alone, he had made five round-trips between Missouri and Santa Fe, along the Santa Fe Trail. Such a schedule might have killed a lesser man.

"Ain't it the truth," William said, laughing. He shook hands with his brother and they embraced, slapping each other on the back.

St. Vrain and William exchanged slightly more reserved greetings, seeing as how the two were only business partners, not family. Ceran St. Vrain had come from good stock, and had no natural distrust of Americans. Indeed, he was such a jolly fellow that he made friends wherever he went, with whatever people he was dealing with at the time. In addition, he was still a good businessman.

St. Vrain looked about the small fort with some distaste. When he and Charles had formed a partnership almost two years ago, they had decided that Charles would make the trips on the Santa Fe Trail, while St. Vrain would open and run a permanent company store in Taos. St. Vrain liked the comforts of Taos, and the many balls and *fandangos* there. He enjoyed the looks of respect he received from the monied Mexican *hacendados*, and the esteem in which he was held by the pert *señoritas*. He had even started looking for one to become his bride since his Mexican citizenship would become official soon.

Still, the short, burly St. Vrain had been in worse places than this little log stockade at the mouth of Fountain Creek.

Both St. Vrain and Charles Bent were dressed considerably more finely than William and his men. They wore clothes of wool or cotton, with fancy braiding on their short jackets, and had beaver-felt top hats.

"You have any trouble on the way up?" William asked as the men entered his cabin.

"Nah," Charles answered. "Ran into a few Jicarillas, but they weren't out to raise hair. A bit of tobacco was enough to send them off."

"Zat and ze fact we had fifteen boys with us," St. Vrain added with a chuckle. St. Vrain might like to think of himself as a gentleman, but a streak of wildness lurked just beneath that dark-eyed, jovial exterior.

William laughed. "Reckon that did take the wind out of their sails a mite." He sat on a stool he had fashioned from a stump. His brother and St. Vrain followed suit. A Ute—the woman of one of William's men —served them bowls of buffalo stew and tin cups of coffee.

"How's Georgie and Bob?" William asked of the two youngest Bent brothers.

"Same as ever," Charles said with a grin. "The both of 'em're hell on women. Or so they'd like everyone to think. George is agitatin' to come on out and throw in with us. Bob too, but not so much."

"And . . . ?" William prompted.

"I ain't so sure. They both seem mighty young."

"They're both older'n I was when you brung me out here."

Charles shrugged. "You're a more level-headed cuss than either of them. Always were."

The men fell silent for a bit, thinking their own thoughts.

"How'd you do this year, Bill?" Charles finally asked after he had finished his stew and tossed the wood bowl aside.

"Good enough, I expect," William answered, then sipped some coffee. "Brought in more than a thousand pelts. Couple hundred buffler robes, plus a fair number of wolf, bear, and other pelts."

"Them others don't mean shit to me, brother, you should know that," Charles said evenly. "Only beaver plews is what we want."

"Zat is true," St. Vrain offered. "But some day, and not too far off, we will want zem odder furs. You watch and you will see."

"Hell, Ceran, I know that. And when that time comes, I'll want buffler and bear and whatever else is in fashion then. Right now, them buffler hides ain't worth shit, either in Mexico or in Missouri. We're gettin' a hell of a lot more for a beaver plew than we are for buffler."

"How much're beaver plews going for these days, Charlie?" William asked as he cut a chunk from his tobacco twist. He tamped the tobacco into his clay pipe and reached for a burning twig to light it.

"Five dollars or so a pound." He had a greedy twinkle in his eyes.

"That shines with this chil'!" William said, grinning widely. "Hell, this calls for a celebration. You bring any Lightnin' with you, Charlie?"

"A tad," Charles said modestly. He went outside, calling for one of his hired hands to fetch a couple jugs of potent Taos Lightning. He returned to the cabin moments later, a large earthen jug dangling in each hand. He set one down and swiftly pulled the cork from the second jug. He tossed the cork away and tilted the jug.

"Prime doin's there," he said after a healthy swallow that made his eyes water. "Plumb prime, I'm tellin' you."

"Well don't hog the goddamn thing," William said in mock anger. "Pass it over this way afore I expire from thirst."

After the jug had made a circuit among the three, Charles lit his small clay pipe, one similar to his brother's. St. Vrain did the same to his long, slightly curved pipe.

The jug continued making the rounds as the men smoked and drank quietly and talked of the past season. Charles and St. Vrain told how business was doing; William recounted the fall and spring trapping seasons and his adventures with the two Cheyennes.

The partners nodded. It was, they figured of the latter, the proper way of doing things. You never knew when you might need an ally.

After a short stretch of quiet William said, "We need to do something about the way we handle our business, Charlie. It's too goddamn hard to get supplies to this pissant fort. Besides, ain't nobody 'round here to trade with anyway, 'cept Utes, and they ain't worth crap. You know that. We need trade with the Cheyennes and the Arapahos. Especially if we're gonna get into buffler robes or somethin' one day."

"What do you suggest?" Charles asked, interested. He had thought the same thing himself not long ago, and had been trying to figure out a way to accomplish it. There was a good chance his brother would have a solution. William might be wild at times. That was to be expected with a man as young as he still was. But William still had a good head for business.

"Build a place on the Purgatoire maybe. Or maybe the Arkansas."

"How're we going to run it, as well as the rest of the business?" Charles probed. "We just opened the store in Taos. Me and Ceran can't be out here as well as in Taos and on the trail too, at the same time."

William shrugged and puffed his pipe a few moments. He did not want his brother to think that he was trying to be the head man of Bent, St. Vrain & Company. "You can handle the supply routes like you been doin'. Hell, after you made five trips on the trail last year you ought to be able to do it blindfolded. Ceran here can deal with the store."

"And the new tradin' post? What about that?" Charles said with a laugh, knowing his brother. "I suppose you want to run it?"

"Not really, but I'll work out of it." He paused. "Unless you want me to run it for you." It was neither a question nor a demand; simply a statement. Charles had brought him out here as a boy barely fifteen years old almost seven years ago; had placed a lot of confidence in him in the interim. William was still trying to pay his brother back. "Or Ceran can run it. You could hire clerks to run the store."

"How're you plannin' to get them to trade with you —us?" Charles asked, accepting the statement his brother had made. He would reserve judgment on all this until he had more information.

"I figure to ride out amongst their villages and tell 'em what we're up to. After savin' those two Cheyennes last year, I expect their people will be willin' to trade with me some.''

"I expect," Charles acknowledged. He glanced at St. Vrain, whose dark brow was furrowed in thought. The plan made a lot of sense to him. He could see himself and St. Vrain—maybe even his brothers too—controlling a vast trading empire.

"I sink ze idea is very good," St. Vrain said in his deep but jovial voice. *"Oui. Très, très bon."*

"I reckon it is a good idea too," Charles agreed. "We can worry later about who's going to run it." He had ideas on that too, but wanted to wait a bit yet, to feel some things out before he made a decision.

Two days later they left the small log stockade, for the last time, William Bent figured, and eased onto the plains. The hired hands stretched out a ways, watching over the mules that were heavily laden with furs and what supplies and trade goods were left. It was a roundabout way of going, but the peaks and high passes of the San Juan Mountains and the Sangre de Cristo Mountains forced it on the men.

Usually St. Vrain would complain about having to go so far out of his way, but this time it was different. The partners figured that since they had to go that way, they would scout out a site for the new post.

Several days out they met a hunting party of Cheyennes that included Winter Hawk and Black Feather. They greeted William warmly.

"Make your camp here," Black Feather suggested in Cheyenne.

William glanced at his brother, who nodded. William then answered Black Feather in the affirmative.

Camp was quickly made, and soon fires of dried buffalo dung were going, meat was roasting, and coffee was boiling. William invited Black Feather, Winter Hawk, and the war band leader—Buffalo Spirit—to share their meal. The Cheyennes accepted the honor with dignity.

As they ate and talked, William told the Cheyennes of his plan. It went smoothly after the Indian invited one of the other members of the band to join them. Rain Beating Down spoke almost passable English.

When William finished speaking, the Indians nodded. "It's a good goddamn idea," Rain Beating Down announced after conferring with his companions for a moment. "We'll trade with you at this tradin' post."

The next morning, Rain Beating Down and Black Feather approached the two Bents and St. Vrain, who had just finished their breakfast. "We know a place for your tradin' post," Rain Beating Down said. "We'll show you. You follow."

Charles looked skeptical, but William nodded without hesitation. When the two Indians left, Charles asked, "You think that's wise, Bill?"

"Hell, Charlie, you know well's I do there ain't many Injuns who'll lie to your face to get you into some trap. I figure they're trustworthy."

"You damn well better hope they are," Charles growled, not angrily, but warily.

William grinned. "You turnin' yellow in your old age, hoss?"

"I could still whip your ass any day," Charles said, pretending to be hurt by his brother's words.

"I'd like to see that."

"Just saddle your horse." But he grinned a little.

Late in the day the Cheyennes pulled to a stop on a low hump of grassland. "There," Buffalo Spirit said, pointing to a well-wooded stretch along the Arkansas. "Big Timbers." He said the three words in English.

"Looks good to me," William said. "What do you think, Charlie?"

Charles Bent sat on his horse, leaning forward some to rest his weight on his hands, which were on the saddle horn. He stayed that way for some seconds. Finally he shook his head. "No."

"No?" William burst out. "What the hell do you mean, no?"

"Just what I said," Charles commented as he resettled himself into the saddle. "It ain't right."

"What ain't right about it?" William demanded.

Charles shrugged. "I don't know," he said simply. "I just don't feel in my bones that it's right."

William snorted. "Dumb notion." He turned to face the Frenchman. "What about you, Ceran? What do you think?"

St. Vrain shrugged. "I defer to Charles in such things," he said evenly. "If Charles says zis is not ze place, zen zis is not ze place."

"Damn," William muttered. "Well, brother, where away?" he asked.

"Follow the river a ways." He moved off, leaving his brother and his partner sitting there. He headed west, the way they had come. Surprised, William and St. Vrain, their men, and the Indians followed.

Some miles upriver Charles stopped and surveyed the rolling, grass-covered prairie. "Here," he said simply.

4

William turned slowly, surveying the land where his brother had decided the fort would be. It was rolling, tall-grass prairie, barren of trees except along the Arkansas River, where cottonwoods and willows grew thick and tall. Across the river, in Mexican territory, sand hills reached out their dusty tentacles.

William rejoined Charles. With William watching him, Charles sat in the shade offered by tall cottonwoods and, with the tip of his knife, drew the outlines of the fort he envisioned.

When he was done, and puffing his pipe, the brothers discussed it in detail, until they were satisfied as to what it would look like.

Then they prepared to leave. St. Vrain had headed to Taos the day before to see to business there. He had stopped here just long enough to see the fort site. Then he and half the men had ridden southwestward, heading for the steep, mule-killing haul across Raton Pass.

The Bent brothers spent two more days there to rest the animals before moving the wagons and mules laden with furs and other goods east toward Missouri.

William had argued about that at first. "Why in hell should I go back to the States with you?" he asked roughly. "Hell, you got more'n enough boys to make sure the goddamn Comanches or any other Injuns don't bother you none. Damn, I should've gone down

to Taos with Ceran and got things a-movin'." He was
the more impetuous of the two, and wanted to get
started on the trading post right away.

"Dammit, Bill, you're my brother, and I can trust
you. I can't trust most of them others not to run off
with a thousand dollars' worth of plews or a sack of
Mexican silver the first damn time I turn my back."

William grunted in acknowledgment, annoyed that
he had not thought of it. Then he shrugged. He was
not the kind of man who would let such minor things
bother him overly much.

Once in Taos, St. Vrain got caught up in business,
and it was two more months before he could think
about hiring men to build the fort. That and the fact
that winter had arrived, and not much could be done
anyway. Indeed, it was even hard to get out of the
mountain valley in which the town of San Fernando de
Taos sat. A small, heavily armed, but otherwise light
traveling group of men could do it, but for a large
group of men, hauling wagons and supplies, it would
be almost impossible.

They arrived at the site where the fort would be built in
late February. The Mexican laborers pitched their
camp among the cottonwoods along the Arkansas
River. Once that was done, they began preparing
adobe bricks. Since William Bent and St. Vrain had
known that straw to use in making adobe was hard to
come by out here, they had arranged to bring wool to
mix with the mud and grass. Making adobe was familiar work for the men, and they pitched into it with no
fuss.

By the next afternoon the workers had converted a
stretch along the Arkansas River into a brick-making
facility. Three huge pits were dug. Into them the workers dropped river clay, marsh grass, and the wool.
Oxen mashed and blended the ingredients before the
men piled gobs of it into wood molds. By the next day

thousands of adobe bricks were hardening under the brittle late-winter sun.

While they were in Taos, Bent had briefed St. Vrain on the details of the fort that Charles envisioned, so the next morning, the two partners stepped off a crude rectangle in the dirt on the north side of the Arkansas River, about a hundred yards from the bank. Then they marked off where the wide gate and the corral would be.

The laborers soon after began building the mud castle. The men worked in two groups—one continuing to make bricks, the other putting them in place to build the walls. All were under the supervision of either Bent or St. Vrain.

That afternoon, Bent and St. Vrain stood on a rise watching the work.

"Ze wintair will not be long in going," St. Vrain said. He shivered almost involuntarily, as he felt a lingering touch of the winter's harsh winds. He looked forward to spring.

Bent looked up at the pewter-colored skies and shook his head. "Spring may be on its way, but winter ain't done yet. I expect it's going to paint its face black against us at least once more before headin' on."

St. Vrain nodded in agreement. Both hoped the dying winter would not run them down and ransack their budding post.

5

An anguished, angry cry brought Bent and St. Vrain tumbling out of their tents. Both had their flintlock pistols in hand. Bent's suspenders sagged around his waist; St. Vrain's drop-front pants were fastened with only one horn button. The morning air was frosty, and their breath formed small clouds from mouth and nose.

The two looked at each other, baffled. Another angry shout drew their attention to the Mexican laborers' sprawling tent camp along the riverbank. Bent spun and ran, moccasins slapping across the frosted grass. The slightly more stout St. Vrain rumbled a little behind Bent.

Bent came to a skidding stop at a wall of Mexicans grouped around one of the few laborers' tents. Like Bent's and St. Vrain's tents, it was a simple vee of canvas, with an open front and back.

"Let me through there, goddammit," Bent growled, shoving men aside, thrusting himself through the milling crowd. He could hear St. Vrain a moment later doing the same thing behind him.

Finally Bent and St. Vrain were through the crowd and standing there. Two laborers were kneeling over another. The stub of a burning candle on a small stool made from a chunk of cottonwood cast an odd orange light inside the flapping sides of the tent. Bent shoved the two men out of the way and knelt in their place. St. Vrain was next to him.

"Damn," Bent muttered.

"Mon Dieu," a worried St. Vrain added in heartfelt agreement.

The man's heavy sweating indicated a high fever, and he writhed as if in great pain. His face was speckled with reddish-pink dots. The symptoms meant only one thing—smallpox.

"Shit, this here's goddamn poor doin's." Bent shook his head.

"Mais oui," St. Vrain said, a vexatious note in his voice. "But zat does not help us now."

"Goddammit, I know that. Shit, I spent all that time talkin' the Cheyennes into comin' here to trade soon, and now this. They come ridin' in now, there's gonna be one hell of a pile of dead Injuns here."

He shut up, trying to think, knowing the laborers were waiting for him to do something. An air of worried excitement permeated the place.

Bent did not want to voice it, but he knew for sure that if the Cheyennes did come and a deadly smallpox epidemic ran through the people, Bent, St. Vrain & Company would be blamed for bringing it. Whoever was left of the laborers and all after the smallpox had run its course would be targets for several thousand angry Cheyennes. He was not worried about his own skin so much as he was that of the workers and the Cheyennes. In a short while he had come to like the Cheyennes. Enough anyway that he did not want them decimated on his account.

St. Vrain glanced at Bent. He could read on his partner's face much of what he was going through. St. Vrain felt the same, but for more practical reasons. A smallpox epidemic would destroy the Cheyennes since they had no protection against such diseases. If that happened, Bent, St. Vrain & Company trade would end before it ever really began. It was not that he didn't care about the Cheyennes; it was just that he thought along practical lines. A man had to get ahead financially, using what tools he possessed or could take. If he could do it without hurting others, so much the better, but he had to think of himself—and by extension, the company—first.

Finally Bent pushed himself up. He stepped outside the tent, facing more than a hundred workers. He rubbed a callused right hand across his face. Damn, he thought in some irritation, it seems mighty warm for this late in the winter. And his head throbbed.

"What're we going to do about this, Señor Bent?" one of the men asked in Spanish. Emiliano Flores, who from the start had been made a foreman of the workers, translated. Bent knew Spanish fairly well, but not well enough for such an important occasion.

Bent glanced at the man who had spoken, trying to put a name to the nondescript face. He couldn't. The man was indistinguishable from the majority of his fellows. He was a small, colorless man in worn clothes of handmade cotton cloth. Sandals covered his feet, and Bent knew the man must be freezing. He held a blanket around his thin shoulders, and an old felt hat in one hand. Bent had tried to provide the men with warmer clothes and blankets, but most of the men sent them home or traded them for cash, which also was sent home to their families.

"There ain't a hell of a lot we can do, boy," Bent said harshly. "Except maybe try and tend whoever's got it until he gets better." He paused. "Or dies." Bent absentmindedly scratched his right temple with the front sight on his pistol. "You should know that."

"We want to go home," someone from the crowd shouted. The voice was worried. The statement drew a growled assent.

"We'll get you there," Bent said sharply, his voice cutting through the rumble of the crowd.

The laborers quieted, reluctantly but surely. Bent

might be a small man, but he always held command in his voice and demeanor.

"It'll take us a little to get everything ready to go. Those who're sick'll need tendin'. The rest of you can help out preparin' the wagons and any other such work as might be needed to get us ready to leave. Might take a few days, considerin' how many's likely to be sick and all that's got to be done. Now go on and do like I told you."

The men looked ready to argue—or revolt—but a few harsh words from Flores sent them on their way. As the men shuffled off, Flores turned to Bent. "Is there anything else I can do for you, *Jefe?*" he asked. His English was far more passable than Bent's Spanish.

Flores was tall and angular. He looked as if he had been hewn from wood by someone who had used a plane that wasn't very good. Like all the other men, he wore simple handmade clothing and a wide-brimmed sombrero that had plenty of holes in it. He wore boots instead of the sandals that were all most of the other men had.

Bent uncocked his pistol and shoved the flintlock into the waistband of his buckskin pants. "Pick two or three boys you trust, Yano—ones that ain't sick or'll get the pox. Then come see me in my tent."

"*Sí.*" Flores said. He ambled off, reminding Bent of a sand crane.

Bent and St. Vrain headed toward their tents. "Are you all right, Bill?" St. Vrain asked. Worry creased his broad forehead.

"Ain't sure. I'm sweatin' more than seems right, and I think I feel the trots comin' on." He paused. "I've had me a powerful painin' in my head the past couple, three days."

"*Merde,*" St. Vrain breathed. "You have not had ze pox?" His worry increased. He knew he had it too, and had hoped Bent was immune. At least one of them should be up and about to deal with the men.

"No, goddammit," Bent snapped. He didn't know whether to be angry or disgusted. Or both. "You?" He looked at St. Vrain, and knew the answer from the sheen of sweat on the portly Frenchman's forehead and the grimace brought by a pounding headache.

"No." The word was harsh and ugly. Both were well aware of smallpox's dangers. Half, maybe three-quarters of the men—including the two partners—could be dead by the time the disease ran its course.

Bent entered his tent and flopped down on the pile of buffalo robes and blankets he used for a bed. He opened an inkwell and picked up his journal. Dipping his quill into the ink, he jotted down what had happened. He got only a few sentences down, though, before he jumped up and bolted out of the tent, heading for the brush down toward the river. He didn't get very far before he had to squat.

Bent felt as weak as a fawn by the time he had wobbled back to his tent. He was coated with sweat, and every muscle in his body seemed to ache. "Shit," he mumbled when he saw Flores and three workers standing uneasily in front of the tent. Bent pushed the aches and pains, the sweating and stomach cramps into a corner of his mind.

"I'm obliged for you comin' here, boys," he said evenly. Except for the sheen of sweat coating his face, it was hard to tell Bent was sick.

"De nada," Flores said. He paused, waiting to see if Bent had more to say. When nothing came, Flores touched each of his companions on the shoulder in turn and said, "This is Manuel, Pedro, and Arturo."

Bent nodded. "You trust these men, Yano?"

"Sí."

"With a very important task?" Bent asked sharply. "One that might be dangerous?"

"Sí."

"Bueno." Bent felt his legs trembling a little, and with

a weary sigh he eased himself down on the robes. "Sit down, boys."

The four Mexicans did, all of them but Flores nervous. It was not often that such men were in proximity to one of the *patróns*.

"You boys afraid of Injuns?" Bent asked. As Flores translated, Bent looked from one man to the other.

"Depends on the Indians," Flores said to Bent after the three had spoken. "Tewas no, Comanches yes."

"Cheyennes?" Bent asked.

"They do not know much about those Indians," Flores translated. "But they have heard the Cheyennes are fierce."

"They are that," Bent agreed. He gave each man another glance. Each gazed back, a little nervously, but evenly. "Would you boys be willin' to ride into a Cheyenne camp?"

The men's eyes got large as Flores translated. None of them shook his head, though they looked afraid. Each spoke a word or two to Flores, while keeping their eyes on Bent.

"They ask why you want them to do such a thing," Flores said.

"I need them to tell the Cheyennes not to come here because of the pox. They come ridin' in here before the disease has gone, there ain't gonna be enough of 'em left to trade with."

Flores talked softly to the three men as Bent spoke, and finished moments after his employer. Bent wondered how Flores could do that. Then the Mexicans spoke among themselves with animation. Their fear was evident, but their voices sounded strong and were determined.

"They will do what you say, *Jefe*," Flores announced.

"Bueno." A spasm clutched tightly at Bent's stomach. "Pardon me, boys," he said hastily as he lurched to his feet. "I got to go." He dashed unsteadily out the back of his tent. He didn't make it even as far as he had the

last time before he had to stop, rip down his pants and squat.

He was considerably shaky as he made his way back to his tent. The four Mexicans were looking at him, worry stamped on their faces. "I'll be all right, boys, don't you fret," he grumbled as he sat.

After taking a few moments to settle himself a little, Bent carefully told the three men exactly what he wanted them to say. He had them repeat it to him so he could make sure they got it right. It was a tricky thing to do, going through an interpreter, but finally Bent was satisfied.

"When should they leave, *Jefe?*" Flores asked.

"Soon's they can saddle a couple of horses." He paused. "No, best make 'em ride mules. I know them Injuns some, but I still don't put all my faith in 'em. Temptin' 'em with a couple of good horses might be askin' too much. They ain't going to be too interested in mules."

Flores nodded. Then he and his three companions stood.

"One more thing, boys," Bent said quietly. When the four turned to face him again, Bent flipped silver dollars at Manuel, Pedro, and Arturo. Each caught his coin and grinned. Then they left.

Bent sighed and stretched out on his robes.

Bent felt a little better when he awoke. Within the next several days, though, more workers began to show unmistakable signs of the disease, and work slowed to almost nonexistence. The few who were left helped the worst cases.

Bent recovered rather quickly, grateful that he had been touched by only a mild case. He peered at his face in a small looking glass. "Not too bad," he muttered when he saw the light sprinkle of pocking. He knew he would have them forever, but he also knew that he was not the handsomest man God had ever created. The pocking did not alter his looks overly much.

St. Vrain, on the other hand, was suffering considerably. Once Bent was back in action, he tended as best he could to St. Vrain, as well as some of the other ailing men. He also drove the men who weren't sick, to get ready for the others to leave.

Nearly two weeks after the smallpox first appeared, Bent watched as the caravan of horses, mules, wagons, and carts pulled out. St. Vrain was among those leaving, lying on blankets in a wagon.

When the caravan disappeared over the horizon, Bent looked around. Fewer than two dozen men remained. None, except Bent, had had the disease. It was eerily quiet, but Bent appreciated it. It was soothing after the hectic pace and all the sickness.

He called to Flores, then spoke with the Mexican a moment. Flores nodded and hurried off. He was back soon with the rest of the men. Slowly they walked through the sprawling camp, trying to pick up the articles that were infected or might have been. Everything suspect was tossed on a bonfire they started near the river, close to the camp. Soon long coils of blackish, acrid smoke were curling into the sky. Bent stepped back, hoping this would exterminate the disease here.

Once that was done, he put the men to work, doing what they had been doing. A few made adobe bricks; the rest put up walls. With so few men left, there was no want of work. The main job besides the work in the fort was keeping the men fed. Bent went hunting every other day or so, usually taking one or two of the men with him. He would ride his horse, while the help brought a flatbed wagon for the meat.

Another chore of Bent's—and one he detested—was keeping the books. He knew it was a necessity, but he did not enjoy it at all. A related task, though one he was slightly more favorably inclined to do, was keeping up his journal. Bent forced himself to write in the journal at least a little, every day, as long as it was possible to do so. He saw it as a builder of character, as he did reading. He had enough savvy to know that educating oneself as much as possible was the way to get ahead. He might be a rough and tumble mountain man, but he was also a *bourgeois*—a company owner. He could not live his whole life in buckskins and fur. The day would come when the beaver trade faded to almost nothing. Reports already were coming out of St. Louis and elsewhere about a reduced demand for beaver hats, which meant less call for beaver plews. That, in turn, pushed prices down. Last year Charles had gotten near six dollars a pound for beaver back in the settlements. This year it was down to less than four dollars a pound. The bottom would fall out sooner or later. Bent wanted to be prepared for that. He had already decided that being a trader was far better than being a trapper. And he was not about to get skunked by some slick banker back in St. Louis, no sir.

A sudden shout of anger caused Bent to jerk his quill, leaving a scrawling line of ink across the page. "Son of a bitch," he snapped. He shoved up and stormed out of the tent, heading for the laborers' camp.

The workers had formed a ragged circle and were cheering and shouting in Spanish. Bent stomped up and shoved his way through the circle of men, and stopped.

"Emiliano!" he bellowed, looking around for the foreman.

"Here, *Jefe*," Flores said. His voice lacked any sign of joy.

"What the hell is going on here?" Bent demanded.

Flores shrugged. He had tried his best to keep Roberto Barrega and Juan Gomez apart. But it had been hopeless. "Juan accused Roberto of taking his knife. Roberto called Juan a liar and said Juan stole a few pesos from him."

"Didn't you step in and try'n' stop it before it got this bad?" Bent asked angrily. Usually he treated the men well, but his temper was never buried too far, and it was boiling over now.

"*Si,*" Flores said with another shrug. He straightened his shoulders. "You might send me away, *patrón,*" Flores said a little haltingly. "But this was going to happen."

Bent squinted up at Flores. He felt a little bad about having given him a hard time. What had happened was inevitable. Bent could not expect things to be peaceful forever. Not with a bunch of men tied to one spot with no recreation, no women, little alcohol. There was nothing for the men to do to have a little pleasure. Trouble could not help but crop up.

During the short exchange with Flores, Bent had cut off a small plug of tobacco and shoved it in his mouth, while mostly keeping an eye on the two combatants. Gomez and Barrega were flailing wildly at each other, but not seeming to accomplish much. Both were of medium height and rather stocky, with muscles built up during a lifetime of hard, physical work. Barrega was a bit shorter than Gomez, but he had a broad chest, matching shoulders, and a wide belly. His bare chest showed the scars of many a fight.

The two appeared to be about evenly matched. At least until Barrega came up with a knife. Bent didn't know where the man had gotten it. It just seemed to have appeared out of nowhere.

He figured it was time to step in and stop this. He didn't much mind if the two men wanted to punch the tar out of each other; he did mind one or both of them getting killed.

6

Bent stepped boldly into the human arena. Gomez had his back to Bent and was warily moving backward. Bent grabbed Gomez's shirt and jerked the man behind him. He planted his feet and glared at Barrega. "Put that knife away, boy," Bent snapped, authority deepening his voice.

Barrega shook his head angrily, his hair snapping back and forth, sending up puffs of dust.

"Now!" Bent roared.

His hoarse bellow quieted the other men. They watched with interest, figuring this would really test their *patrón*. Paying good wages was one thing, but to win these men's respect and admiration, a man had to prove himself. Tall tales about the mountains would not do; it had to be done in their sight.

"No," Barrega snarled, lips curling back in a sneer over a mouth full of rotten teeth.

Bent spit. "Drop the knife, boy, or I'll shove it up your ass."

"You don't scare me, Bent," Barrega said with bravado. Barrega looked angry enough to chew down one of the walls of the burgeoning fort. He looked at the anglo and figured Bent was not all that tough. Not without all his stinking Americano friends around to save his miserable hide. Barrega was suddenly feeling good. He was at least three inches taller and forty pounds heavier than Bent. He figured he would have no trouble at all taking on this short, thin Americano. "I think I'll just carve you up, Señor Pollo." His voice had strong overtones of derision, which filtered through even his thick accent. Eyes gleaming, Barrega crouched and began moving slowly forward.

Bent scratched at the stubble on his face.

Barrega advanced a few more steps.

Bent stood, seemingly unconcerned. The men began muttering amongst themselves. Most appreciated Bent, since he was the man who paid them such good wages. A few disliked Bent for what he stood for—a wealthy Americano holding in his hand the well-being of the Mexicans. Many disliked Barrega, though, since he had bullied them.

Bent cared little about any of that. He knew he would have to stand up to this man, and show everyone what he was made of.

Barrega was almost within reach now, his knife slicing threatening circles in the air. He wondered why Bent had not moved, other than to spit tobacco juice again. He shrugged mentally. So much the better, if Bent considered himself above getting in a fight.

Barrega smiled again as the tip of his knife neared Bent's cotton shirt. *"Adios, bastardo,"* he said quietly. He thrust the knife toward Bent's flesh, expecting to cut through tissue with agonizing ease.

Bent suddenly spit the whole wad of tobacco on Barrega's face. Some got in Barrega's eyes. He lurched back involuntarily, trying to wipe the stinging mass from his eyes.

As Barrega stumbled backward, still frantically trying to clear his vision, Bent stepped up and smashed a fist into Barrega's chest twice. The impetus of the blows shoved Barrega back even faster. Bent stalked Barrega and pelted his face, chest, and stomach with punches, driving Barrega back and back. Then Bent grabbed the Mexican's right arm—the one with the knife—at the wrist and biceps. He jerked it down hard while bringing his knee up. The arm snapped like a rotten twig.

Barrega screeched and dropped the knife. He grabbed his broken arm and looked up, hate burning in his eyes. He muttered some Spanish that Bent could not understand but knew was not complimentary.

"You got one chance to live, amigo," Bent said calmly.

"Go to hell, you son of a bitch," Barrega said in Spanish.

Even if Bent was not able to understand that simple sentence, he would have known the gist of it when Barrega grabbed for his knife on the ground. When he came up, Bent also had a big butcher knife in his hand. "Don't," he warned.

Barrega's response was to bellow something incoherent and lunge at Bent. The American blocked the knife thrust with his right forearm. In his left, he grabbed Barrega's broken arm and twisted it.

Barrega screamed in pain as the radius and ulna ground together. At the same time, Bent's knife ripped upward into Barrega's belly.

Bent stepped back and let Barrega fall. After wiping his bloody blade clean on the back of Barrega's dirty shirt, he straightened and looked around the circle of dark, suddenly serious faces. "Any of you others want to come against me?" he asked loudly.

He had no takers. He nodded and slid the knife into the hard leather sheath. Then he walked away, pushing through the ring of men, heading for his tent.

The men crept around the camp warily for some days, keeping an eye on Bent when he was around, and feeling a lifting of gloom when he was off hunting. Gradually, though, over the next several days, the men lost their fear of Bent. He was the same as ever, a hard man but fair.

Since Bent had seen no Indians, he figured that

Manuel, Pedro, and Arturo—the three men he had sent out to warn the Cheyennes—had done their jobs well. He hoped to see them back soon, just to know for sure how successful they had been.

There was little excitement in the camp. Because there were so few men, they were kept busy with work, and in the evenings they generally were too tired to cause much fuss.

About the only excitement they had was when a wandering grizzly bear strolled through the camp one day, sending men scrambling for safety up in the trees. The bear rifled through some supplies and ambled off, seemingly pleased with his plundered deer haunch.

Bent had stood out front of his tent, attracted by the yells of fear from the men, and watched with some amusement as his workers tried to claw their way up the cottonwoods.

A week later Bent rode off on one of his hunting trips. As was usual, he took one of the Mexican workers with him. It was unusual, however, that he took Emiliano Flores. The man had proven himself to be a good and loyal worker, and Bent thought it right that he be treated well. So he took Flores to give him a break from supervising the laborers.

Less than an hour out Bent stopped near a small cluster of buffalo. He dismounted and with quick efficiency dropped two cows. As Flores's wagon creaked toward the herd, the other animals snuffled in irritation and then wandered off.

The butchering did not take long, and before noon Bent and Flores were done. "Hell, Yano," Bent said, "it seems a shame to waste some of this fresh meat. Go get us some *bois de vache*, and we'll have us a few bites."

"*Si, Jefe,*" Flores said eagerly.

Not long after, they were chewing down hunks of buffalo hump that were still running with blood on the inside, though the outside was seared black. Between bites they sipped at harsh, boiled coffee.

As he and Flores ate, Bent spotted two riders on a ridge a half mile or so away to the southwest. The Indians had half a dozen horses trotting ahead of them. Bent jabbed Flores's arm with an elbow and pointed with a piece of meat.

Flores nodded. "Can you tell what they are?" the Mexican asked.

"Nope. But, damn, I hope they're Cheyennes 'stead of Comanches."

The two continued eating quietly, though both made sure their rifles and pistols were ready.

The Indians had disappeared in one of the innumerable gullies, and then floated up on a ridge a hundred yards from Bent and Flores.

Bent nodded. "Cheyennes," he said with some relief. He knew they could still be trouble, since he had not met every Cheyenne warrior in all the bands. He just hoped that word of him had spread enough to make this encounter a friendly one.

As the Indians neared, Bent stood and wiped his greasy hands on his old buckskin pants. The Indians stopped, and Bent held out his right hand, palm outward, and traced little circles in the air with the hand. *"Hola,"* he said in welcome, though his stomach was suddenly knotted. "Come, sit at our fire," he added in signs.

The Cheyennes returned the greeting. After hobbling their horses, they sat and took some meat and ate hungrily.

Bent had trouble taking his eyes off the Cheyennes' faces and the telltale tainting of smallpox. Not knowing what to say, he went to his horse and pulled out the extra tin mug. He resettled himself and held the cup toward the warriors. "It ain't but the only extra I got," he said dully. "You can share it, if you're of a mind to have coffee."

The Cheyennes did.

"What's your name?" Bent asked in signs, looking at

the slightly older warrior. Both were yet young, perhaps in their mid-twenties, Bent figured. Their backs were straight, but their otherwise handsome faces were screwed up in pain, and a film of sweat covered their foreheads.

"Yellow Arrow."

"Your friend?" Bent pointed to the other warrior, who held the mug of coffee.

"Eagle Heart."

Bent nodded. "You know who I am?" he asked.

Eagle Heart answered, since Yellow Arrow had taken the cup back. He was sweating heavily. "You are the Little White Man who is building the mud lodge for trading."

Bent nodded. "Didn't one of my people come to your village to tell you not to come to the fort place?" Bent asked in signs and Spanish.

Yellow Arrow shrugged. It seemed to take a great deal of effort. "We have been making war on the Comanche," he answered in kind.

"You didn't go to the fort place, though?" Bent asked. His worry grew, as he realized that the epidemic might be far more widespread than he had figured.

"Not in some time," Eagle Heart answered.

Bent's stomach fell. He paid no heed to Flores, who had stood and moved off toward the wagon a few feet away. Bent was about to say something else, but Flores called, *"Jefe, por favor."*

Bent looked at him in some annoyance, but then realized that Flores was considerably agitated. He pushed up and walked to the wagon. "What is it, Yano?" he asked, trying to keep his fear in check.

"You see the shirt Yellow Arrow's wearing?" Flores asked, worried.

"Yeah. So?"

"It was José Morales's."

It took Bent a moment to conjure up the look of

José Morales, one of the workers at the fort. "You sure?" he finally asked.

"*Si, Jefe.*"

"But how . . . ? When . . . ?"

"I don't know," Flores said. "But I'll find out damn soon after we get back."

Bent nodded, his worry having evolved into a sick, empty feeling in his stomach. "You know what them being here means, don't you? I can't let them get back to their village. There's too much at stake."

"*Si,*" Flores said quietly. "Business will be hurt."

"Hell, Yano, you know me better'n that. Sure it'd hurt business, but I've come to like the Cheyenne people." It was said flatly, as a matter-of-fact. "That's why I can't let them two back to their village. It'd kill the Cheyennes off quicker'n anything."

"I understand, *Jefe*, but—" Flores stopped and stared at Bent, horror growing in his eyes as he realized just what Bent was saying. He tried to speak, but no words would come, and even if there had been words there, they would have been inadequate for the occasion.

"No one—no one!—must know about this," Bent hissed. "You understand me, Yano? Answer me, Yano," Bent said harshly when he got no response.

Flores nodded numbly. He stared at his boss, and it suddenly hit him how much pain Bent was in over the decision. Yet it could be no other way, Flores knew. It was something that had to be done. Flores did not envy Bent's position. "When?" he asked after several attempts.

Bent pulled a sliver of wood from the wagon and picked his teeth. He had no desire to do this, but he had to. There was no other choice. What would otherwise happen was far more sickening to him than what he planned to do. "No reason to delay, I expect." He glanced over at the Cheyennes. They looked ghastly. "At least they'll go out on a full stomach."

"Is there anything I can do, *Jefe*?" Flores asked quietly.

Bent paused, looking thoughtful. "I expect not, Yano. Just be ready in case somethin' goes wrong."

"Si," Flores said. He hesitated, then, "I could help you in this task."

"No call for that, Yano." He looked directly at Flores. "I'm obliged you made such an offer, but this is somethin' best done on my own." He sighed and reached into a box in the open bed of the wagon. He grabbed a small bottle of whiskey. He hesitated only a moment before he pulled the cork and, shading what he was doing, took a healthy swallow. Then he capped the bottle. "Well, shit," he muttered, "this ain't gonna get no easier with me standing here playin' with my pizzle, now is it?"

Bent headed back to the fire, which was only embers. "I have news for your people," he said. He felt sick but didn't show it. When neither said anything, he added, "I have whiskey." He held the bottle out.

Both warriors were sweating, though it was a cold day, and they seemed almost ready for the grave. They looked at each other and grinned weakly. Bent handed Yellow Arrow the bottle. He uncorked it, sniffed suspiciously at the opening, then smiled. He took a healthy drink before handing it to Eagle Heart.

"When's the last time you boys was at the fort place?" Bent asked.

Eagle Heart shrugged. "Ten suns maybe."

"You trade for anything there?" Bent was so tense he thought pieces of him might snap off.

Yellow Arrow nodded, and plucked at his yellow calico shirt. "I give a knife—damn good knife—for this."

Bent shook his head. "It's doomed you two," he said almost to himself. More loudly he added, "We had sickness there. Bad sickness."

"What kind?" Yellow Arrow asked nervously. He knew, but he hoped it was not true.

"The spotted sickness. Smallpox," Bent said in Spanish, voice a flat monotone. He waved a hand vaguely at their faces.

The Cheyennes looked worriedly at each other. After a few moments Yellow Arrow looked back at Bent. "We don't have this sickness," Eagle Heart said with bravado.

"Like hell you don't," Bent snapped. Then he shrugged. "But whether you boys want to admit it or not don't matter," he said. "What matters is you boys can't ever go back to your village." He did not need to tell the Cheyennes why. With the Indians' lack of immunity to white men's diseases, they were doomed.

"No," Eagle Heart snarled.

"Hell, you two know what'll happen to your families you go back there now."

Yellow Arrow's face grew hard. "No," he said in Cheyenne, sweeping his hand away from his body, palm coming to rest face up. He angrily grabbed the bottle of whiskey from Eagle Heart and drained it. He threw the bottle away as he stood. Bent and Eagle Heart also rose.

Yellow Arrow placed a hard palm on Bent's chest and shoved. "We will go now," he announced in English. He and Eagle Heart pushed past Bent, heading for their ponies a few feet away.

Bent turned toward them. He was sick at what he had to do, but he had no choice. If they got back to their village, the Cheyennes would be decimated. He could not face that. "Sorry, boys," he said, choking the words out past a constricted throat, "but I can't let you do that."

The two Cheyennes looked at him over their shoulders, smirks curling up their lips. Each grabbed the reins to his horse.

With a heaping dose of nausea and disgust, Bent pulled his two pistols. He fired one, hitting Yellow Arrow fairly high in the back. The punch of the lead ball shoved him forward. The Cheyenne bounced off his pony and went down.

Bent did not wait to see Yellow Arrow fall. As Eagle Heart swung in surprise toward him, Bent fired his other pistol, and Eagle Heart fell.

Bent stood there for what seemed like an eternity, seeing nothing, feeling a horror so deep that he was not sure he could live with it. Finally he put his pistols away and woodenly took the small shovel from the wagon. He began digging a hole, hoping the physical work would keep him from feeling too much. Flores tried to take the shovel from him, but Bent growled at him. Flores was worried about Bent.

As Bent flung dirt this way and that, he partially managed to assuage his conscience by telling himself firmly, over and over, that Yellow Arrow and Eagle Heart would have been dead in a few days anyway. The fact that Bent was fairly certain that he had just saved a sizable portion of the Cheyenne people didn't hurt either.

As they neared the fort an hour after finishing the graves, Bent warned, "You remember, Yano, that nobody can ever know about this."

"*Si, Jefe,*" Flores said firmly. No one would be able to tear Bent's secret from his lips, he vowed silently.

{7}

St. Vrain was his usual jovial self when he returned from Taos. His broad, beaming face brightened the otherwise gloomy work camp. He was accompanied by more than one hundred workers, quite a few of whom had been among the original detail.

Winter no longer lay heavy over the land. The coat of snow and frost was gone. But thick, iron-gray clouds kept the sky's blue at bay, as it had the past two days. It had not rained, though it seemed imminent.

Not much had been accomplished in the two months or so since St. Vrain and the rest of the smallpox-suffering workers had ridden off toward Taos. But with the return of the men, work quickly progressed. It helped that spring had finally arrived, breaking winter's harsh grip over the land. Leaving St. Vrain in charge, a melancholy Bent rode out. Bent had said nothing to St. Vrain, but the Frenchman knew something was wrong with his partner. As Bent was saddling his horse in preparation for leaving, St. Vrain stopped by. Looking at Bent across the horse's back, he asked quietly, "What is wrong, *mon ami?*"

"Ain't none of your concern, Ceran," Bent said flatly.

St. Vrain stared at Bent for a few moments. Then he nodded and left. He could understand another man's need for solitude. But as soon as Bent rode off, St. Vrain started nosing around. No one seemed to know anything, though. Or if they did, they were staying mum.

Bent was gone more than a month, and when he returned, he seemed to have mostly gotten over what was haunting him. To St. Vrain, though, Bent retained a certain air of discontent or despair. It would be a long time before St. Vrain saw that disappear entirely from his friend.

Bent put aside his melancholy as best he could, again trying to convince himself that he had done right by killing the two men a few days prematurely to save hundreds of others. He began making forays into Cheyenne and Arapaho country again, telling them the smallpox epidemic had run its course and it was safe to come to the fort site. Between each village, Bent fought with the rising bile of his hypocrisy.

When he rode back to the fort almost two months later, he was astounded at the progress that had been made.

"It's about time you come back," St. Vrain said, feigning anger.

"Miss me?"

"Hah! Zat will be ze day." He paused to let some chuckles run their course. "How did your journey go?" To St. Vrain, Bent seemed more nearly his old self.

"Good enough, I suppose," Bent said with a nod. He began unsaddling his pinto as a laborer took his two mules.

"You seem troubled, *mon ami*," St. Vrain prodded. He might look jolly, but he had a mind as strong and sure as a bear trap.

Bent dropped the saddle and *apishamore*. He faced St. Vrain, leaning an arm on his horse. "It's nothing," he said.

Bent began brushing the horse's sweaty sides.

"I must get to Taos, Bill," St. Vrain said hastily. "Our business zere has been too much neglected."

Bent nodded, slowing his work. "Why don't you figure to leave in the mornin'." Bent went back to his chore with renewed purpose, if not vigor. He was hungrier than a starving wolf. He was tired too, but not the physical tired of too much exertion, rather a mental exhaustion brought on by trying to do too much, of being tense from riding into Indian camps, of being constantly on the alert for hostile Indians, of too many things happening in too short a time.

He shook off the gloomy feeling some. He did not have the time or energy for such dark thoughts. Finishing with the horse, he headed to his tent, which had been left standing while he had been gone. One of the Mexican laborers had started a fire just outside the tent as soon as he saw Bent riding into camp. By the time Bent arrived at the tent, there was coffee boiling and fresh buffalo meat cooking.

He felt a little refreshed after he had splashed some water on his face and then ate. Two cups of harsh, black coffee helped too, and he was feeling much more like himself. He leaned against a willow backrest and pulled out his journal, ink, and quill.

He was still writing in the journal when St. Vrain arrived and sat across the fire from him. Bent put the book aside and capped the inkwell. Then St. Vrain asked, "Do you need anyt'ing from Taos?"

"Nothin' I can think of. We have enough DuPont and Galena? Sugar, coffee, and other such fixin's?"

"Enough to last until I get back," St. Vrain said with a nod. "But you might have to ration salt and a few odder t'ings."

"We'll make do. The hunters makin' enough meat?"

"*Oui.*"

"Give my regards to Charlie, Bob, and George."

St. Vrain nodded. There was nothing more to say, so he rose, brushed the dirt off the seat of his pants, and strolled away.

St. Vrain and several men were on the trail shortly

after Bent rose. He bid his friend farewell and watched as the group got smaller and smaller before disappearing into the horizon.

As Bent stood there alone watching the caravan, Emiliano Flores slipped up alongside him. Bent glanced at him, surprised at the hard but sad look on Flores's face. "Somethin' eatin' at you, Yano?"

Flores's long face drooped a little more. "*Sí, Jefe,*" he said sadly.

Bent waited, wondering, but not wanting to pressure Flores.

"We have one less man on the work crews, *Jefe.*"

"Oh?" Bent responded, surprised.

"Señor José Morales has had an accident."

Bent looked blankly at Flores, trying to pin a face with the name. He couldn't, but the name rang a bell in his head. "The shirt Yellow Arrow was wearing," he said more than asked.

"*Sí.* He was telling the others he had given the shirt to two Indians, hoping it was infected and would kill many Indians."

"Why?"

"His family was killed by Indians. Or so he told some others."

"Cheyennes?" Bent asked. He knew how the Cheyennes would act on the war path.

Flores shrugged. "It doesn't matter." Seeing Bent's sudden look of anger, Flores added, "To him it doesn't matter."

Bent nodded, understanding. "So how'd he meet this accident?"

"We were walking along the river, looking for a new source of clay for the bricks when he fell in," Flores said flatly. "But poor José, he couldn't swim, and so he drowned."

"Then that's what all the commotion was about this morning, eh?"

Flores nodded. "I did everything I could to save

him, but . . ." His shoulders lifted, as did his hands, palms up.

Bent stared across the prairie. "I reckon we both got a little secret now, don't we?"

"*Si, Jefe.*" Bent's calmness reassured Flores. If Bent could deal with his terrible secret, then Emiliano Flores could do the same with his own.

Just over a month later, St. Vrain and his group rode back into the work camp. Behind the small group trailed several mules, their backs loaded with supplies for the workers and bosses, plus some trade goods. Both Bent and St. Vrain knew the Indian trade well enough to make sure there were always some small trinkets—small mirrors, inexpensive knives, beads, cloth—among their packs.

The trading post had its shape now, at least on the outside. Though to St. Vrain's eyes there was still plenty of work to be done, the end was in sight.

Bent rode out, heading for Gray Thunder's village once more. There, he had long talks with the aging chief, and spent a considerable amount of time addressing the councils of warriors. He also spent some time watching Gray Thunder's two youngest daughters—Owl Woman and Yellow Woman. The former was about thirteen, Bent figured, almost ripe for marrying, and the latter barely twelve. Both were about Bent's height, with broad, full faces that were quite attractive. Under their simple buckskin dresses, their forms held promise.

In his travels since helping Black Feather and Winter Hawk, Bent had come to know the Cheyennes some, but not well enough to make advances on the chief's daughters—yet. Business had to come first, and alienating Gray Thunder by being overly attentive to his daughters was a sure way to foul potential business, especially when they were yet so young. So he contented himself with surreptitiously watching them and thinking about what it might be like to marry one of them.

That would have to wait, at least for a while, he figured. Otherwise, he was pleased with his trip. With the assistance of Black Feather and Winter Hawk, he had talked Gray Thunder into promising to bring his band down toward the fort for trading. Bent figured that if Gray Thunder kept his word, quite a few of the other Cheyenne bands would follow, since Gray Thunder was well thought of by all the bands.

Feeling satisfied, he climbed up on his horse and headed south on the long journey back to the fort.

It took almost two weeks to make the trip. He would have made it a little sooner, except he stopped off at the rendezvous for a couple of days of carousing, drinking, and raising hell. Gray Thunder's daughters had turned his mind toward the thought of how long it had been since he had had a woman. The rendezvous, with its large compliment of willing Indian women, helped to slake that hunger, at least for a while.

As he crested the small ridge just north of the fort's entrance, Bent saw more wagons and mules than had been there when he left a little more than a month ago. He stopped and stood in the stirrups to give himself more of a vantage point. Then he grinned.

Voicing a whoop, he swatted his horse with his hat. The startled animal bolted, dragging a loudly protesting mule behind. Bent continued his whooping and hollering as he bore down on the camp. He grinned into the rushing wind as he saw Mexican laborers scattering like chickens at the noise he was making. He spotted St. Vrain coming out of his tent to look up the ridge, curious about what was raising such a ruckus. When he saw it, he yelled at the fleeing workers. His voice floated up to Bent, as he stood there with his hands on his hips.

Bent was pleased when he reached the fort. The outside walls had been plastered over with adobe, giving the brown mud castle a clean, uniform look. There was much to be done inside, though. Workers were building up walls to the rooms that would surround the *placita*, but all in all, the fort would be mostly done by summer's end, Bent figured.

He felt even better when he saw his brother Charles giving him loud hurrahs as he rode hell-bent into the campsite.

Bent stopped his horse sharply, sending a cloud of dust billowing up before being swept away in the wind. He pulled his right leg over the saddle horn and slid out of the saddle, facing Charles and St. Vrain, who were walking quickly toward him, grinning like devils.

The Bents embraced happily, slapping each other on the back. Then William shook St. Vrain's hand and handed the reins of his horse to one of the laborers who had rushed over. Then the two Bents and St. Vrain headed toward St. Vrain's tent.

As they passed the fort, William suddenly stopped, staring at the adobe over where the entrance doors would be hung.

"You like it?" Charles asked, chuckling.

"Suits this chil'," William said, still in wonder as he gazed on the hastily painted sign that announced the trading post as Fort William. "But why name it after me?"

"Hell, you supervised most of the buildin' so far," Charles said.

"Ceran's done as much," William said. He was proud as could be at the honor, but he wasn't sure he deserved it.

"That's true, I reckon," Charles said. "But you kept things rollin' whilst Ceran was in Taos tryin' to get over the goddamn smallpox."

"Reckon that's true. But he's stayed here whilst I was out traipsin' 'round the countryside talkin' to Cheyennes."

"Well," Charles said evenly, "whilst you was out

traipsin' 'round, me and Ceran was talkin' some. Seems like you been elected to run the damn fort." He suddenly burst into laughter.

They resumed walking, and in a few moments were sitting around the small fire outside St. Vrain's tent. In silence, they poured themselves coffee and cut off chunks of roasted meat. Finally each poured another cup of coffee and lit his pipe.

"Ceran says things've gone well, Bill," Charles asked. "That true?"

"True enough, I expect." William blew out a stream of smoke. "Only ones reluctant to come on down here to trade with us was Gray Thunder and his bunch. They'd gotten mixed up in some war with the Pawnees. But he finally come 'round."

"Good," Charles said with a nod. "When do you expect 'em to take a *paseo* on down this way?"

"Some—the ones I talked to first—ought to be comin' in soon, I'd say. You got goods to trade?"

"Hell, yes. Brought a whole caravan just to here, whilst sendin' another down to Taos and Santa Fe."

"Good thinkin'. You plannin' to set here awhile?"

"Nah," Charles said. "Now you're back, I can head to Taos and see to things there. I want to get another caravan to Missouri soon. That way we'll be able to bring another load out this way before winter sets in."

Within a month Cheyennes began to arrive. At first it was a trickle, then more like a flood. Each evening, Bent rode through the Cheyenne camps, trying to get a count of how many lodges were there. He also took the time to speak with some of the war leaders and civil chiefs, getting to know them. Nights, he often would sit at the fire with some of the warriors and trade stories with them.

Soon there were camps running for miles along the river, in both directions. A few Comanches showed up occasionally across the Arkansas. Each time they were spotted, several young, hotheaded Cheyenne warriors would leap on their ponies and ride into the river. But by the time they reached the other bank, the Comanches had fled.

And still the camps kept growing.

Bent and St. Vrain stood atop a pile of boxes piled on a stack of adobe bricks which were sitting on the flat bed of a big freight wagon, which was parked a foot or two from the fort wall. In doing so, the men could get an idea of what it would look like when the second floor of the fort was completed. The two men gazed out to the north and east. It seemed as if Cheyenne and Arapaho lodges stretched to forever in any direction the men looked. Bent had counted at least three hundred of them in one ride though the forest of tipis.

"I reckon we ought to open for business," Bent said quietly.

"But ze fort, she is not finish. Zere is much work to be done, *non?*"

"Yeah, there's a heap to be done, but hell, we ain't gonna be able to hold these Cheyennes off much longer. We promised them boys trade if they'd come on down here, and by God they're gonna get trade."

"It will be dangerous, *non?*" St. Vrain countered. "Ze trade room is not finish. If we trade in ze *placita,* too many Indians will get in here."

Bent scratched the stubble on his chin. "It shouldn't be hard to figure out a way to limit how many of 'em can get in here at one time."

St. Vrain lifted his bristling black eyebrows.

"Hell, just park a couple of these big ol' wagons in

front of the entryway. Leave 'em hooked to the mules.''

"They could get in under ze wagons," St. Vrain said, playing the devil's advocate. Since he was a practical sort of man, he was all for opening up the trade. He just wanted to make sure that Bent had foreseen all the potential problems.

"Shit, how many of 'em could get in here at a time?" Bent said with a snort of derision that was only partly feigned. "Besides, we'll have a cannon aimed at the front gate and the other facing the back. That and our own boys should be able to fend 'em off."

"It should work," St. Vrain said. "But we must answer an important question first." He looked levelly at Bent. "Do you trust zese savages?"

Bent thought about that for some moments. When he answered, he chose his words carefully and spoke slowly. "I don't know as if I trust 'em exactly. But I ain't ever seen a one of 'em go against his word. They been friendly to us since we kept Black Feather and Winter Hawk from the Comanches that time. I don't see that we shouldn't trust 'em." He paused. "Besides, we ever want to start tradin' with 'em regular, we're gonna have to put at least some of our trust in 'em sooner or later."

"But is zis ze time to do zat, eh?"

"You gettin' scairdy in your old age?" Bent joked.

"Zat will be ze day, when I am afraid of trading wit' Indians. Hah!" He paused, running his stubby fingers through the tangled black mass of beard. "When will we start zis trading, eh?"

"It won't do us no good to put it off." He looked over at St. Vrain, who was watching him. It was difficult for Bent to discern what the Frenchman was thinking; the man's face was blank, serene.

"Tomorrow, zen?" St. Vrain asked.

"Suits this chil'." He knew now that all of St. Vrain's

questions had been answered. He would endorse the project wholeheartedly.

Bent and St. Vrain climbed down from their rickety perch. When they were solidly on *terra firma* again, St. Vrain went to take another count of the trading merchandise; Bent went to saddle his horse.

Soon Bent was riding toward Gray Thunder's camp to spread the word among the Cheyennes that trading would begin at daylight. He had come to enjoy being in Cheyenne camps. He was welcome, and there was something comforting about the way these tall, handsome people lived. Their camps were beehives of activity, much of it joyful.

Children ran crazily, unfettered, through the camps, playing games that would serve them well in the years to come. Their noise fought for attention with the din of barking, yapping dogs. Hundreds of horses grazed on the rich prairie grass just outside the camp, under the watchful eyes of boys too old to play children's games but not old enough to join the men on the hunt or in war.

Warriors sat outside their lodges, near the tripod racks on which their weapons rested. They talked, made or repaired weapons, gambled. Their laughter and friendly arguments provided a deep bass line to the higher-pitched noises of the youngsters and dogs. Adding to the overall cacophony were the chattering women, who helped each other with their many tasks. Racks of drying buffalo meat were ubiquitous.

Bent stopped in front of Gray Thunder's lodge. The chief, who was still vigorous despite having seen more than sixty winters, greeted him warmly. He had taken to the young trader, seeing Bent as brave, strong, and a man of his word.

Bent sat cross-legged across the fire from Gray Thunder, whose oldest wife, White Flower, served Bent a bowl of buffalo stew. Bent slurped it down, though it was poorly made. As he did, he tried to keep an eye on

Gray Thunder's two daughters. From his trips to Gray Thunder's camp, he had come to look more favorably on Owl Woman than on her sister, Yellow Woman. The latter was too young yet. He wondered if he had any chance of courting the attractive Owl Woman.

He finished the stew and gently set the bowl down. He packed his pipe, lit it, and turned his mind to business.

"I am grateful that the great chief of the Cheyennes, Gray Thunder, has come to the big stone lodge to trade," Bent said, mostly in sign language. He knew some Cheyenne, but he was not well-versed in it. He hoped to rectify that soon.

Gray Thunder said nothing, and Bent continued. "I bring the great chief, Gray Thunder, a token of my friendship." Bent pulled a silver pendant out of the possible bag at his side. He held the pendant out.

Gray Thunder nodded and with a wave of his wrinkled hand directed Owl Woman to fetch the prize. Owl Woman took it tentatively, but as her hand touched Bent's she felt a sudden thrill. Bent felt it too, and though his calm demeanor never changed, Owl Woman could see in his eyes that he was very interested in her. Flushing with the sudden heat that flooded her, Owl Woman took the pendant to her father.

Gray Thunder turned it in his hands, enjoying how the firelight played off the design etched into the silver. Finally he placed the silver chain around his neck and patted the pendant lying on his bony chest.

"With this small gift," Bent said in signs, "I invite the great chief Gray Thunder to my stone lodge to trade."

"When will this happen?" Gray Thunder asked.

"When the sun breaks next," Bent signed.

Gray Thunder sat as if in deep thought. Bent felt sure the chief would not refuse to come. Not after he had made the trip here from the small Black Hills far to the north. Bent figured the old man was just putting on a show for anyone who might be watching. After all, a chief as great as Gray Thunder would not be rushed into things.

Finally Gray Thunder nodded. "I will come to your stone lodge," he said in Cheyenne. As he said the words, his hands sculpted them in the air. "I have many furs to trade to Little White Man."

"And we have many things to trade to the People," Bent said. "Knives, looking glasses, pots, bolts of cloth, burning glass, iron for arrowheads, beads, many more things."

"Guns?" Gray Thunder asked. "You will trade guns to my people?"

"For the great chief Gray Thunder, there will be a gun. And some powder and lead to go with it."

"Only one?" Gray Thunder seemed slighted.

Bent nodded. "Later, when the Cheyennes have shown that they are worthy, there will be more guns."

Gray Thunder looked deep into Bent's brown eyes and saw honesty there. He nodded again, accepting the statement. It would do no good to press anyway, he knew. And why should he make an enemy of a man who so obviously wanted to be a friend to the Cheyennes? No, Gray Thunder was wise enough to know that if he befriended this small, hard-looking white man, it could have valuable rewards sometime later.

"Whiskey?" Gray Thunder asked in English. The word was garbled but unmistakable. "You have whiskey?" He waited, his face composed.

"No," Bent said in English, and signing it. "No whiskey."

Gray Thunder sat stone-faced for a moment, and Bent's heart sank. Then Gray Thunder grinned. "Good," he signed. Then he said it in Cheyenne, so Bent could learn the word.

* * *

As darkness closed softly over the fort, Bent sat in his small tent, writing in his journal by the light of a candle lantern. He was feeling good about things for the first time in a while. Even the time he had been forced to kill Yellow Arrow and Eagle Heart had faded from a sharp, guilty pain to a dull, morose ache.

He had just closed his small pot of ink when all hell seemed to break loose. "What the . . . ?" Bent muttered. He tumbled out of his tent and looked over at St. Vrain, whose tent was only a few feet to Bent's left. They headed into the fort.

Wolves howled seemingly from all directions. Dogs in the Cheyenne camps added their own nervous barking and yelping.

Bent and St. Vrain climbed onto the wagon on which they had stood earlier in the day. As they peered over the fort wall into the darkness, shouts and screams of fear erupted steadily from the Indian camps up and down the Arkansas River. Though Bent and St. Vrain could not see them very well in the firelight, the Mexican laborers were swearing or praying, some of them doing both at the same time.

The horses were spooked too, but Bent was not sure whether it was all the howling and noise or something else.

"*Mon Dieu,*" St. Vrain breathed. He pointed to the sky. "Look."

"Jesus holy Christ almighty," Bent said in an awed whisper. He rubbed his eyes several times, not sure that what he was seeing wasn't a dream—or a nightmare. "The stars are fallin'."

Afterward Bent walked through the Mexican camp, and he heard more than one laborer pleading with the Virgin Mary and the Holy Spirit and a half-dozen saints to rescue them from the doom they expected at any moment.

He drifted toward the closest Cheyenne camps, navigating by starlight, moonlight, and firelight. The warriors were spooked by the strange event. Bent realized that none of the men—Cheyenne, Mexican or Anglo—remembered ever having seen such a thing before.

"Them there was some powerful strange doin's," Bent muttered to St. Vrain as the two of them discussed the night over a pipe and some coffee. They sat in the dirt at a small fire between their tents.

"Mais oui!" St. Vrain agreed. "I nevair see such a t'ing." They fell silent, listening to the noise that reverberated across the land. Finally St. Vrain asked, "You t'ink zis will make trouble for ze trading tomorrow?"

Bent shrugged. "Hell, Ceran, I got no idea. I do know that these here doin's ain't settin' well with the Cheyennes nor the Mexicans."

The area remained restless throughout the night, and Bent and St. Vrain had trouble sleeping, what with all the continued howling of wolves, baying of dogs, and other assorted, unearthly noises.

{ 9 }

In the light of the morning, most of the Mexicans'
fears had fled. They figured that if the Apocalypse had
not arrived, they were safe.

The Cheyennes were not so easily mollified, however. Bent awoke early and rode out to talk with Gray
Thunder. Though the old man tried to hide his nervousness, Bent could see it in the small things Gray
Thunder did—the way his callused fingers plucked at
the blanket draped around him, the furtive movements
of his dark eyes, the twitch of a leg. The meteor shower
had affected the Cheyennes deeply, and they were
making ready to leave.

"You aim to pull out?" Bent asked in signs. If the
Cheyennes did leave now, the company's trade might
be seriously impaired before it even got started. Besides, he wanted to try to stay close to Gray Thunder,
so that he could stay close to Gray Thunder's daughters.

"Yes," Gray Thunder signed, hands trembling
slightly. Bent saw it, and wondered if it was from age or
fear. He decided it didn't matter.

"Why?"

"We must make medicine," Gray Thunder signed,
his agitation growing. "The spirits are displeased with
the People. We must find our medicine again." He
knew the explanation was inadequate, but he could

think of no way of getting across to Little White Man the depths of his feelings in such matters.

Bent nodded. He knew he did not fully understand, but he accepted the Cheyennes' need to reconcile themselves with their gods. Still, he had to make a stab at keeping Gray Thunder's people here. "What makes you think your medicine's gone bad?" he asked. He knew the question was foolish, but it was all he could think of at the moment, and it would serve, even if only for a few moments, to keep Gray Thunder sitting at his fire.

"The stars fell from the sky last night," Gray Thunder said, suddenly wondering if Bent had become touched in the head by last night's startling event.

"Yes. Yes they did," Bent said, hands flying. He slowed down, adding, "But the sun came up this morning—from the east, as it should. None of the People have been hurt."

"All this is true," Gray Thunder said thoughtfully, though he still had his doubts. "But the others want to leave."

"Call a council," Bent said eagerly. "I'll talk with the warriors. Maybe I can make them see things as they are."

Gray Thunder thought about it for some moments, then nodded. He enjoyed Bent's company, and did not wish to leave this place yet. Still, he had been quite troubled by the previous night's strange occurrence. Gray Thunder had seen many things in his long life, but never anything like that. "It will be as you say." Gray Thunder pushed himself up. "You come back when the sun is straight overhead," he said in passable English.

Bent left, as if afraid that by lingering even for moments, Gray Thunder would change his mind.

Sitting and waiting at the fort was not easy. Having St. Vrain constantly nagging him to light for a while did nothing to ease Bent's anxiousness. At the appointed time, he rode back to Gray Thunder's camp.

Sitting at a large fire were almost forty Cheyennes—medicine men, war chiefs, civil chiefs, warriors. Each represented a different band. They all smoked a long ceremonial pipe until it had completed the circuit. Gray Thunder nodded at Bent.

The trader stood. He quickly explained to the warriors what he had told the chief that morning. The Cheyennes did not seem impressed. Bent took a deep breath, eased it out, and then continued.

"I saw many of your warriors last night when the stars were falling. The Cheyenne are the greatest warriors, and when I saw the men of the People last night, they were fearless, painted for battle with the sky and the night. Yes, this was a strange thing to happen. But the People's warriors ended the strangeness, chased away the evil spirits who fell to earth last night." He paused, unsure if he should go on. He had lathered his praise mighty thick and did not want to overdo it.

Gray Thunder stood and spoke quickly in his own language. Bent could understand perhaps a third of what the old man said, but Gray Thunder appeared to be supporting Bent.

Each warrior then stood to say his piece. Most made short, succinct speeches, though a few rambled on. Bent sat and listened, trying to pick out as much as he could. Two hours later the parley was still going on, but it seemed evident that the Cheyennes were pretty much coming around to Bent's favor.

Still, it was late afternoon before each man had had his say, and they decided that they would stay to trade with Little White Man.

With great relief, Bent told them to come to the as yet uncompleted fort in the morning. The others nodded. Once more the ceremonial pipe was smoked, sanctifying their words and decision.

* * *

Bent woke some of the laborers as soon as the first faint stripe of pink split the eastern sky. They groaned and complained, but set to their duties swiftly and quietly when Bent growled at them. When he did that, they knew right off that he was tense, and they adapted.

The men ate a hurried breakfast, then went into the fort's enclosure and began setting up for the trade. Bent had told them the evening before how he wanted things laid out, and the men found no trouble as they swiftly did what was needed.

St. Vrain joined Bent inside the fort. It was eerie in there, with just the blank walls staring at them. "Well, *mon ami*," St. Vrain asked softly, "are you ready for zis?"

"Reckon I'm about as ready as I'm ever gonna be," Bent responded flatly. He looked around, at the wagons blocking off the entrance, the wagon full of goods to be traded, the makeshift counter of wagon timbers on two large kegs, the armed men standing guard at various places, the cannon pointed toward the doorway. He sucked in a breath and released it. "Let the first group in, Mr. Flores," Bent said.

Things went smoothly. Dispensing all sorts of goods, checking pelts and hides from the Indians, marking everything in a ledger, kept Bent and St. Vrain busy.

Then along about midafternoon, one of the Cheyenne warriors began baiting the young grizzly bear chained to a wagon in one corner of the *placita*. Sam Butler, one of Bent's friends from the mountains, had come by with the bear a couple weeks before. Butler said he had found the animal the last summer as a cub and had kept it over the winter. He asked Bent if he could keep the bear at the fort for a while, as he rode down into Mexico to see about selling it. Bent had agreed.

Bent was only partly aware of it, so pressed for business was he. It only caught his attention when the bear's growling began to interfere with his working. He spun, saw what was happening and shouted, "Hey, boy, get the hell away from that b'ar."

Bloody Arm—a cocky young man whose handsome face and thigh-length hair were mighty attractive to many women—looked at Bent and sneered. But Bent had already turned back to his work.

Suddenly there was a loud, angry growl, and a short, sharp scream. Bent whirled. "Dammit," he muttered. The bear had broken loose from the wagon and had the warrior on the ground. The bear was clawing and biting Bloody Arm. The big paws slapped Bloody Arm back and forth as the warrior scrambled to get away from the ferocious beast.

The bear was only about two years old, as best Bent and Butler had been able to figure, but it was a big one nonetheless. It was effortlessly mauling Bloody Arm.

Bent had two big flintlock pistols in his belt. He jerked both free and ran toward the bear. Ten feet away from the animal, he stopped and fired both pistols. A heartbeat later more than a dozen arrows suddenly appeared in the bear's shaggy coat.

Bent looked around and saw about a dozen Cheyenne warriors firing arrows. The bear reared up, swatting ineffectually at the many points of pain, and then fell. Four Cheyennes edged up toward the bear, two of them with arrows nocked. The other two crept in, grabbed Bloody Arm, and hauled him away from the bear.

The animal made one more feeble attempt to get to its feet, but two more arrows knocked it down for good.

Calm began to descend on the fort. As several warriors carried Bloody Arm toward the gates, Bent saw that the young man was injured quite severely. Bent did not think Bloody Arm would live out the day.

Bent went back to his table, wiping sweat off his face. He set one of his pistols on the makeshift counter and reached for his powder flask to reload. The flask was not there. Angry, he turned to St. Vrain. "You see who it was took my powder flask?" he asked harshly.

"*Mais non,*" St. Vrain said apologetically. "I tried to watch all our t'ings, but I could not . . ." He shrugged.

"Dammit all." Bent was livid, and he considered calling off the rest of the day's trading.

Gray Thunder, who had been around the trading area most of the day, walked up and slapped a hand on Bent's shoulder. "You have others," he said.

"I know that. But dammit, it don't shine with this chil' to have someone makin' off with my things when I'm tryin' to help here."

"Ending the trading here now will do no one good," Gray Thunder said in Cheyenne, slowly so that Bent could understand. "To hurt many people for the actions of one is wrong."

Bent nodded, temper still hot, but in control. There was no more trouble that day, nor in the next few days. Finally the trade began to dwindle enough so that Bent and St. Vrain could have a breather.

As the last few Cheyennes walked off, Gray Thunder and a young warrior stopped near Bent. "My son, Smoke Wind," Gray Thunder said.

Bent nodded. "Pleased to meet you, boy," he said pleasantly. He looked at Gray Thunder. "You plannin' to leave here soon?"

Gray Thunder nodded. "Two suns." He paused, then announced, "We must go now."

Bent walked them to the fort entrance and saw them off. He went back to the counter and saw his powder flask. It had been about half full when he had last seen it. Now, however, it was full. He turned to look through the gate, tossing the small can in his hand, shaking his head. He smiled ever so slightly.

He and St. Vrain spent most of the next day taking stock and toting up all their ledgers. It was dark by the time they finished, working the last hour or so in torch-light. But Bent at last slapped the ledger book closed. "We done good, Ceran," he said. His voice reflected his tiredness. He hated doing the books and other clerklike duties, and it was always tiring for him.

"Oui, mon ami." The Frenchman seemed none the worse for wear.

The next morning, Bent stood outside the fort, lean-ing against one of the adobe walls, and watched as the Cheyennes rode slowly north. He was sad as the proces-sion dwindled in the distance. Gray Thunder had stopped by once more to say good-bye.

"I will miss the great chief Gray Thunder," Bent signed, but he thought, *I will miss your daughter Owl Woman.*

10

Though Bent was more than a little sad to see the Cheyennes go, there were more than enough things to be done to keep his mind and body occupied. St. Vrain was preparing to return to Taos again to check on things, so all the supervising of the work on the fort fell on Bent's narrow, though strong, shoulders.

In addition, some of the men he had trapped with or employed as trappers and hunters in the mountains began arriving at the fort. One of the first was Seth Walsh, one of Bent's best friends.

"Ho, Seth," Bent said, a smile brightening his dark face, "what brings you to these parts?"

"Come to see what all the fuss was about at Bent's Fort."

"It's Fort William," Bent said, not angry.

"Fort William my ass," Walsh said with a chuckle. "Ain't a one of the boys calls this place Fort William. It's known as Bent's Fort, and, by God, you best get used to it bein' called such."

Bent shook his head. He wasn't upset; he just wondered how St. Vrain would take it. "Well, that'll have to do," he allowed.

The work on the fort was just about finished when St. Vrain returned. He was, as usual, ebullient, especially when he saw Walsh, Honnicker, and some of the others. But he took a serious tone when he and Bent sat at Bent's fire. He would not even wait until they had eaten. He just poured a tin mug of coffee, took a sip, and then said, "Charles has run into some trouble."

Bent was instantly alert, nerve ends tingling. "What's wrong?" he asked, trying to keep the worry out of his voice.

"He's all right," St. Vrain said reassuringly. "He just had some horses and mules stolen."

Bent breathed a heavy sigh of relief and took a sip of coffee. He set the mug down and began filling his pipe. "How'd you find out?"

"He sent Red Water—one of those damn Delawares you brother is so fond of hiring—up to Taos. I sent Red Water and a couple of Mexicans out with enough horses for Charles to make it to Santa Fe."

Bent nodded. "Ain't the first time we've had animals took from us," Bent said nonchalantly. "Who took 'em?"

"Snakes." St. Vrain almost smiled.

"Down here?" Bent demanded. That worried him a little. They were far from the Shoshonis' normal haunts, though it was not unknown for them to visit the Comanches, their distant relatives. It was also a little surprising, since he and his brother had had little trouble with the Shoshonis, whom all the men called Snakes.

"*Oui,*" St. Vrain said flatly. "Charles"—St. Vrain could never bring himself to call the older Bent "Charlie"—"was taking a large 'erd of horses and mules from Taos to Santa Fe, when ze Snakes struck."

"Anyone hurt?"

"*Non.* Neit'er ze Snakes or our people."

"At least that's something," Bent grumbled. "How many head we lose?" It was always "we" among the partners. Most of what each did was a part of the company. If Charles Bent had lost horses and mules, then William Bent and Ceran St. Vrain also had lost livestock. It was, they all had agreed, though never vocally, the only way to run their enterprise.

"Just over two dozen." St. Vrain grimaced. He hated to take a loss of any kind, especially this way.

"That gonna hurt us much?" Bent asked. A loss always hurt, but there were degrees to it.

"Non," St. Vrain admitted. Then he grinned. "But your brother is hoppin' mad. *Très, très faché."* He almost laughed.

"I reckon he is," Bent said with a chuckle. Then he grew serious again. "But there's gonna be some sorry Snakes comes time for me to trade with 'em," he said tightly.

St. Vrain nodded. It was the only way to teach these savages anything, he reckoned. It often was unpleasant, but if not addressed, only meant more trouble in the future.

St. Vrain took several days to restock the fort with the goods and provisions he had brought up from Taos. He complimented Bent on the work that had been accomplished. "She is finish, *non?"* St. Vrain asked after a tour of the trading post.

"Almost," Bent said. "Got a little bit here and there yet to be done. I figure that when you get back to Taos, you can talk Charlie into comin' up here to open the place in style."

"Zat will be good," St. Vrain said.

"Hell, Ceran, it'll shine. And I want you to invite all the boys you can find. Kit, ol' Bill, any of the ol' boys we've seen starvin' times with. Bring 'em all up for a real doin's."

St. Vrain grinned, his teeth gleaming whitely against the black furriness of his beard. *"Bon,"* he said energetically. *"Très bon."*

St. Vrain left a few days later, heading back to Taos. Bent, watching the short Frenchman riding away, figured his partner must be getting plumb sick of all the traveling between the fort and Taos. But it had to be done, and St. Vrain was probably the best one for it. He turned and walked back into the fort, to his room. His was in the southeast corner on the ground floor, at a right angle to the kitchen and dining room. Quarters for St. Vrain were above, a sort of solitary blockhouse sitting on the second floor of the fort.

Several days after that, Bent was working in his small room when Seth Walsh called for entrance. Bent looked up, blinking at the bright sunlight that poured through the open door.

"Injuns comin', Cap'n," Walsh said, almost eagerly.

"Cheyennes?" he asked.

"Snakes."

Bent's eyes narrowed and he felt a quickening in his pulse.

"I ain't certain they're the ones," Walsh said softly. Like all the other mountaineers who were still camped outside the fort, Walsh knew what had happened to Charles Bent.

"Well, we'll sure as shit find out, won't we, Mr. Walsh." It was a statement, not a question, and Bent's tone was harsh.

"Yessir, Cap'n." The eagerness had crept into his voice again. "I expect we will."

"Call *levé* on the boys, and have 'em gather in the *placita*. But don't give nothin' away."

"Yessir." Walsh lumbered away.

Bent stood. With two swift steps he grabbed two pistols from their hooks on the wall. He quickly checked the weapons and stuck them into his belt. Then he walked outside, stopping under the portico to let his eyes adjust to the sunlight before actually going into the open *placita*.

Bent stepped into the sunshine of the dusty little courtyard. "Are they comin' in, Mr. Walsh?" he asked.

"Miller," Walsh called to one of the men watching over the wall, "those Snakes comin' in?"

"Nope." The wizened old man spit out tobacco juice, not caring that a large dollop of it splattered on his muslin shirt.

"What're they doin'?" Bent asked in some exasperation.

"Just settin' there." Miller was a crusty old man who had been trapping most of his fifty-eight years. He wasn't about to be pushed around by some young snot who was his boss in title, not in experience.

Bent shook his head at the old man's obstinacy. Then he climbed the ladder to the catwalk and looked out. "Mr. Walsh," he called down, without looking that way, "my spyglass, please."

When he had the long tube in hand, he peered through it. The Shoshonis were a quarter of a mile off, to the northwest.

"They the ones?" Walsh asked quietly, standing at Bent's elbow.

"Yep," Bent said angrily. "I can see that sorrel mare Charlie's so fond of. And dammit, the bastards are tauntin' us."

"Such doin's don't shine with this ol' chil'," Walsh growled.

"Nor with me, Mr. Walsh," Bent agreed.

"We ain't gonna let 'em get away with these doin's, are we?"

Bent looked up at Walsh. "You've been ridin' with me for what, five, maybe six years now?" Walsh nodded. "Have you ever knowed me to let the savages get away with such doin's?"

Walsh's grin spread. He was happy with the prospect of a battle looming. "No, sir," he said almost joyfully.

"Trouble is, it don't set right with me somehow."

"What don't?"

"Them just settin' out there makin' faces at us. Bastards seem to want us to come down on them."

"You ain't known any Injuns who set out a challenge for some ol' hosses like us?" Walsh asked sarcastically.

"Reckon I have at that, Seth," Bent said with a tight grin. He looked through the telescope again. "A couple of 'em's moved in a little closer," he said. Then he nodded curtly. "Mr. Walsh, I want you to go and have some of the men saddle their horses back in the corral. You'll see that my mare is ready."

"We going to chase those sons a bitches?"

"That we are, Mr. Walsh." He paused. "I don't know why they're settin' us a challenge, but I'm damn well certain I ain't gonna stand here and not do nothin' about it."

"Yessir." Walsh turned and nonchalantly clambered down to the *placita*. He walked among the gathered mountain men, speaking a few words to each. In ones and twos the men began to drift casually toward the "tunnel" under the second floor that led to the shops and the corral. Before long the men were returning to the *placita*, each towing a saddled horse behind him. The last one back was Seth Walsh, who held the reins to two horses—his own and Bent's.

Bent had spent the time watching the Shoshonis through the telescope. He was furious at their taunting. It was bad enough that they dared to attack his brother and steal his horses and mules, but if they were not held to account for this, they would be emboldened. This was, in a way, the first challenge to the fort and the company. If he did not make them pay, there was a good chance that Bent, St. Vrain & Company would lose this gamble, for the Cheyennes and Arapahos might not trade with men who could not protect themselves.

"All set, Cap'n," Walsh called. His voice was soft but carried well.

Bent closed the collapsing telescope and dropped it into his bag. He spun and went slowly down to the *placita*. He took the reins of his horse from Walsh and climbed into the saddle. He checked the pistols in his belt, and the other men, who were mounted by now, did the same.

"Let's get them sons of bitches, boys."

There was a soft, deep chorus of grunted assents.

{11}

Bent and his eleven men charged through the wide front gates of Fort William. By the time they had cleared the fort, they were going full out, quirting their horses hard. Some of the men howled and screeched.

The dozen Shoshonis sat there a few moments before whirling their horses and racing away. They herded stolen horses and mules—many of them taken from Bent, St. Vrain & Company—ahead of them.

The men urged their horses to a fraction more speed. The sturdy prairie mustangs were the same type the Shoshonis used, but they had an advantage in having been rested and well fed the past few days. Bent figured the Shoshoni ponies were tired from having been on the move.

Gradually the mountain men drew closer to the fleeing Shoshonis. Though they were slightly outnumbered, the Americans were not worried. Most considered the odds about even. Walsh and one or two others thought they had the upper hand.

One warrior, looking back over his shoulder, shouted something in his own language. Three other Shoshonis looked behind and also shouted. The four swung around in a small circle, stopped about three hundred yards from the racing Americans and jumped off their ponies. Holding their rope reins in one hand, they nocked their bows.

The charging mountain men spread out so they

would not be too bunched up, and thus more vulnerable. One fired his rifle. The crack was barely heard in the rush of the wind and the thump of hooves, nor were Jim Willoughby's annoyed oaths at his poor aim, but they all could see the ball kick up a puff of dust in front of the Indians.

The Shoshonis let loose a barrage of arrows. They hit none of Bent's force, which was still two hundred yards or so away. Bent's men fired their rifles. They didn't figure to hit any of the Shoshonis, seeing as how they were still far off, as well as not being able to aim much from the back of a galloping horse. Balls kicked up bits of dirt and grass.

The four warriors leaped up and onto their saddleless ponies. Firing a couple more arrows each, they whirled and sped off, looking back over their shoulders at times. They began to pull away from Bent's force, and then stopped again. They fired several more arrows, three of which hit home. Willoughby tumbled off his horse and bounced in the dirt, snapping off the arrow shaft that stuck out of his left thigh.

Bent glanced back and saw Willoughby getting up. The trapper was shaking a gnarly fist at the Shoshonis. Bent grinned and looked ahead.

Suddenly he went flying buttocks over teacups. In the second or so before landing, he thought he saw several arrows buried in his horse's chest. Then he hit the ground hard. As he was bouncing and flopping, he hoped no one else's horse would run over him.

Finally he came to a halt, and he rose gingerly, testing to see if anything was broken. Everything seemed to work right, except one hand. He looked at it and saw that the middle and ring fingers of his left hand were canted at an odd angle. He figured they were broken, but he wasn't about to let that bother him now. What did slow him some was a wrenched knee, and his chest felt like it had been scraped raw.

He turned to look toward the Shoshonis. They had

disappeared over a grassy ridge, with the mountain men in close pursuit. Bent moved forward quickly, favoring the right knee. A stolen pony was standing nervously not far away, and Bent headed toward it. The horse was having none of it, though. For every step Bent took in its direction, the horse moved back a little. "Damn stupid beast," Bent snarled. He shrugged and moved on as quickly as he could, wanting to get in on the action.

As he hobbled along, though, something ate at him, a small, nagging thought telling him that something was wrong. He wasn't entirely sure what, but it was tied to the Shoshonis taunting the men in the fort. Why? It made no sense for them to be trying to draw the men out of the fort. It was almost as if . . .

"Jesus," Bent muttered. He ran as fast as his wrenched knee would permit. Up ahead he saw his men top another ridge several hundred yards away. Two of the men vanished over the far side, but the others stopped short as they reached the crest.

Bent lost sight of his men as he limped up a knoll. He stopped at the top, out of breath. His knee was giving him more than a little pain, and his broken fingers throbbed.

Bent saw his men whirl and begin racing back toward him. Moments later more than three dozen Shoshonis roared up over the grassy ridge, charging hellbent after the mountain men.

Bent brought his rifle up to his shoulder, trying to protect his broken fingers. As soon as his men were heading up the ridge on which he was standing, Bent fired over their heads. One of the galloping Shoshonis fell off his horse.

The mountain men jammed to a hard stop around Bent, who was almost finished reloading. As his men slid out of their saddles, Bent fired again. A pony went down, throwing its rider as the animal skidded along on its chest for some yards before coming to a stop.

As Bent reloaded again, half his men fired. The other half waited a few moments before laying down a fusillade of their own. Several Shoshonis went down, bouncing on the hard-packed earth.

Old man Miller fell, an arrow sticking entirely through his neck. The first group of men fired again at Bent's hurried order. Two more Indians and another pony died, and the others pulled up and swept to their own flanks before racing back toward the safety of the other knoll.

"How do, Cap'n?" Walsh said, a humorless grin splitting his mustache and beard.

"Passable. Couple of busted-up fingers and a stove-up knee is all," Bent said. He still stood, keeping an eye out for the Indians. "Looks like we're in a tight spot here, Seth," Bent commented wryly.

"Hell, we been in a lot tighter doin's than these," Walsh said with a grin. "You mind the time a couple years back you and me and a bunch of ol' boys had them doin's with the Gros Ventres?"

"Hell'll be turned cold as a virgin's thighs before I'd forget that goddamn *fandango*," Bent said tightly. "We sure as hell made 'em come that day, didn't we?"

"Sure did." Seth Walsh was always happy when he was in the midst of a battle. Then again, Walsh was generally happy wherever he was, whatever he was doing.

"Wagh!" Willoughby said. He had arrived just after Bent had. "I still got me some hair was raised against them coons."

"Me too," added a long, scrawny old fellow named Enoch Eubanks.

"None of that hair you all raised so long ago is gonna help you save your asses now, boys," Bent said without rancor.

"Hell," Willoughby snapped. "We showed them a thing or two."

"Buffalo shit," Bent said harshly. "Them bastards suckered us clean as you please."

"You figured that out, huh?" Walsh said with some annoyance. He hated being made a fool of.

Bent nodded. "How many of 'em are there?"

"Must've been forty of 'em come after us this time here, plus there was still some back down in that gully watchin' all the horses and stolen plunder." He paused. "Hernandez and Finnegan was first over that goddamn ridge," he added solemnly. "They didn't make it back."

"We're in some deep shit here, boys," Bent said.

"Up to the eyes," Walsh added.

"What do ye suggest, Cap'n?" Art Honnicker asked.

Bent shrugged. "It rubs my nuts the wrong way to be made to run by any goddamn Injuns," he said angrily. "But I reckon the best thing we can do is to get back to the fort as soon's we can manage."

"That might be a spell," Walsh said, pointing.

Everyone looked. The Shoshonis were coming hard, quirting their horses for all they were worth.

"Take 'em down if you can, boys!" Bent shouted.

Rifles roared, followed by pistols. Shoshonis and horses fell, and a thick cloud of powder smoke covered Bent and his men. When the smoke drifted away, the men could see the Indians scampering back to the safety of the far ridge.

It also revealed that Caleb Salton was dead, as were three of the whites' horses. The men looked angry as they stood or knelt on the grass, reloading or wiping down their weapons.

"What's your pleasure, Cap'n?" Walsh asked quietly.

"Same as it was before."

"We're short on horses now, Cap'n, even with Miller and Salton gone under. We try doublin' up on our horses, and them Shoshonis'll catch us easy."

Bent stood there, thinking. "Well," he finally said, "we can't stand here forever. Sooner or later those bastards're gonna throw everything they got at us. And most likely some of 'em'll circle 'round our backs. They do that, and the whole damn bunch of us'll be gone beaver.''

He scratched at the stubble on his narrow chin as he thought some more. ''This ain't gonna be easy for none of us, but I reckon those boys still got horses ought to ride out.''

''And us others?'' Eubanks asked. He was one who had lost a horse.

''I figure to lay a trap for them. Hell, they done it to us, this chil' figures we can give 'em the same in return.''

''What's your plan, Cap'n?'' Honnicker asked.

''We slip down the ridge here on our bellies, spreadin' out some.'' He paused and spit some of the dust out of his mouth. ''When them boys come over that ridge there, we'll give 'em a nice little surprise.''

''It don't shine with this ol' hoss to go slinkin' about like a goddamn serpent,'' Eubanks said. His comment drew a small growl of agreement.

''Ain't a none of us wants to do that,'' Bent said evenly. ''But once we send 'em packin', we can crawl to safety before makin' our way back to the fort as best we can.'' He knew that none of the ones who stayed behind would live, but he did not want to announce that to his men.

''Buffler shit,'' Eubanks said, bringing forth another chorus of assent. ''I ain't crawlin' around on my meatbag for nobody.''

''Me neither,'' Willoughby snapped. ''I'd as soon bite the ass of a buffler bull as crawl away from a bunch of goddamn Injuns.''

All the men but Bent murmured in wholehearted agreement.

Bent grinned tightly, proud of his men. Then he nodded, mind made up. ''First off, we got to get off this ridge. Them Snakes ain't fools, and I expect they'll be comin' at us a different way, seein' as how comin' straight at us ain't done 'em no good. We can ride double for that.'' He paused. ''Luis—you and Art take the bodies with you. Quickly.''

The two nodded. Working together, they none-too-gently tossed the bodies of Miller and Salton across their saddles and then climbed on behind the corpses. The others who had horses mounted up. Each held out a hand to give a comrade a hand up, though not all were necessary. Bent figured his wrenched knee would give him a little trouble, but big Seth Walsh pulled him easily up behind him.

''Where away, Cap'n?'' Walsh asked.

''See that knoll down yonder to the southwest? There.''

In minutes they were on the far side of the new ridge. Honnicker headed to the bottom of the gully away from where the Indians had been. Everybody else stayed below the rim of the ridge, though Eubanks lay on the top of the mound, watching for the Shoshonis.

''I saw a couple of Snake ponies gone off loose over yonder,'' Bent said, pointing. ''Mr. Walsh, take one of the boys and see if you can round 'em up. If our medicine ain't all gone to shit, we might be able to make it back to the fort without losin' any more men.'' He paused as he heard shouts and war cries. He smiled. ''Outwitted them bastards—for now,'' he muttered. Swinging back to Walsh, he said urgently, ''Hurry.''

In the short time between Walsh and Honnicker leaving and returning, the other men reloaded and then waited, sweating under the hot sun. Eubanks still lay on the top of the ridge, watching for the Shoshonis. Minutes later he called, ''Them Snakes're comin'.''

''Chargin'?'' Bent called up.

''Nope. Slow, like they're tryin' to figure where we've got off to.''

''All right, boys, up the hill,'' Bent said. He began hobbling up the grassy little hill, knee getting worse.

And his hand throbbed as his blood thumped hard in his veins.

"There ain't near as many of 'em as there was before," Willoughby said. "I tol' y'all we did 'em some damage."

Bent surveyed the group of warriors coming toward them, moving slowly. He knew he and his men had killed several Indians, but not twenty or so. Yet there were fewer than two dozen Shoshonis out there. From where he lay, he called urgently, "Cleve, Jim, each of you go watch our flanks. One to a side."

In less than five minutes gunfire broke out on their western flank. At the same time, the Shoshonis out front charged.

Gunfire popped and arrows flew. The puffs of powder smoke mingled with dust. Sweat trickled into men's eyes, blurring vision. The shouted curses of men and the whinnying of horses competed for loudness.

Walsh and Honnicker suddenly appeared in the midst of the inferno of heat, noise, and death. "Time to go, Cap'n," Walsh roared.

The sudden appearance of the two men coming from behind had startled the Shoshonis. The warriors on the southwest flank raced up and over the hill toward their companions out in front of the mountain men. The resulting confusion sent the Shoshonis running. They stopped just out of range of the white men's rifles to regroup.

In the brief peace, Bent's men mounted up. They paused just long enough to make sure the bodies of Willoughby and Cleve Townsend, who had been killed in the assault on the flank, were on horses.

Then they turned tail and ran, whipping their horses. Behind them they could hear the charging Shoshonis. They rode hellbent straight into the fort. The Mexican workers, having heard the noise and seen what was happening, had made it into the fort just before the riders. The big, double oak doors were slammed and locked.

The Shoshonis stopped three hundred yards away or so and were once again shouting taunts.

Bent was livid. "Son of a bitch bastards," he bellowed, pacing. Finally he stopped. "Seth!" he bellowed. "Grab that goddamn two-pounder. He headed up to the second floor, which was almost finished.

Walsh followed him and set the small cannon—with the stump on which it rested—down. Luis Saltillo followed with a burning twig. "Try this on for size, you sons a bitches," Bent muttered as he put the twig to the touch hole. Moments later the cannon roared.

Bent was not sure if any of the Shoshonis were actually hit, but they skedaddled straight off. Still, the loss of six men because of his rashness would haunt Bent for a long time. Combined with the remorse for killing the two Cheyennes several years ago, Bent had a deep well of guilt eating at his insides.

12

"Raise 'er up, Mr. Walsh," William Bent said while holding in check the emotion that flooded through him.

Twenty yards across the rippling prairie and ten or twelve feet above it, Seth Walsh tugged on ropes, and an American flag soon was fluttering above the small belfry atop the blockhouse over the entryway.

"Sure is some sight, ain't it?" Charles Bent said quietly, though there could be no mistaking the pleasure in his voice.

"Plumb shines to this chil's eyes," his brother said gruffly.

"Let's go on inside and start the doin's," Charles said. He sounded eager. It was rare that he felt a rush of excitement these days. He usually considered himself a little old, as well as too much of a businessman now for such displays. Still, he thought it was good to get back to the way things used to be, when he was wilder.

The three partners had dressed for the occasion in bleached tan buckskins covered with fringe, beads, and porcupine quills. They headed toward the trading post. The fort was finally finished, and the partners, along with a passel of their friends, were here to celebrate the official opening of Fort William—the name used by no one but the partners.

The Cheyennes and Arapahos had come out in force

too. Their camps spread for miles up and down the Arkansas. Gray Thunder's camp was nearest the fort, the place of honor.

It had been, William thought as he walked toward the gaping maw of the fort, one hell of a year: the flood of Mexican workers, thousands and thousands of adobe bricks drying in the sun, the smallpox epidemic, rains slowing the work, the fight with the Shoshonis, two smaller engagements with Comanches.

That was all behind him now, though. The future stretched out as far as one could see across the plains. He walked through the portal and into the fort. To his immediate left, its outer wall forming one side of the entryway "tunnel," was the Indian trade room. At a right angle to it were the council room and the main trade room. He looked at all three rooms, making sure the doors were closed and locked. That was all they would need—a bunch of drunken mountain men rooting through them. Or worse, having some thieving Cheyennes roaming around loose in the trade rooms. He had no illusions about his Cheyenne friends. They were like any other Indians, as far as theft went. They would take anything they could lay their hands on, and then, with a straight face tell you it was your fault for not taking care of your property. To them it was a game.

Helping keep people from getting to the trade room —after all, a pistol shot would make quick work of the lock—were tables laden with food. Whiskey was kept out of sight in a room at the southwest corner of the *placita*. The Bents didn't care how much their white friends drank, but they were dead set against letting the Indians have any.

In fact, Bent, St. Vrain & Company did not want to use whiskey in their trade with the Indians. All three partners were adamant about that. They had seen far too many instances of unscrupulous traders handing out rotgut whiskey to the Indians with a free hand.

Once the warriors were staggering drunk, they would do just about anything to get more whiskey. The traders then would be able to buy beaver plews, buffalo robes, and other hides for practically nothing. Trading in such a way disgusted the partners, who believed in paying a fair price for plews. Only after the trading was done would they perhaps bring out the Taos Lightning and hand it around.

Somebody suddenly shoved a tin cup into William's hands. He nodded thanks, not even sure who it was. Then he sipped. "Damn, that shines with this ol' hoss."

His brother and St. Vrain grinned at him. They too had mugs brimming with alcohol. All three looked up at the sound of a high-pitched whoop. A tall, cadaverous buckskin-clad man yelled again, and then began scratching on a fiddle once he had everyone's attention.

A young, gaudily dressed Mexican joined in with a guitar, and another mountaineer piped up with a tin whistle. A few of the men began dancing, pairing off with each other since none of the Indian women were around, other than a couple wives of some mountain men.

William wandered around the fort greeting men, stopping to chat a moment, sipping from the cup of whiskey. He finally piled a tin plate high with buffalo tongue, sourdough bread, and prairie turnips.

Just about the time Bent was finished eating, he saw some Cheyennes venturing into the fort. They were unafraid, though cautious, and stopped just inside the "tunnel" past the double-wide gates.

Bent got up and hurried toward them. "Welcome, Gray Thunder," he said in Cheyenne. Bent had learned much of the Cheyenne language in the past year or so, most of it from Gray Thunder himself.

The Cheyenne leader nodded and solemnly returned the greeting. But his eyes were on the festivities.

He was not quite sure what was going on here, but it certainly intrigued him.

"Come in, Gray Thunder," Bent said, grinning. He switched to English, some of which he had taught Gray Thunder in payment for having the old leader teach him Cheyenne. "These're shinin' doin's, goddamn if they ain't."

The Indians moved forward a little, proud of their finery. The men wore soft, tanned buckskin leggings and breechcloths of buckskin or blanket. Their long war shirts were decorated with shells, tin, painted porcupine quills, beads—and scalps. Their hair was greased and braided, the braids wrapped in otter fur and hanging down on their chests.

The women were no less fancified. Their creamy buckskin dresses were decorated with geometrical shapes of beads, quills, shells, and feathers. The bottom hems and the yokes were festooned with small tin cones that clacked softly. Their hair was loose, flowing in black cascades onto their shoulders, the parts painted with vermilion.

The whites inside the fort had gradually slowed in their dancing as more and more became aware of the Indians. They looked on with eager interest in their eyes. It wasn't that they had never seen an Indian before; it was more the presence of the women.

"Come on, boys," someone yelled, "let's have some music."

The impromptu band started another reel, and mountain men began moving toward the small, tight-knit knot of excited Cheyenne and Arapaho women. Within minutes the women, old and young, were being whirled around the *placita* by often clod-footed mountain men. All the while, other men tried to muscle their way into the women's embraces.

Bent talked with Gray Thunder and several other warriors for a little before drifting off, leaving the Cheyennes on their own. He was not worried. He had told Gray Thunder earlier in the day that only so many warriors could be inside the fort at any one time. With the number of mountain men inside, and by keeping alcohol out of the Indians' sight, Bent figured there would be no trouble.

Bent walked to the room that housed the fort's cistern, and he dipped up another cup of whiskey. He sipped appreciatively before stepping outside. Dark was coming fast, and workers were moving around the fort lighting torches and lanterns. Bent set his cup on a bench. He pulled out his pipe and slowly stuffed it with tobacco. Just as he finished that, a worker came up with the candle with which he was lighting the torches and lanterns. Bent grabbed it and lit his pipe.

He picked up his cup and then leaned back against a thick wood post that held the balcony up. He alternated between comforting puffs of the strong, harsh tobacco and sips from the equally strong and harsh liquor. He watched as couples twirled around the *placita*, kicking up a godawful amount of dust. It was some sight watching the clumsy, bearish mountain men doing something more akin to a war dance than a minuet with the Cheyenne and Arapaho women.

Suddenly there were shouts that the revelry couldn't quite drown out. The music petered out until it was no more. Men stopped dancing and looked for the source of the acrimonious voices.

"Shit," Bent muttered. He pushed away from the wall.

Bent shoved his way through the milling horde of men. Being shorter than many of them, he could not see what was happening, but he heard the increasing volume of angry voices.

"C'mon there, goddamn it, out of my way," Bent roared. The authority in his voice made a path between the bodies. He wondered, though, as he hurried forward, where Charles and St. Vrain were.

Finally Bent was through the forest of men and in a

small clearing near the main trade room. White men and red stood in a circle around two small knots of men. A group of whites held a mountain man in their grasp. A few feet away a group of Cheyennes held a warrior in a tight grasp. The two men being held struggled and shouted. Charles and St. Vrain stood between the two groups, each facing one.

"Shut up, goddamn it!" William Bent roared. "All of you!"

"That's a goddamn 'nough," he bellowed, when the men stopped fighting and shouting. "That's better." He looked from one group to the other. "Now, what the hell is all this ruckus about?" he demanded.

No one answered, and Bent walked up to the mountain man who was being held. "Well, Ollie?"

Ollie Clark glared at him. Clark was tall and slim except for a fairly new potbelly. His skin was leathery and crinkled from a lifetime in the harsh sun and wind-whipped snows of the mountains. He wore a plain osnaburg shirt that was splattered by grease drippings and spilled whiskey. His bear-fur hat with the leather brim was askew on his head.

"Let me go, goddamn sons a bitches," Clark growled at Seth Walsh and Tom Fitzpatrick, the only two who still had a good grip on him. They ignored him.

"Answer Mr. Bent, Ollie," Walsh suggested, twisting Clark's left arm up around his back.

"Goddamn you, Walsh," Clark snapped, "I'll have your hair hanging from my lodgepole, you son of a bitch."

"You don't answer Mr. Bent's question, you ignorant piece of shit, I'll tear your arm off and beat you to death with it."

"You don't scare me, Walsh, you son of a bitch. And I don't have to answer no goddamn questions. This's my own goddamn affair."

Bent's eyes snapped with the fires of rage. He

stepped up and glared up at Clark. "This is my god-damn fort," he said in a low voice full of threat and warning, "and what goes on in it is my concern. Now," he added after a moment, "what the hell's goin' on here?"

"Ask that son of a bitch," Clark snarled, jerking his pointed, jutting chin toward the Cheyenne.

Bent stared at Clark a few more moments, letting Clark feel the heat of his anger. Then he spun and went to where the Cheyenne was being held. Bent took note that the one being held was a young, headstrong warrior named Iron Shield.

As Bent neared the Indian, the smell of whiskey grew quite strong. He had smelled it before, but figured it was either himself or Clark. Looking at Iron Shield, he knew that the Cheyenne was drunk.

"Where'd you get the firewater?" Bent asked, thrusting his anger-wrinkled face within inches of the warrior's.

Iron Shield burped, loudly, and a few men tittered. Bent felt a chuckle rising up, but he battled it back down. Bent backed off a step and looked at Gray Thunder, who was tight-lipped in anger. "Please ask Iron Shield where he got the firewater, Chief," Bent said in Cheyenne.

The old warrior did so. When Iron Shield was not very responsive, Gray Thunder snapped out clipped words in his own language. His face displayed the anger and disgust he felt.

Iron Shield laughed and drunkenly said something in Cheyenne.

Bent couldn't understand the words, but he suddenly realized where Iron Shield had gotten the whiskey. He whirled and walked to Clark. "You give him whiskey, you dumb bastard?" he asked harshly.

"And what if I did?" Clark responded arrogantly.

"You were told to keep the whiskey away from Indians, dammit."

"Hell, one little drink ain't gonna hurt 'em none," Clark said. His words were slurred only a little.

"You just give him a taste out of the goodness of your stinkin' goddamn heart?" Bent demanded.

"Hell no," Clark boasted. "This ol' hoss ain't that goddamn stupid." He chuckled a little, hoping it might lull Walsh and Fitzpatrick enough to let his arms go. Then he'd raise hair sure as hell. The two guards did not ease their grip even a fraction.

"What'd he give you for it?" Bent asked, still fighting his temper.

"Four beaver plews a cup." He sounded proud of it all.

"And how many goddamn cups did he get?"

Clark shrugged.

"How many plews you take?"

"Twenty," Clark said proudly. "Ol' hoss over there had him some thirst, I tell ye. Thought he had two hollow legs."

"Why do you two idiots have your faces painted black against each other?" Bent asked calmly. He knew damn well that Clark was trying to fool with him, and he was not about to join the game.

Clark grinned crookedly. "He wanted another snort, and I could see he was some sheets to the wind. So," Clark began to laugh, low and wobbly, "I upped the price to five plews."

"You're even more goddamn stupid than I thought, Clark," Bent said, amazed at Clark's foolishness. He turned back to the Cheyennes.

"You said no whiskey," Gray Thunder said in accusatory tone.

"I know," Bent replied with regret. He felt bad about all this, since it had been his word that had been broken. "But he'll be punished," he added, jerking a thumb over his shoulder toward Clark.

"How?"

"Floggin'," Bent answered matter-of-factly.

Gray Thunder nodded, but from behind Bent, Clark roared, "You ain't floggin' me, you little son of a bitch. You try floggin' me, you little bastard, and I'll cut your goddamn liver out and feed it to ye."

Bent ignored him. "Come back at first light, Gray Thunder."

Gray Thunder didn't look happy about it, but he accepted it—for now. He and William Bent had spent much time together, and had come to trust each other. This would be a good time, Gray Thunder reasoned, to see how strong Bent's words were. He nodded. With his people in tow, he turned and walked majestically toward the gate.

The mountain men cleared a path for the Indians. Most regretted seeing the Cheyennes and Arapahos leave, since the women were leaving too. Many was the chil' here who had set aside a little foofaraw with which to buy some robe time with one of the Indian women.

Bent watched the procession leaving, and he could see the disappointment and even anger on the men's faces. "You boys're free to start up the *fandango* again," he shouted.

"Such doin's don't shine with this chil'," one of the men roared back. "Not when them women's waltzed out on us like they done."

There was a general round of agreement. Bent sympathized. "These could've been some shinin' doin's here if yonder asshole hadn't of pulled the shit he did. You got him to lay these troubles on."

Clark gulped a little. It was one thing to get drunk enough to feel the blood racing through your brains, to take in a few plews, to banter with the fort's partisan. It was entirely another to have forty or fifty hard-ass mountaineers blacken their faces against you.

"It's up to you boys if you want to go back to havin' a spree. This chil's gonna get some robe time."

{13}

A large contingent of Cheyennes and Arapahos was outside the fort's huge oak doors in the morning. They stood waiting patiently.

William Bent came out of his small room and looked up at the sun, checking its new glory against the large pocket watch he often carried. He looked up at the guard standing near the guardhouse.

"There's a heap of Injuns out there, Cap'n," the guard called.

"They look troublesome, Mr. Collier?"

"No, Cap'n," Lee Collier said. "They're just standin' there quiet."

"How many are there?"

"Forty, fifty maybe."

Bent nodded. He looked around the *placita*. A few drunken men were still sleeping on the dusty ground. Most of the others were coming out of the small rooms on the second floor along the west wall. Some looked terribly hungover. Charles Bent and St. Vrain strolled up, both in their city finery. William was clad in his well-used buckskins.

"You think I'm doin' right, Charlie?" William asked.

His brother nodded.

"Either of you want to take charge?" William asked.

Both partners shook their heads. "Zis is your fort," St. Vrain said without enmity. He was stating a fact, no more, no less. "You must do what you t'ink is right."

William nodded. He had figured as much, but he wanted to make sure his partners didn't think he was trying to run them, too.

"We'll be watchin' from up there by Ceran's room," Charles said, pointing toward the walkway above. St. Vrain had a small room up there, away from the others.

William nodded again. "Open the gates," he ordered. He turned. "Fetch the prisoner, Mr. Walsh. Take another man with you, if you see the need."

"He won't be no trouble, Cap'n," Walsh said matter-of-factly.

Bent nodded and turned to watch as the Indians filed into the *placita*. He noted that there were no women in the entourage. Iron Shield was there, looking thoroughly miserable.

"Welcome, Gray Thunder," Bent said in grand style.

Gray Thunder nodded once, curtly.

Walsh arrived with the prisoner. Bent pointed to a post. "Chain him there, Mr. Walsh."

"Yessir, Cap'n," Walsh said. He sounded almost gleeful.

"How many lashes you gonna give 'im, Cap'n?" one of the men standing on the second floor shouted.

"Twenty-five," Bent said after a moment's thought.

"Hell, that ain't nowhere near enough," another man growled. "That sumbitch pissed on our *fandango* last night."

Bent glanced around at the men assembled in the *placita* and on the walkway above. They were all grumbling in agreement with whoever had spoken. He stood there, running a hand across his bony chin, thinking. Then he finally nodded. "Fifty, then," he said.

He was surprised when the men seemed unplacated. A slow smile grew across his lips. "Any of you boys want to raise hair on this son of a bitch?" That brought a rousing round of agreement.

Bent nodded again, his mind made up. "The gantlet," he said loudly enough for all to hear.

The men whooped and hollered. Some jumped from the second floor walkway; others charged down the stairs, jostling each other in their haste. They formed two ragged lines across the *placita* from near the gate to the workrooms. Some slapped pieces of wood against their hands, others held a pistol or quirt. A few hauled out stone war clubs.

Things began to quiet down, though the feeling of expectation was almost palpable. "How many times ye gonna run him?" Honnicker asked.

"I reckon twice'll be about right—once up and once back." He turned toward Walsh and nodded.

Walsh had chained Clark to the post. With the prospect of a gantlet, he did not mind the extra work of unchaining Clark again. He soon had Clark loosened, and held him tight by the shirt collar, facing the lonely alleyway of violence. The men looked even more eager.

Suddenly Gray Thunder appeared at the other end of the line. Bent was ready to give Clark the word to go, but he wondered why everyone was looking the other way. Turning, he saw Gray Thunder. He walked down the gantlet and stopped in front of the Cheyenne.

"I am ashamed of Iron Shield," Gray Thunder said in his quavering voice. "He has brought shame to all the People."

Bent translated for those who couldn't follow the Cheyenne.

"He too will run the gantlet."

Bent nodded, as did most of the other white men. They thought it a fair punishment. "So be it," Bent said evenly.

Cheyenne and Arapaho warriors wormed their way into the two lines of white men, most of whom thought it only right that the warriors join in doling out the punishment. Two warriors escorted a sullen, sulking, hungover Iron Shield to the other end of the line. There they waited with him just behind Walsh and Clark.

Bent looked up and down the twin lines of men. Some of the men looked joyful, others just eager. Bent nodded.

Walsh shoved Clark's back, sending him staggering forward.

Men whooped and hollered as they hit, kicked, punched, whacked, and chopped at Clark. He mostly kept silent, only occasionally hissing or emitting an involuntary grunt. He fell twice, but pushed up and onward immediately. It seemed to him that the two lines of men went on to infinity. Finally he made it past the last men and sank down to the ground at Bent's feet. He was covered with blood from hair to waist and his shirt was in tatters. He breathed hard, trying to ignore the pain.

"Gray Thunder," Bent said.

The chief nodded. He looked up and waved his hand. The two warriors shoved Iron Shield, and he went down the gantlet. The young warrior managed to get through the line without falling, but he was still a mass of blood and bruises when he stopped, standing in front of Gray Thunder. He was breathing hard, but showed no signs of the pain he must have been feeling. Bent and all the rest of the men respected that.

"All right, Mr. Clark," Bent said firmly, but without rancor.

Clark looked up at him, hate covering up what pain he felt. He pushed himself to his feet and squared his shoulders. He figured he had at least two cracked ribs and a broken finger. He also figured that a couple of the cuts he had received would need stitching. But he'd be damned if he would let Bent or any of the others see him cringing.

Clark took a deep breath and almost fainted from the pain in his ribs. It took several moments to recover. Then he charged forward, weaving from side to side, slamming into anyone he could, trying to knock them down. He succeeded in a few cases. Between that and his frantic weaving, he was hit fewer times than he had been the first time.

No one was more surprised than Clark when he ran into Walsh's solid frame. He shook his head, as if waking.

Walsh gave him a jug, but said nothing.

Clark nodded and took the jug. His hands shook some as he tilted the jug up, but the harsh whiskey settled him some.

Clark heard a whoop and turned, spilling some of the whiskey. The sudden turn sent shafts of fire up his legs and back, but he ignored them as he watched Iron Shield charging down the lane of human flesh.

Then Iron Shield was standing by Walsh and Clark. He was as bloody and bruised as Clark was, but he seemed less affected by it.

The men moved off in small groups, most of the whites heading toward the kitchen, where Charlotte Green—one of Charles Bent's two slaves—had pots of coffee, plates of buffalo meat, flapjacks, hominy, corn bread, and more. The Indians left the fort, heading for their camps.

Just before the "tunnel," Gray Thunder turned back and looked at William Bent. He nodded once and smiled a little. Bent returned it.

Within a few days most of the mountain men had drifted off, moving on to various locations. Even Ollie Clark had pushed on, after having taken the time to get over the worst of his injuries. As Clark gingerly loaded his mule with supplies, William Bent strolled up. Clark, who was trying hard not to show the intense pain he encountered with every movement, refused to look at him for a while.

Bent, never the most patient of men, would not be ignored. "You come back to this fort, Ollie, you best come ready to live by my rules."

"Don't figure to be comin' back here," Clark grunted grudgingly.

"Don't make me no never mind you don't." Bent spit tobacco juice. "But if you do, you best heed my warnin'."

"Piss off, you snake-fuckin' son of a bitch," Clark rasped. He was of no mood to listen to someone preaching good behavior at him.

"Was I you," Bent said slowly, trying to keep a cap on his anger, "I'd not come back to these parts at all." He spit again. "The Cheyennes ain't likely to see you in a kind light, ol' hoss."

"I ain't afeared of no fuckin' Cheyennes. Nor no goddamn Comanches or Arapahos or any other fuckin' Injuns."

"Suit yourself," Bent said stiffly. He was of half a mind to put a pistol ball into the infuriating Ollie Clark. He drew in a breath and then let it slide on out. "But be mindful, boy, that if you ever cut my trail again, I'll peel your goddamn hide."

"Shit, you and what fuckin' army?"

"I won't need no army, hoss." Bent strolled under the portico and leaned against the wall, keeping an eye on Clark. He wouldn't put it past the man to try and steal something just to annoy him.

Clark didn't, though, and within ten minutes he was riding out, his pack mule behind him.

Later that day, Charles Bent and St. Vrain left. Bent headed east toward Missouri in the company of half a dozen men. St. Vrain rode for Taos in the company of several mountain men.

The Cheyennes and Arapahos were for the most part gone too. A few lodges remained, but that was about all. They were the lodges of men who had crossed the Arkansas and headed south to raid the Comanches. The Indians, led by a middle-aged warrior named Yellow Wolf, figured their families would be safe here in the shadow of the brooding mud castle. Bent didn't mind that they were there, as long as they didn't cause trouble, which he thought unlikely. Winter Hawk and Black Feather were among the warriors who rode with Yellow Wolf.

In the past couple of years, Bent had come to know the Cheyennes pretty well. They were a tall, proud, handsome people, expert horsemen, fierce warriors. The Cheyenne women were comely and well-versed in womanly arts, both inside the lodge and outside. These days, Bent spent a considerable amount of time in Cheyenne villages, trading or visiting.

After breaking his fast, Bent had a horse saddled and he rode out with Seth Walsh, who had a pack mule trailing behind. They rode through the remnants of the Cheyenne village, making sure everything was well. Then they cut a little east, looking for buffalo.

They found a small herd several miles out. With a whoop and a holler, they gave their horses free rein. The animals raced after the buffalo. Bent always enjoyed running buffalo like this. It represented a freedom the likes of which were unequaled.

Walsh shot two buffalo, Bent only one. As the two were carving out chunks of meat, Bent said, "Damn, I sure miss that ol' pinto them Shoshonis killed in that little ruckus we had there a couple months ago. That mare plumb shined as a buffler pony."

"Reckon you'll need to train you another," Walsh said as he threw the buffalo's tongue onto a piece of hide he had peeled off the animal.

"Well it sure as shit ain't gonna be this goddamn bag of bones." He pointed his bloody knife at his horse.

"Hell, with all them horses you got, you mean to say you can't find a one of 'em worth makin' a buffalo pony?" Walsh chuckled.

"Shit," Bent growled in mock anger. They finished their bloody work and rode slowly back to the fort.

Three days later a shout from one of the guards brought Bent out of the trade room, where he had been inventorying his stock. He walked outside into the harsh, hot sunlight and looked toward the guard.

"Cheyennes're comin', Cap'n."

"From the south?"

"Yep."

"It's Yellow Wolf's war party, then. They bein' chased?"

"Doesn't appear so. There's a heap of dust, but I expect they've got theyselves a passel of horses took from the damn Comanches."

Bent nodded. He went back in the trade room and handed his paperwork to his clerk, Ramsay Mac-Gregor, and then went back outside. He climbed up to the walkway and pulled his telescope from his pocket. He surveyed the scene across the river. "Jesus," he breathed, "looks like they cleaned the Comanches out of horses."

The Cheyennes worked across the wide, swift Arkansas and turned their stolen herd toward the village. Seeing that, Bent headed back to his work. He hated doing it, but it had to be done. Still, he took any excuse to get out of the burdensome work.

Soon after, Winter Hawk, Black Feather, and Rain Beating Down came into the fort. They strutted around the *placita*, boasting in Cheyenne and in mangled English about their exploits.

Bent thought it was a great excuse to go chat with the Cheyennes. He headed outside. The Cheyennes spotted him, and with chests puffed out in pride, they walked toward him. Bent kept a straight face as the four men sat in the dust. He handed each of them a twist of tobacco. He reached into his belt pouch, pulled out some more tobacco, shoved some into his mouth and chewed.

"Seems you boys made 'em come on these raids." As usual, the men spoke in signs, English, Spanish, and Cheyenne.

"We are mighty warriors," Winter Hawk exclaimed.

Bent was not sure if the man was serious or boasting. He chuckled. "Hell, most likely you stole 'em from some wrinkled ol' squaws."

"We took them from many warriors!" Winter Hawk insisted.

"Probably all nags couldn't even pull a dog travois anymore," Bent said, battling back a grin. Winter Hawk was so sincere in his convictions that he could not see Bent was joshing him.

"They are good horses. Mules too."

"You're full of buffler shit." He grinned.

Black Feather and Rain Beating Down's eyes twinkled. They could see that Bent was not serious.

But Winter Hawk could not. He grew angry. "I will show you," he said roughly, leaping up. "You will see that the horses and mules I took were the best. Even better than the ones Yellow Wolf took." He puffed out his chest. "So great a warrior am I, that I will lead the next raid on the Comanches." He whirled and strode off, the ends of his breechcloth flapping with his long strides.

Bent finally released his chuckles, and his two companions joined in. They joked about Winter Hawk's sensitivity and his lack of maturity. Dick Green—Charlotte's husband and also Charles Bent's slave—brought three mugs of coffee, those for the Cheyennes thick with sugar.

They had finished that and were chatting casually when Winter Hawk returned. He walked through the fort's doors. In each hand he had a horsehair rope. One was attached to a mousy-gray mule; the other was looped around the neck of a beautiful spotted stallion.

Winter Hawk stopped where Bent, Black Feather, and Rain Beating Down sat. The three uncoiled, standing. "For you," Winter Hawk said, holding out the ropes to the animals. "You will see that I took only the best animals." He puffed himself up again, bronze chest gleaming with sweat. "These I took from Bull

Hump, a mighty warrior of the Comanches." He spit in contempt.

Bent took the ropes and moved between the two animals, looking at them closely. "Lord a'mighty," Bent breathed. "This here is plumb shinin' horseflesh. Damn if I don't say so."

Bent finished checking the animals. Then he had Green take them to the corral that was part of the fort but out of sight behind the workshops. "Sit," he said to Winter Hawk. Then he went inside the trade room. Moments later he was back with a blanket in hand. He sat cross-legged and leaned over, placing the blanket in the dirt in front of Winter Hawk. "This I give to you," he said solemnly.

"I have no need for a blanket," Winter Hawk said haughtily. "I have many buffalo robes."

"Open it," Bent said with a wink.

Winter Hawk stared at him a moment, trying to see if Bent was trying to fool him. He couldn't decide, but he had not known Bent to be such a man. Bent might be a white-eyes, but he spoke true and kept his word. Winter Hawk flipped off the top flap of the blanket and saw a flintlock pistol. He picked it up almost reverently. It was a fine thing to have, though he could see little use for it in war. Still, many a warrior would envy him this prize.

Suddenly Winter Hawk looked at Bent, face showing puzzlement. "I'll need lead and powder," he said in an accusatory tone.

"I'll see you get some before you leave, Winter Hawk," Bent vowed.

"It is good," Winter Hawk said gravely. Then he grinned.

14

Bent fired his rifle as he edged up on the south bank of the Arkansas, wanting to alert his brother Charles and St. Vrain that he was coming. He stopped and let his horse drink from the sluggishly moving river, while he checked things out across the water. He was not surprised to see Cheyenne and Arapaho tipis over there on the flats near the fort. He was, however, surprised at the sheer number of them. He was even more baffled when he saw what seemed to be canvas tents upriver a little way. He responded in kind when he saw someone waving from the battlements of the fort.

He turned in the saddle and looked behind. A billowing cloud of dust was approaching. His men, with the large herd of horses and the pack train of mules, would be here in minutes. He pulled off his large-brimmed, floppy felt hat with his right hand and ran the right sleeve of his calico shirt across his forehead. "Damn, it's hot," he muttered.

The rumble of the animals was very close. Bent glanced back again and then eased his horse into the water. It was not the Comanche horse Winter Hawk had given him, the one the Cheyennes had stolen from Bull Hump. Bent had not thought it wise to ride that spotted stallion through Comanche country when he was trying to establish a trade with those Indians. Much to Bent's surprise, the Comanches and Kiowas had sent an emissary to the fort asking for Bent to send a trader into their lands. The envoy—a half-breed named Bear Dancer Gagnon—had always been trustworthy, so Bent agreed. Still, he was wary and decided it would be best to lead the expedition himself—with Gagnon guiding.

And what a trip it had been too. Behind him, rapidly approaching the river, were hundreds of buffalo robes packed on large, hardy mules, all gotten for goods that cost Bent, St. Vrain & Company only pennies.

Bent pulled up on the north bank of the river and stopped, facing the south. The huge herd of loose horses had hit the river, and heads bobbed as the animals swam across.

Several *vaqueros* suddenly charged out of the fort, racing toward Bent, who nodded and waved his hat at them. Cheyennes moved up warily, then more boldly, watching gleefully as the horses—then the heavily laden mules—bucked their way up the bank.

The *vaqueros* whistled and snapped whips to keep the animals moving, heading the horses toward pasture a mile or so away and guiding the mules toward the gates of the fort.

Bent's men brought up the rear. The five of them were dark and leathery from the harsh sun, and they were coated from head to toe in dust. Sweat carved small ravines on their faces.

Finally all the horses were gone and all the mules in the *placita*. Bent rode into the fort and stopped next to the men who had been with him these past several months.

"You boys done good," he said as he dismounted. "Go on and cut your dry. I reckon you can find some Lightnin' around somewhere."

The five men needed no more encouragement. They walked their horses back to the corral and let a few Mexican boys take the animals. They headed for the bar up on the second floor over the workshops.

Charles and St. Vrain were waiting for him in front

of the trade room. An army officer stood with them. "*Hola*, little brother," Charles said with a grin.

"Charlie. Ceran." William ran both palms over the cheeks of his rear end. "Goddamn if that ride didn't rub my ass raw from the day I left. Christ, I swear, I ain't got nothin' left back there."

He hawked up some spittle, though he could not find much, and expelled it on the ground. "And goddamn if I didn't eat twenty pounds of dust this trip." He looked up at the tall army officer. "And who's the general here?" he asked. He was in no mood to deal with some soldiers. All he wanted was a couple good-sized tankards of Taos Lightning, a wash-up, a decent shave. And some robe time with a willing woman—Cheyenne, Arapaho, or Mexican, he didn't much give a damn.

"Colonel, son," the officer said. "Colonel Henry Dodge." He held out his hand.

Bent took the proffered hand and shook. As he did so, he took stock of the officer. He was tall, rather handsome, Bent supposed, what with his iron-gray hair and unlined face. Bent figured the man to be in his late forties, maybe even early fifties. He had a stiff-backed military mien about him. His handshake was strong and resolute.

"We've been entertainin' the colonel here and a few of his officers," Charles said without enthusiasm.

"What brings you to these parts, Colonel?" William asked after a questioning glance shot at his brother.

Charles laughed. "He come here to see that all the Injuns make peace with each other."

"Shit," William snorted.

"It's true, son," Dodge said, his voice full of dignity and purpose. "And we've had considerable success so far."

"Yeah? With who?" William was bored, hot, hungry, and tired.

"The Pawnees, Osage, Arapaho, and," he smiled, "the Cheyennes."

"You got the Cheyennes to make peace with the goddamn Pawnee?" Bent asked, more than a little surprised.

"Yes, indeed, son." The colonel beamed.

William was getting quite tired of being called son. He had no liking for people who took such liberties. "Old Gray Thunder agree?"

Dodge shrugged. "Can't say as I know him," he admitted without apology.

"Gray Thunder wasn't here," Charles said. "When he heard about these doin's, he took it into his head to ride out to some Pawnee village. Said somethin' about fetchin' back some medicine arrows or some such."

"Shit," Bent breathed, worried. "That ol' fart's gonna get himself put under sure as hell. Goddamn fool."

"He'll be fine, son," Dodge said placatingly. "The Pawnees have agreed to live in peace with the Cheyennes. They have given their word, and so it shall be."

William cocked an eye at Dodge. "I sure as hell hope so," he said. "Them Pawnees raise hair on Gray Thunder and all hell'll break loose."

"Oh, pshaw," Dodge remonstrated. "What would the death of one more Indian mean? They've been killing each other for years."

William felt like punching the pompous colonel. "That might be true, Colonel," he allowed. "But Gray Thunder is powerful medicine amongst the Cheyennes. He's the keeper of the sacred arrows."

"And just what does that mean?" Dodge asked. He was trying to be polite, but somewhere in the back of his mind he was actually curious.

"It'd take too goddamn long to explain it, Colonel, especially to some ol' hoss what ain't likely to believe anyway."

"But Mr. Bent, I am interested in knowing about these savages."

"Good," William said more than a little sarcastically. "I'll have Winter Hawk or one of the other Cheyennes pay a visit to you tonight."

"That won't be necessary," Dodge said without rancor. He was intelligent enough to know when he was being insulted. He had also been around long enough not to be antagonized by the statements of a head-strong young man who had just spent several months traveling by horseback through hostile Indian country. He paused, then nodded. "I understand you have just spent time in . . . Mexico?"

"That ruffle your feathers?"

"By no means."

Dodge's calmness was infuriating to William Bent.

"I also understand that you have been trading with the Comanches?" Dodge asked evenly.

"Yep." He nodded thanks as slave Dick Green shoved a large pewter mug of *aguardiente* into his hand. He took a healthy slug.

"Looks like we done all right, Bill," his brother commented, waving a hand at the mules.

Workers—most of them Mexican—were swarming around the mules, unloading the heavy bales of robes. Each young man would place a leather strap around his forehead and then heft the bale off the mule, balancing the hundred-pound packs on his back, and trudge off to one of the many storerooms. Other workers would take the unloaded mules back to the corral to feed and water them.

"Yep," William said after several deep draughts of whiskey. "This shines," he said, grinning. "But a hailstorm'd be even some better."

Charles and St. Vrain grinned in acknowledgment.

"Hailstorm?" Dodge asked, interested despite himself. "What in hell is a hailstorm?"

"You ain't give him a hailstorm, Charlie?" William

asked, feigning shock. "Jesus, what kind of host are you?"

"We give him some," Charles said with a chuckle. "Just didn't tell him what it was."

"Was that that bilious, mint-flavored concoction you poured into me?" Dodge asked, smiling. He could still be one of the boys, he figured.

"One and ze same, Colonel," St. Vrain said, his throaty laugh reverberating up out of the barrel chest.

The joyful sounds wound down. "You have any trouble down there, Bill?" Charles asked.

"Things got touchy once or twice, but that was about it," William said with a shrug. "You think I had troublesome times?"

Charles shrugged. "Kit was here a little time back. Said he and a bunch of the boys was takin' the Cimarron Cutoff when a passel of Comanches come on 'em."

"Sounds like poor doin's," William said wryly.

"No shit. Kit and five other of the boys kilt their mules right there and used 'em for a barricade. They held off nigh on to a hundred of them screamin' red devils. Kit said they put more than forty of those bastards under before the rest of them critters run off."

"Forty?" Dodge snorted. "Six of them held off a hundred Comanches, killing forty of them?" He shook his head in disbelief. "I think this Mr. Carson is spinning one of those mountain yarns I've heard about." He seemed somehow pleased to make the pronouncement. Colonel Henry Dodge was not a man to be fooled so easily.

Charles saw the look in his brother's eyes and thought for a moment that he would step between William and Dodge. Then he decided against it. He would just wait and see how this played out.

William angrily tossed his almost-empty mug aside and then wiped a shirtsleeve across his mouth. Then he pulled out his butcher knife. "I've known Kit several years now, you fancified bag of wind," he snarled, edging closer to Dodge. "And Kit speaks with a straight tongue. If he was to tell me the sun come up in the west this morning and was goin' down in the east, I'd believe him. Leastways when it comes to such doin's as fightin' Injuns. Now, was he settin' 'round a fire somewhere, just a bunch of the boys jawin', then maybe he'd spin a few tales that was a mite exaggerated."

Dodge stood his ground, looking down his nose at the shorter man. "Put that knife away, Mr. Bent," he said sternly.

"Supposin' I don't?" William asked. He placed the tip of the knife on Dodge's blue-clad breast.

"You would be killing an officer of the United States Army," Dodge said. He sounded just a mite uncertain.

William Bent shrugged. "Don't make me no never mind."

"You'd be arrested and hanged," Dodge offered, trying to retain his dignity.

"You think that passel of dysentery-ridden critters you got out there'd come against this fort? Shit."

Charles figured this had gone on long enough. He knew his brother was not about to carve up an army officer, though William would not be averse to scaring the bejeebers out of Dodge. "Sheath your blade, Bill," he said. "Colonel Dodge has enough problems of his own without you waving that goddamn knife under his nose."

"Just watch who you call a liar, Colonel," William warned. He slid the blade away and stepped back.

Dodge hadn't lost any composure, at least none that could be seen.

William looked at his brother. "What's his troubles?" he asked, nodding in Dodge's direction.

St. Vrain and Charles were fighting back chuckles. "He aims to go south and talk the Comanches into bein' peaceable critters."

William looked at his brother, incredulity spread

over his face. Then he laughed. When he finished that, he looked at Dodge, his respect for the officer having grown a little. "You either got more balls than I gave you credit for," he said, "or a lot less brains than I figured."

"And why is that?"

"The Comanches are about the meanest bastards you'll ever face."

"But you just returned from a successful trading trip with them."

"Wasn't no church social neither," William said with a touch of pride. "We was just a few boys with some trade goods. You go marching an army down there, they might not look as kindly on you."

Dodge acknowledged that. Then he smiled a little. "Well, son, look at it this way, you went and softened them up for us."

William looked at his partners, then shook his head. "Good luck, Colonel," he said dryly.

"We got other visitors too, Bill," Charles said. "George and Bob are out here now. For good, from what they tell me."

William grinned. "We best lock up all the women," he said. He turned and strolled off, heading for his apartment.

❦{ 15 }❦

If it wasn't one thing needed to be done at the fort, it was another. The work seemed never-ending to William Bent. Two days after he arrived from the trading trip to the Comanches, the army left. When they did, Bent thought he would get some peace and quiet. With Charles and St. Vrain, plus the younger Bent brothers George and Robert, William figured he'd get a least a little time to have himself something of a spree. He looked forward to that.

But Charles and St. Vrain rode out the morning after the army had left. Charles never had spent much time at the fort, what with being on the trail much of the year, and that was not likely to change. St. Vrain was spending far less time there, leaving the running of it to William.

George and Robert Bent and St. Vrain's youngest brother, Marcellin, remained at the fort. They were young and inexperienced, and they had been left behind to benefit from William's tutelage. He generally didn't mind, but the responsibility of it wore on him of a time. He wanted the freedom of the mountains and the plains, where a man could ride for days without being bothered, where the air was fresh and clean, instead of foul and stinking of manure, mud, grease, and more.

"Damn," Bent muttered to himself as he watched his older brother and St. Vrain riding away. He didn't have much time to dwell on his annoyance, since his clerk, Ramsay MacGregor, was at his elbow, thrusting papers under his nose.

"Goddammit, Ramsay, back off," Bent growled good-naturedly. "Christ, I don't even let a squaw take such liberties with me." When MacGregor had taken a step back and let the arm holding the papers fall to his side, Bent asked, "Now, what's got you all in a lather?"

"We were shorted on the gun locks we ordered." He was in high dudgeon, and so rolling his r's even more than usual. "We ordered two hundred fifty, but received only two hundred twenty-five."

"You just found out now?" Bent asked. He didn't much care that a few gun locks were missing, and he just plain flat-out could not get so edgy over it. Still, he had to seemed concerned.

"Aye," MacGregor said with a long, wheezing sigh. "I should've found out a lot sooner, but I had little time, what with Charles and Ceran here, and then all those soldiers. Och, mon, what a time it was."

"Well, don't concern yourself overly much about it, Ramsay." He had no hope that the Scotsman would do so.

"Och, I canna do such a thing, Bill."

"Hell, Ramsay," Bent said, releasing some anger, "Charlie must've just miscounted, or dropped some of 'em while they were bein' loaded."

"But this is thievery, Mr. Bent," MacGregor responded formally.

"Ramsay," Bent said with a sigh of exasperation, "we shipped, what, twelve, fourteen thousand robes, plus a few hundred buffler tongues, and a pile of other furs?" When MacGregor nodded, Bent said, "A couple gun locks missin' don't mean a damn thing to our business. Now, had we been shorted on twenty-five or so of everything in our merchandise, I might've worried some." He turned away. "Now, go on back to your work.'' He could hear MacGregor muttering as he walked away.

Bent almost smiled. He was, if not a king, certainly a prince, with a whole kingdom laid out before him. But he had no one to share it with, he thought almost wistfully. He was twenty-six now, and he figured it was time to start thinking about a wife. Charles and St. Vrain had been granted Mexican citizenship, and seemed to be looking toward Taos for their future. William, though, while he liked Taos and the Mexican people, did not seem to feel the same pull of it that his brother did.

William gazed over the wall of the fort. There were a few Cheyenne lodges out there, as there usually were. It was there, in those painted buffalo-hide tipis; that's where his destiny lay, he thought.

A minor scuffle attracted Bent's attention, and he looked over to the small room on the second floor of the fort, on the south wall. Enoch Eubanks was spouting off at someone inside the small room, which was the fort's saloon and billiards parlor.

Eubanks had always been a cantankerous old fellow, but since the fight with the Shoshonis, he had turned intractable. He was drunk much of the time, and more often than not he was belligerent. Bent shook his head. It was a pity seeing Eubanks like that. It was another life wasted, a life sucked out by the demands of the high mountains and wide plains, by too much drink and too little common sense.

Bent continued watching as Eubanks stumbled down the corner stairs into the *placita*. He ran smack dab into Solomon, who had just come from the cistern room with a bucket of water.

"Oh, shit," Bent muttered. He headed quickly toward the corner stairs, keeping an eye on the scene unfolding in the *placita*.

"Get outta my way, you goddamn big, ugly ape,"

Eubanks bellowed, shoving the burly man. "Just get out of my way."

Solomon stood firm. He was not tall, hardly taller than Bent, but he was well-muscled. He wore only a pair of cotton pants, held up by a rope. The bottom of each pant leg was ragged. He wore no shoes. He had more clothes; he just didn't like wearing them when it was this hot.

Solomon was born a slave, but became a free man by fleeing a Mississippi plantation. He had drifted west and north, finding trouble wherever he worked, until he got out into the far reaches of the West. He had hired on with Bent, St. Vrain & Company more than two years ago.

He had worried at first, when he took a job with the company. The Bents owned slaves, had come from slave-holding areas. They told him that if he was a free man, that's what they considered him, no matter how he got to be that way.

"We ain't in the business of returnin' slaves," Charles had said.

Solomon relaxed, and found the Bents excellent employers. Here he was allowed to live in peace, and use the blacksmithing skills he had learned in Mississippi. Within a few months he had become Seth Walsh's assistant in the blacksmith shop. He had learned to read from a Bible, and from that he took his name. He used no other name—the whites with whom he associated could not pronounce his African name, and he refused to take the last name of his former owner.

With the hard life he had lived, and the success he had made from it, Solomon was not a man to take being pushed around lightly. Especially not when the man doing the pushing so obviously disliked anyone with black skin. He backhanded Eubanks, knocking the man flying. "You just watch yo' mouth and who you be pushin', goddammit."

Solomon turned and continued on his journey

toward the blacksmith shop, the water sloshing a little out of the bucket.

"You goddamn black bastard," Eubanks screamed. He scrambled up, jerking out his flintlock pistol. By the time he was standing, he was fumbling, still trying to cock the pistol. The hours, days, months of continuous drinking had taken their toll.

Bent stopped on the stairs and pulled his pistol. Without hesitation he fired, not wanting to give Eubanks even a small chance to kill Solomon.

Eubanks had finally managed to cock the pistol a moment before Bent's bullet slammed into his chest. His own shot went wide, the ball plowing into one of the big support timbers holding up the portico.

"I be obliged, Mistah Bent," Solomon said quietly.

"It was my pleasure, Solomon," Bent said. "Enoch was gettin' to be a royal pain in my ass anyway."

"I still be obliged." Solomon picked up his bucket and turned, once more heading for the blacksmith shop.

William looked at his brother George. "Have Crutsinger haul Enoch out of here with his next load of trash. Have a couple of the boys go along to dig a grave somewhere." It was better than Eubanks deserved.

George nodded and walked off. With a sigh, William headed for the saloon. He felt the need of a hailstorm.

The weeks passed in dreary monotony, broken only with the occasional arrival of some Cheyennes or some wagons, and old friends. Kit Carson, Bent's good and longtime friend, arrived several weeks later. Once he had unsaddled his horse and thrown his gear into one of the rooms set off as trappers' quarters, he headed for the trade room.

William was working diligently, though with no enthusiasm. Until Carson walked in and whooped. "Hyar now, ol' hoss," he roared. "I got me one powerful case

of thirst, and I aim to quench it if there be any chil'
hyar thinks he can keep up."

Bent beamed. " 'Bout time you showed up, you ol'
buffler fart. You got the specie to back up them
bodacious claims?"

"Damn me to hell, or a Blackfoot village, if I don't,
goddamn it." He was laughing now. "I expect all this
fauncin' around by you is 'cause you knowed goddamn
full well that you can't keep up with this chil'."

"Shit, I can outdrink, outtalk, and outfornicate the
likes of you, and do it with a hangover and with a Comanche arrow in my lights."

"Hell, quit this jawin' then, and let's go lift a cup."

When Carson left two weeks later, normalcy returned to the fort. But normalcy generally did not
mean peace and quiet.

16

Bent stood in the corral running a hard brush over the red roan's long mane, as he had done just about every day since Winter Hawk had given him the stolen Comanche horse. He already had found it to be one of the best horses he had ever seen. The reddish roan had a powerful neck and a deep chest and would, Bent figured, have good speed, but more importantly, stamina.

"That ol' hoss has the makin's of bein' one shinin' buffalo pony," Walsh said to Bent the day after he had gotten it.

"Yep," Bent said. He patted the horse's neck and ran his fingers through the roan's mane. "He's been treated well too." Bent paused as he ran a hand along the horse's flank. "Them damn Comanches might be sons of bitches, but they do know how to handle horses."

Over the next several days, Bent had spent a lot of time with the horse, getting the animal accustomed to his riding style. He found that the horse had an easy, rolling gait—once he got used to the saddle, bridle, and bit. Within a week Bent was ready to give him a real test, out on the prairie. So far he had just ridden the horse easily, first in the corral, and then in the immediate area outside the fort.

With Walsh riding with him and towing Bent's new mule, Bent rode out through the fort's gates and headed northwest. Both men had their rifles across their saddles in front of them. They rode quietly, seeing no need to talk. It was too hot for jabbering anyway; waves of heat shimmered off in the distance a little, dancing atop short, browning grass. It could make a man see crazy things. With nothing solid to latch your eyes onto, a man often saw strange and eerie things as plain as day. Like the time Bent had seen an army of Mexican lancers, hundreds of them, each ten foot tall or so, mounted on gigantic horses. Bent, barely seventeen then, thought he was going crazy, until he found out everyone else in the party led by Charles Bent had spotted it too.

He had been spooked by that, but over the years he found that such things were commonplace. Many times the visions were lovely ones. It was strange, at first, but Bent had come to be used to them.

Such things were sometimes funny, sometimes annoying. One could never be absolutely sure that what one saw was real. Like a herd of buffalo. Bent and Walsh saw a herd to the northeast, and they moved in that direction. Neither said anything, wanting to make sure they had seen a real herd and not some mystical vision.

The thick, heavy grunting of bulls let the two men know the herd was real. They came up on it from the downwind side, moving slowly. When they were within fifty yards, Walsh said quietly, "Call it, Cap'n." He dropped the mule's rope.

Bent nodded. "Reckon we'll see for sure now just what this ol' horse can do." He checked his rifle, then grinned. Abruptly, he tore off his battered felt hat. Letting go a boisterous whoop, he slapped the horse's rump with the hat. The animal bolted. The bison, hearing the sudden, sharp noise, looked up in befuddlement. Then one began lumbering off, the others quickly following. Within moments the prairie echoed with thunder as the buffalo churned across the grass-land.

Bent and Walsh whooped and hollered in pure joy as they charged across the plains after the rumbling buffalo. Each picked out a plump cow and went for it. In only minutes each man had brought down two buffalo. They pulled to a stop, watching as the racing bison dwindled in size, and then they were gone, most likely in one of the ubiquitous dips between the interminable swells.

"How'd he do, Cap'n?" Walsh asked as he rode up to Bent. He pointed at the roan.

"Like he was born to it." Bent patted the animal's sweating neck. "He's been trained considerable. I reckon ol' Bull Hump is powerful pissed off at having such an animal took from him."

Walsh chuckled. "Hell, Cap'n, was he watchin' that hoss more closely, he wouldn't have lost that roan."

Bent joined in laughter. When they settled down and their horses quit blowing, Bent said, "You go fetch the mule. I'll start makin' meat."

After that, Bent figured the horse needed no more training. The animal seemed to have adapted to him, and was clearly well-trained for the hunt. There was nothing more Bent could teach it. So, with reluctance, he had gone back to his more mundane duties, though he almost always put aside a bit of time for the roan.

When he had to perform such loathsome chores—inventory, toting up the books and such—he used any excuse he could find to get away from them even for a bit. When not with the horse, he often would walk the second-floor walkway and gaze wistfully across the prairie.

This day, he wanted very much to be on the roan, riding hard across the prairie. That was impossible today, though. There were too many things to be done. He sighed as he handed the roan a lump of sugar. He patted the animal's strong neck and left.

Still loath to go back to work, he headed up onto the second story. This was a rare day—there was not a Cheyenne lodge in sight.

Something caught his attention, though he was not even sure what it was. He only knew that something out there in the emptiness had intruded into his consciousness. He turned and looked eastward. A few minutes of staring made him realize there was nothing that way. He made a quarter turn and gazed to the south.

"Shit," he muttered as he spotted the small dust cloud moving slowly north. He pulled out his telescope and stared through it a while. Nothing coalesced, so he waited a bit before looking again.

He walked to the edge of the wall, looking down over the *placita*. "Mr. MacGregor," he shouted. He repeated it more loudly a few minutes later, when his first call brought no response.

The tall, thick-waisted clerk poked his head out of the trade room, finally realizing that his boss had beckoned from above. He looked up. "Aye, Mr. Bent. What can I do for you?" His burr was prevalent.

"Find Seth, and tell him I want to see him. And be quick about it."

MacGregor looked at Bent in surprise. The small trader was feisty, to be sure, but rarely was he this testy. It worried the Scotsman. He turned and scurried off in the direction of the blacksmith shop. Seth Walsh had been a trapper and trader with the Bents for some years, but he also was a trained blacksmith. When Bent opened the fort, he asked Walsh if he would like a job. Walsh, who had been with the Bents for several years, nodded and was immediately made the fort's blacksmith.

MacGregor called for Walsh, who stepped outside of the shop. He was covered with sweat and soot.

"Mr. Bent wants you, Mr. Walsh."

"Hell, I'm in the middle of something."

MacGregor might be a clerk and a shopkeeper, but

he had held his own in brawls from Glasgow to St. Louis. Walsh did not intimidate him, even though he was getting a mite long in the tooth. "He said now."

Walsh looked pointedly at MacGregor, who stared back evenly. Walsh knew from MacGregor's face that trouble was brewing. "Where?"

MacGregor pointed. Walsh nodded, spun and yanked off his long, leather apron. Tossing it aside, he grabbed his two pistols. He was shoving the weapons into his belt as he strode outside. In moments he was standing next to Bent, looking through the telescope.

"Comanches?" Walsh asked as he handed Bent's telescope back.

"It's got to be," Bent said. "I'd have knowed if the Cheyennes were sendin' a war party down there."

Walsh nodded. The Cheyennes would be sure to stop at the fort for powder, lead, and such. None had been there since Yellow Wolf's war party stopped a week and a half ago on their way back from Comanche country.

"You expectin' trouble, Cap'n?"

Bent shrugged. "They might just be comin' to trade." He didn't sound very convincing, even to himself. Still, the Comanches had come to the fort on a few occasions to trade. Bent had made some inroads in trade with them. The main stumbling block to establishing a flourishing trade with the Comanches was Bent's friendship with the Cheyennes. The Comanches and the Cheyennes were bitter enemies. Until that was resolved, Bent would not turn the Comanches away if they came to trade, but he'd be damned if he'd drop his business with the Cheyennes just for the Comanches.

"On the other hand, they just might be comin' up here to raise hair on the Cheyennes," Walsh said quietly.

Bent nodded. He had already considered that possibility. The cloud was close to the far bank of the river now, and through the telescope, the Comanches became real figures bobbing dimly in the heat. "There anyone out?" he asked.

"Ol' Crutsinger's out with his water wagon. And the Mexicans have the horses out to pasture."

"How far off are they?"

"Half a mile, maybe a little less."

Bent nodded again. "Send somebody after 'em. And make it fast. I want them horses and mules inside the corral by the time them goddamn Comanches get across the river."

"That's gonna be cuttin' it mighty slim, Cap'n."

"Then don't stand here jawin' at me," Bent said tensely.

Walsh knew that Bent had the welfare of the fort in mind, so he was not bothered by his employer's terseness. Instead he spun and hurried down the stairs, shouting orders as he went. Men scurried about, knowing that Walsh's commands were Bent's.

Up on the walkway, Bent watched as a lone rider raced out of the fort, heading northwest, where the herds of the fort's animals were grazing. Another rider hurried down toward the river. Bent could see Crutsinger's wagon now, a dark–grayish splotch against the browns and greens of the cottonwoods along the river.

The Comanches got closer and closer. Crutsinger and the man sent out to get him were hurrying back to the fort, the barrels of water in the back of the wagon bouncing loosely, spilling water all over.

Bent smiled grimly, figuring that the rider must have told old Crutsinger that Comanches were just about ready to take his hair. Crutsinger was medium big, medium old, and completely crotchety. No one knew his first name, where he had come from, or what he had done in his life. He seemed to have no trade nor any talents. He had shown up one day in Taos, and a sympathetic Charles Bent gave him a job sweeping up in the store and doing other small chores. Just before the fort was set to open, Charles had brought Crutsinger, using him on the trail for minor chores—gathering firewood, bucketing up water and such. At the fort he had been given the boring though necessary job of bringing barrels of water from the river to the fort every day, since the fort's well could not handle all the fort's needs. Crutsinger also was responsible for hauling out the tons of manure produced by the fort's animals. Both were jobs that required little intelligence and considerable brawn, jobs that fit Crutsinger perfectly.

Walsh rejoined Bent, and they saw the Comanches creep across the sand hills. They arrived at the river and began edging into the water. About the same time, Bent heard the rumble of hooves. He turned and saw the Mexican wranglers pushing the fort's horses and mules toward the fort. Before the Comanches were across the river, the animals were in the corral. Bent nodded.

"They don't look like they're half froze to raise hair," Walsh said.

"That's a relief," Bent said dryly. He had no fear of any band of Indians attacking the fort. The walls were three feet thick, the two big doors of iron-reinforced oak. Weapons were hung all about on the inside walls, waiting to be grabbed by anyone in defense of the fort. There were two small cannons, the guardhouse, and the two circular bastions, which gave the men an unobstructed view of the prairie in all directions.

The Comanches were on the river's north bank. They did not stop, though they slowed as they approached the fort.

"Time to go meet them, I suppose," Bent said. He was not exactly thrilled with the idea. Not now, only a week and a half removed from the return of Yellow Wolf's successful raiding party.

"Shit," Walsh muttered. "These doin's don't shine at all."

"I wonder if that's Bull Hump," Bent said, pointing

to a warrior wearing a bonnet of a buffalo head with the horns still on and part of the hide flowing down his back. He wore only the hat, a breechcloth, and moccasins. "I've never dealt with him, but the talk in the Cheyenne and Comanche camps is that he is one tough son of a bitch."

{17}

The Comanches were very close to the fort now. Bent spun to face his big friend. "Have someone get my roan and the mule Winter Hawk gave me and hide 'em. Bring 'em into the shop, if need be. If that is Bull Hump, I don't want him seein' his horse here. If it ain't, a heap of those Comanches might know the horse and word'll get back to him."

Walsh nodded. It was the prudent thing to do. Why risk an attack when that could so easily be avoided? Not only was the latter safer, it made good business sense. Bent did trade with the Comanches, and planned to expand that trade, if possible.

Of course, Bent could just give the roan back, making a great show of it, and thereby gaining the goodwill of at least one intractable Comanche. Bent was known to buy horses from anyone, no questions asked. He could just tell the Comanches he had bought the horse to return the stallion to its rightful owner.

But Walsh had seen the way Bent cared for the roan. The horse was one of a kind, and one of the finest buffalo ponies he had ever seen. The animal had instinct, speed, and stamina. Walsh could understand why Bent would not want to return it. Walsh also knew from long experience that Bent had a streak of perversity in him. He might keep the roan just to annoy the Comanches.

Bent came down into the *placita* and waited for the

Comanches. Armed men stood on the second floor and in rooms around the *placita*.

The one Bent thought might be Bull Hump led the way into the fort. He looked regal, despite the coating of dust and grease. His buffalo headdress was crooked and his moccasins had holes in them, but that did not detract from the royal mien.

In sign language Bent said, "I welcome the Comanches to Fort William." He looked perplexed. "You have brought nothing to trade?" A stern look crossed Bent's face. "I cannot just give away my goods to you," he signed. "I must have furs to trade."

The Comanche slid off his pony. "I'm not here to trade," he signed. "I come for horses."

"I have many horses," Bent signed. "But I won't give them to you. Or to anyone. They're good horses. The best in all the plains."

The Comanche spit. In Spanish and extremely cracked English he said, "My horses." He looked ill-at-ease.

"Why do you think your horses are here?" Bent asked sharply.

"They were taken by Cheyennes," the Comanche said in his language. The last word was drenched in hatred and disgust.

Bent knew enough Comanche to understand the man. He allowed a small smile. "Then you weren't watching them very well, were you?"

"Bah," the Indian snarled. His honor was impugned, and he did not like it. That the statement was true in no way lessened his anger.

"Well, I might let you look at my herd. You find any of your horses in it, we'll talk about it, eh?" Bent said boldly.

"We won't smoke?"

Bent nodded. "You're right," he said. "I'm a poor host. Sit." Bent sat cross-legged. The Comanche tossed the rope rein of his horse to one of his men. He sat facing Bent, less than a yard separating them.

A moment later Charlotte Green brought out two bowls of buffalo stew. Her sudden appearance startled Bull Hump, and he stared at the hefty woman with a combination of awe, fear, and bafflement in his eyes. He had never seen a person with black skin before. It was startling. To cover his confusion, he took the bowl and slurped it down, never taking his eyes off Charlotte until she was gone into the recesses of the kitchen.

Bent said nothing. He just poured the stew into his mouth, using the bowl to hide his amusement.

When the food was gone, a young Mexican brought a pipe to Bent. When Bent put it into his mouth, the youth lit it with a candle.

Bent got the pipe going to his satisfaction, then blew smoke to the east, north, south, and west, then to the sky father and the earth mother. He passed the pipe to the Comanche, who performed the same rite.

When the ritual was done with, the Comanche asked, "Do you know who I am?" He was such a great warrior among his people, he just assumed he would be known throughout the land.

Bent decided to take a risk. He didn't know this Comanche from Adam, but he had his suspicions. "Doesn't everyone know the great Bull Hump, the mighty Comanche warrior?" he responded calmly.

"I didn't think the white-eyes would," the Comanche commented.

"Not all white-eyes are fools."

Buffalo Hump nodded. "Then you will know that if you speak with a snake's tongue, I will kill you," Bull Hump said matter-of-factly.

Bent turned his head a little to his left. Closing his right nostril with a finger, he expelled snot out the other side. He reversed sides and did it again. Then he turned back to face Bull Hump. "You ain't gonna do shit, Bull Hump, and you goddamn well know it," Bent said in English. He figured the Comanche would get the gist of what he was saying, even if he didn't understand most of the words.

Bull Hump was livid. "I'll kill you and all the white-eyes who come to my land," he said angrily.

"You ain't gonna do no such thing, you stinkin' bag of wind."

"I will," Bull Hump said. The voice was dark and low with menace.

"Buffler shit." Bent held up a hand to forestall more protests. "You can't take this fort," Bent said reasonably. "Sure you could kill my traders and hunters. Maybe even make it hard for the wagons to get by on the Santa Fe Trail. But you do that, and you're gonna have a passel of folks come down on you hard. But more than that, you'll be cuttin' your people off of things they need. You think I'm gonna trade with you folks after you've killed off a bunch of my men?"

"No," Bull Hump said grudgingly.

"Goddamn right, no." Bent paused. "Now, if you'd come in here sayin' you thought maybe the Cheyennes had brought in some horses was took from you, and could you please see if any of 'em was here, I'd have had every piece of horseflesh in this fort brought out for your inspection." He spit. "But no, you aim to bully me. You make threats against me and those in my employ." He shook his head. "I'm of a mind to toss you out of here on your ass, you dumb son of a bitch."

Bull Hump's eyes looked like they would pop out of his head, and veins knotted in his forehead and neck. Then suddenly, out of nowhere, he laughed. "I like you," he said. "You're brave for a white-eyes."

Bent shrugged. He liked the fact that Bull Hump had suddenly gotten reasonable, but he certainly wasn't going to acknowledge that he cared anything for what the Comanche had to say.

"So, what's it gonna be?" Bent asked.

Bull Hump sat in thought. Then, "Are any of my horses here?"

"How the hell should I know?" Bent retorted. "I get horses from all over." He chuckled a little. "Besides, nearabout any horse you had was stole from someone. Most likely from me and my *compadres.*"

"We haven't taken any horses from you," Bull Hump said with a straight face.

"Like hell," Bent said, but he smiled a little to take any real sting out of it. He bought any horses or mules brought to the fort, and he cared not a whit where they came from. Many were stolen by the Cheyennes from other tribes, or even from whites in some of the settlements. He bought animals from his old friends, many of them stolen from Mexicans somewhere. He could understand Bull Hump's reluctance to admit he had taken horses.

Bull Hump shrugged and then grinned. It was the way of things, and he accepted it. Growing serious then, he said, "I care only for one horse," he said quietly. "The finest buffalo horse on the plains."

"Everybody thinks he's got the best buffler pony on the plains."

Bull Hump acknowledged that many men would make such a boast. "But you should see this one when he is running after the buffalo." His eyes gleamed wistfully.

"A good buffler horse is one of the best things a man can have," Bent said nonchalantly.

Bull Hump nodded. "Yes, that is so. But this horse was special." He held up his hands, as if he could not find a way to adequately explain the horse's attributes.

"What's this old nag look like?" Bent kept his face blank, though he was pretty sure he knew what was coming.

"A red roan," Bull Hump said, gazing intently at Bent. He was sure the horse had been brought here.

He didn't know why he was sure, but he was. He hoped the small, fierce-looking man would give himself away.

"Lots of red roans in these parts," Bent said non-committally.

"This one had a white star on his forehead."

Bent had not taken his eyes off the Comanche's. He shook his head. "Ain't seen no such horse," he offered.

Bull Hump was sure Bent was lying, but he had no way to prove it.

"I would've noticed such a horse," Bent said soothingly. "But you're welcome to look over my animals."

Bull Hump was surprised this time. He had not expected it. "Where are your horses?" he asked warily.

Bent jerked a thumb over his shoulder. "Back there in the corral."

"They're not out grazing?" Bull Hump asked suspiciously. His warriors had watched the white man's fort on occasion, and he knew that the horses were brought out every day under the watch of Mexican *vaqueros*. He was sure Bent was lying now.

"We had 'em out to pasture—till we saw you boys comin'," Bent said, half smiling. "Hell, we know how good you are at stealin' horses. I ain't gonna leave my herd out there to make 'em easy pickin's for you."

Bull Hump nodded, pleased at the praise. Still, he could not entirely trust the white man—or any of the pale-skinned people. "Such a thing is wise," he admitted. He paused, staring deep into Bent's brown eyes. "I will look at your horses," he finally said.

"I already said you could." Bent rose, knocking the cold ashes from the pipe, scattering them to the wind. It was one of the few things he disliked about the plains: the wind. It never, ever stopped. It might be less blustery on some days than others. But it was always there, sometimes just a little puff; sometimes a driving force that could make a man loco if he thought about it.

There was nothing he could do about it, though. Charles and St. Vrain had found lives and homes in Taos. But Bent had unconsciously, if no less firmly, chosen the plains. He wasn't sure he would ever leave them. The wind might be an annoyance, but for him it blew in freshness every day. Then, too, here was where the buffalo ranged, great giant herds of them, many times stretching as far as the eye could see.

Also, this was the home of the Cheyennes. Sometime in the past year or so, Bent had concluded that he was as one with the Cheyennes. He had spoken with Gray Thunder about the possibility of courting one of his daughters. The old chief had not given his consent, but on the other hand, he had not turned Bent down either. Yes, the southern plains were home for William Bent. He might wander into a town or city of a time, when the need arose, but for the most part he was sure he would spend the rest of his life on these broad, grassy prairies.

Bull Hump stood too, and was staring at Bent, who seemed to have gone off somewhere. Bull Hump suspected that Bent was having a vision, though he didn't think white men were capable of that. Still, Bent had that slack, dreamy look that might come with a pleasing vision.

Bent snapped back to reality. "Tell your boys to stay here and not to cause no trouble," he warned. "They act up, I'll have 'em thrown out."

Bull Hump nodded.

"Come on, then," Bent said, turning. As he walked toward the small alley that separated the *placita* from the workshops and corral, he hoped that Walsh had hidden the roan well. If not, there would be hell to pay, that was sure.

Bent waved a hand as they reached the corral. "There they are. You see this buffalo pony of yours out there?"

Bull Hump made a quick scan and then shook his

head. If the horse was at the fort, it was hidden, he figured, and he had no way of checking that short of declaring war on the fort. And that would not be wise. Silently, he headed back to be with his warriors. A few feet from his men, Bull Hump stopped and turned to face Bent.

"I told you that horse wasn't here," Bent said.

Bull Hump nodded.

18

"**Y**ou lie!" another warrior shouted harshly. He shoved through the other warriors and stopped alongside Bull Hump.

Bent gazed balefuly at the warrior. Something about him was mighty familiar, Bent thought. Then recognition dawned. "You're that damn fool who come to the old fort up on Fountain Creek tryin' to stir up trouble, ain't you?" Bent said more than asked. "Your name's Fartin' Buffalo or some such."

A number of the men—of both sides—sniggered.

"Singing Buffalo," the warrior snapped angrily.

"Yeah, that's it," Bent said unapologetically. "I remember now. You're the one who's always pissin' on someone else's doin's and then not havin' the balls to finish off what you started."

Singing Buffalo was livid, and he yanked out a tomahawk. The sound of several dozen guns being cocked froze him where he was. He cautiously slid the weapon back into his belt. Being insulted in front of everyone like this did nothing to improve his humor.

Bent looked at Singing Buffalo with hatred and anger in his own eyes. "That's the second time you called me a liar, boy," he said flatly. "I'm of a mood to end your troublesome ways here and now." He paused. "Being a man of reasonableness, I'll let it pass this time. But don't you ever dare do such a thing to me again." He felt no need to continue the threat. It was evident enough.

Singing Buffalo looked as if his eyes would explode out of his head, so angry was he. The hatred and rage kept him from thinking clearly, and he moved to rip out his tomahawk again. This time, though, Buffalo Hump stopped him.

The warriors talked feverishly in Comanche. Bent could understand little of what was being said. But from that and from watching the two, he figured Buffalo Hump was trying to keep Singing Buffalo from getting killed. It would be, Bent knew, suicide for the Indian—or even all of them—to try something here. The whole war band might get a few of the whites, but there was no doubt that all the Comanches would die.

Singing Buffalo seemed disinclined to listen, though, and finally Buffalo Hump's face was as enraged as Singing Buffalo's was. Then Buffalo Hump pointed toward the horses and shoved Singing Buffalo.

Singing Buffalo hesitated only a moment, then angrily walked back to his pony. He could hear the derisive laughter from the white men along the walkway.

"Best keep your boys in line you ever come back here, Buffalo Hump," Bent said fiercely.

Buffalo Hump nodded. His own anger was bubbling, but he was not sure who he was angry at. Certainly Bent for his rude insults to him and Singing Buffalo. But Buffalo Hump also was angry at Singing Buffalo for inviting ridicule here, where he and his warriors were heavily outnumbered. Buffalo Hump was a brave warrior, one of the fiercest of all the Comanches. He was not used to having to swallow such insults. He also was intelligent, and so knew that any show of force here would end in the deaths of all his men.

Buffalo Hump was not afraid of dying. Nor were his men. But to die for no good purpose, such as would happen here, was foolish.

"We'll meet again, Bent," Buffalo Hump said in English.

"We do, you best keep your men in line," Bent said angrily.

Buffalo Hump nodded once. Then he turned and walked to his horse. Moments later the Comanches were out of the fort and heading toward the river.

The men inside the fort finally began to relax and drift away, already telling each other what they would have done had the Comanches wanted to battle.

Bent watched for a bit, then turned to head back to his room. Suddenly he heard a galloping horse. He looked over his shoulder and then began turning. Several gunshots rang out, hitting the pony. No lead ball hit Singing Buffalo, though. As his horse went down, Singing Buffalo flung himself off the pony, slamming into Bent.

Both men hit the dust, each scrabbling for a handhold on the other. They rolled through the embers of a cook fire, hardly feeling the heat. They came to a stop, with Singing Buffalo partly atop Bent. As he tried to hold Bent down, Singing Buffalo also tried getting to his knife. But Bent was struggling too much.

That gave Bent a small opportunity to slam Singing Buffalo in the side with a forearm, knocking the Indian off. He lay a moment, hurting in several spots. Not only had he hit the ground, but he had been hit by Singing Buffalo flying off his horse. He also had taken the brunt of the heat in rolling through the fire.

Singing Buffalo was already on his feet. As Bent tried to get up, Singing Buffalo kicked him in the stomach. Bent fell, doubled up. Singing Buffalo screeched a war cry and lifted his tomahawk over his head, for just a heartbeat savoring the victory that was his.

Half a dozen gunshots rang out. Singing Buffalo did a death dance as the lead balls smashed into him. Then he fell, bloody and broken.

Seth Walsh and Solomon rushed over and helped

Bent up. "About time you boys come to my rescue," Bent wheezed.

"Hell, Bill," Walsh said, laughing, "you was doin' so good, me 'n' Solomon was caught up watchin' you so's we might learn something."

He and Solomon laughed. Bent tried, but realized right off that such a notion was foolish. He decided a weak smile would have to do.

Many of the other men had come over to see how he was doing, but then Bull Hump led his Comanches back into the fort. Most of the whites aimed rifles at the warriors. "Say the word, Cap'n," someone said.

Bent straightened. He saw Sam Butler kneeling to take Singing Buffalo's scalp. "No," he gasped. His breathing still was not right.

"Why the hell not?" Butler asked, surprised. It wasn't as if it was the first time a white man had ever raised hair on an Indian.

"Because I said so," Bent said weakly.

"Hell, this chil' put the fatal ball in the red son of a bitch," Butler snapped, "and, by Christ, I'm gonna get his hair."

Luis Saltillo moved quietly up behind Butler and placed a cocked pistol lightly against the back of Butler's head. "You touch that Injun, señor, and I'll splatter your brains."

Butler hesitated only a moment. Then he released the grip he had on Singing Buffalo's hair and very slowly moved his knife away. As he pushed up he muttered, "Jesus Christ, it ain't bad enough with an Injun-lovin' *bourgeois*, now I got goddamn greasers goin' agin me."

The other men parted, creating a lane for Bent. With help from Walsh and Solomon, he walked through it and stopped near Bull Hump. At least two dozen of Bent's friends were aiming guns at the Comanches.

There were some moments of silence, then Buffalo

Hump spoke, quietly and with dignity. "Singing Buffalo was a fool. He was also a great warrior for his people. He will be missed."

Bent nodded. He figured that Singing Buffalo had acted on his own, not under Buffalo Hump's direction. "If you think you can do so without your people causin' any more trouble, Buffalo Hump," Bent said with more strength, "you can take that sack of shit home with you."

Buffalo Hump nodded. He waved a hand and two warriors slid off their ponies and nervously moved through the group of white men. Then they retraced their steps, carrying Singing Buffalo's corpse.

Seeing that the Comanches had no extra horses, Bent said, "Art, go get a mule. . . . no, make it a horse. That little bay mare come in the other day. Then give it over to the Comanches." He looked up at Buffalo Hump, who was still sitting on his pony. "You can use it to take Singing Buffalo home. And then you can do with the pony what you want."

Buffalo Hump nodded.

When the pony was brought up, the two warriors set Singing Buffalo's body over it. Then they mounted their own ponies. At a word from Buffalo Hump, all the warriors headed out the fort. Buffalo Hump waited, though. When his men were gone, the war leader looked at Bent. With signs he said, "You must be a good man, if all these men"—he waved a hand around, encompassing the fort—"will do battle for you."

Bent nodded. There was nothing more could be said about it.

"You come trade with my people again?" Buffalo Hump asked in English.

"Long's your people ain't gonna go to war with us for what happened here today."

"I can't promise that all the Comanches will leave your traders in peace," Buffalo Hump signed. "You

should know that I have no control over the men."
When Bent nodded again, Buffalo Hump continued,
"But you have my word that around my village they will
be safe."

"Can't ask no more than that." He wished the Comanche would go. He wanted nothing more than to lie
on his bed with a jug of whiskey to deaden the pain of
his injuries.

Buffalo Hump turned and rode out of the fort, back
straight. Bent watched until Buffalo Hump was out,
then turned. As Walsh and Solomon helped him
toward his quarters, Bent noted that the other men
were a lot more wary than they had been the last time
those Comanches had gone through the fort gate.

⟦19⟧

It seemed to take three-quarters of the way to forever for winter to pass. But it finally did, its arrival heralded by Kit Carson and a dozen other trappers who rode into the fort with whoops and roaring guns. It was a facade, though, quickly dispelled at the season's paltry take.

"Damn," Carson said, "beaver don't shine no more, it seems." He was more mystified than angry.

"Hell, I told you that last year," Bent told him. They were sitting in the dining room over mugs of whiskey-laced coffee and plates of *machaca de huevo*.

"I know," Carson said around a mouthful of the egg and buffalo jerky dish. He looked up, stabbing his tin fork in Bent's direction. "What I didn't know was it was gonna be so bad, so soon." He shook his head. "And now you're payin' out less'n three bucks a pound for plews. Jesus, a man could find himself in starvin' times easy now."

Bent shrugged. "I'm payin' you better'n you'll get in Independence, or St. Louis, or Taos."

"Damn, that just fries my ass."

Bent smiled and shoved more food in his mouth. When he was done chewing, he said, "You gonna give up?" He looked at Carson with a question in his eyes. "I ain't ever known you to quit anything before."

"Hell no, I ain't about to quit," Carson said defiantly. "I'll make beaver come again, sure as you're sit-tin' there." He chomped down another mouthful, then snapped, "I'll be damned if'n I'll set here and have you call me a quitter. Son of a bitch."

"Don't get yourself all a-boil, boy," Bent said with a chuckle.

"Bah," Carson growled, then he grinned and poured a heaping helping of whiskey-laced coffee down his gullet. "Shit, I suppose it's got to come to an end one day," he surmised. "I'd best get used to such a thing." He paused, fork suspended in air, dripping bits of egg. "But not yet," he said quietly, though fiercely, as if talking to himself. "No, goddamn it, not yet. I'll make beaver come again. Damn sure I will. Might not be shinin' like in the old days, but I'll make do."

Bent nodded, not wanting to disturb Carson's reverie.

Carson came out of his self-imposed trance and shoved the forkful of food between his teeth.

Moments later Charlotte bustled in, carting a wood tray on which sat a pot of coffee and a plate of tamales. She set the tray down, beaming at the men, as she always did, and filled the two men's mugs. "I figured you two'd still be hungry," she announced as she set the plate of tamales in the center of the table. Then she left.

"You ought to set ol' Charlotte free, Bill," Carson said as he slugged down a mouthful of coffee followed immediately by half a tamale.

"She rightly belongs to Charlie," Bent said, tearing into a tamale.

"He'd never say anything against you was you to do such a thing."

"I expect not," Bent admitted. He polished off a tamale and reached for another. "I've thought of doin' so for Charlotte, ol' Dick too. Even talked over it with Charlie. But . . ."

"But what?" Carson had downed three tamales already and was doing serious damage to another—the last on the plate.

Bent's brothers George and Robert strolled in and sat at the table.

Charlotte suddenly swept out of the kitchen with another pot of coffee. Her husband followed along with another tray, on which were two platters of tamales and some Indian fry bread.

Bent and the others broke off their conversation until Charlotte and Dick had left again.

"But what?" Carson asked again as he reached for a tamale.

The two younger men then grabbed a tamale each, knowing that if they didn't help themselves, no one would offer.

William Bent took a moment to compose his thoughts. He sipped coffee while he did so. Then slowly, as if the words pained him, he said, "We figured they'd be worse off bein' free than they would bein' with us." He looked like he just swallowed something foul.

"That ain't right," Carson said, reaching for a piece of fry bread. His appetite was prodigious for so small and slender a man, but he made no apologies for it. Most of the men who made their life out of trapping in the Rocky Mountains were the same way. William Bent could still do it, Carson knew, if he was of a mind. But Bent had been out of the mountains for some time now, and was slowly losing some of the ways that set mountaineers off from the rest of humanity.

"I didn't say it was right," Bent said reluctantly. "I reckon they'd just stay on with us, and we wouldn't mind that in the least. But what'd happen to 'em if I went under, or if Charlie did?"

"They'd get by," Carson offered, the wad of food in his mouth garbling the words. "Hell, you know that. Solomon's done it, Jim Beckwourth, and a heap of others too."

Bent nodded. "True enough. But if we set 'em free and somethin' was to happen to me and Charlie, they might come to a bad end."

"Hell," Carson snorted, coming close to spraying the table with mashed pieces of fry bread, "that could happen to 'em any time."

"Damn, where'd you learn to eat. Your ma know you eat like that?"

"You leave my ma out of this, Bill Bent," Carson said in mock anger. "And don't you try changin' the subject. You ain't answered me."

Bent shrugged and swallowed the bite of tamale. "It's out of my hands, Kit. It's all up to Charlie." He paused. "What in hell's got you so all fired up over freein' slaves?" he asked.

Like the Bents, Carson was from slave-holding territory. Also like the Bents, he was a bit uncomfortable about it. Not that he owned any. Unlike the Bents, his family barely had enough simply to live. It was Carson's turn to shrug. "I dunno," he offered. "It just seems the right thing to do. After all the service Dick and Charlotte's given you, they ought to have a payback."

Bent thought about it for a little, then nodded. "You might be right, ol' hoss. I'll take it up with Charlie again next time I see him."

"Speakin' of Charlie," Carson said with a short, hoarse laugh, "I understand the ol' hoss had hisself a hell of a honeymoon."

Bent started to chuckle. "It's the truth." He shook his head. "Damn fool gets hitched and then leaves his new bride settin' there all on her own whilst he goes trapisin' off down the trail."

The laughter almost shocked Bent's two younger brothers. When it wound down, Carson said, trying again, "What about you, Bill?" He cast a sly look at his friend. "Ain't it about time you spread your robe over some lovely *señorita?*"

"None of your damn business." Bent laughed. "What about you?"

"I got me a woman," Carson said proudly. "Singin' Wind. And she's as pregnant as hell too, by God." He burst into laughter.

"No!" Bent exclaimed. "When?"

"Hell if I know," Carson said with a shrug. "Couple more months, I figure, judgin' by her size and when she realized she was with child."

"Well that shines, boy. It purely does."

"Now, back to you. It's about time you took yourself a wife."

"Goddamn, leave off with it," Bent said with a laugh. "Charlie harpin' on it at his weddin' was bad enough. I don't need it from you."

Carson looked at him, wondering why Bent was so uncomfortable. Then he decided that Bent most likely had someone in mind and had either been unable to convince her—and her father—that he was right for her, or had not yet been able to make his intentions known.

"So, who is she?" Carson asked boldly.

Bent glared at him. Only a friend—a very good friend—could get away with such a thing. "That ain't none of your concern," he said stiffly, filling his mouth with food.

"Hell," Carson chuckled, "maybe I can help. Let her pa know of your intentions. You know, maybe give you a good word or something down in Taos."

"I don't need no goddamn help from the likes of you," Bent half growled. "And I don't want no help."

Carson shrugged. "Suits me." He was eager to find out who it was—Charles Bent's wife had two sisters, and it would not be unthought of for the next younger Bent to marry one—but he knew he would find out sooner or later. Still, he was not one to give up so easily, whether it was taking beaver or eliciting information.

Carson was still eating, though he stopped stuffing food into his mouth long enough to pour himself another mug of coffee. "You're what, twenty-five, twenty-six, Bill?" he asked innocently.

"Twenty-seven," Bent said a little sourly.

"See," Carson said with a grin, "soon you'll be so old you won't be able to get it up no more, and then where'll you be?"

"Still here, you parsimonious little fart," Bent said somewhat heatedly. "Whilst you'll be planted in the ground."

"You think some Injun's gonna get me with an arrer, eh?" Carson said, still chuckling.

"Hell, no," Bent said, lips curling up just a bit. "I'm gonna put a lead pill in your goddamn meatbag."

"This chil'd like to see that," Carson said, thrusting out his chest.

"Any time you're ready." He only half meant it.

"Think I'll just have me another tamale," Carson said, unashamed.

{ 20 }

With all the work, Bent found himself with little time to spend with his friend, except in the evenings. It was the one thing he missed since he had stopped trapping —the camaraderie of the men around a fire.

Carson tired of sitting around doing nothing, so when several trappers stopped by on their way to Taos, Carson hooked up with them.

Bent missed his friend, as he missed his older brother. True, he had the two younger brothers around, but it wasn't quite the same. George and Robert had no experience in the mountains, as he himself did. It was not their fault that they had come of age after he and Charles had left the trapping end of things and become more settled. William did not fault them, but he did miss having family around who had shared his experiences.

Thinking of such things also brought thoughts about what Carson had said—and what Charles had too— about marriage, since Charles had gone and married the daughter of a wealthy Taos *hacendado*.

He realized, though, that he had been waiting—unconsciously to be sure, but that did not lessen its truth —for Gray Thunder's two daughters to come of age, particularly Owl Woman, the older of the two.

For the first time, he felt a need to get married; to find Gray Thunder and see what the old chief would take for his daughter. Trouble was, he had no idea where Gray Thunder's camp was these days, and he had to get out on his trading route before the Indians had traded away all their pelts to others.

In some ways, he looked forward to getting away from the fort. There was a good chance he would find Gray Thunder's village somewhere out there. Then he might be able to talk with the old warrior for his daughter's hand.

All the work required of him kept him too busy to entertain thoughts of marriage more often than not. But it was in the quiet times that he most often thought about Owl Woman.

Finally he left the fort on his annual trading run. He would cover hundreds of miles with his mules heavily laden with trade goods that the Cheyennes, Arapahos, Comanches, Kiowas, and any other Indians he came across who seemed peaceable would want. He would make a wide circle, first hitting the Cheyennes and Arapahos north and east of the fort. Then he would swing around toward the south, into Kiowa country, and then into the barren, harsh Llano Estacado.

He had had no luck in finding Gray Thunder, and he took that as an omen. He could not spend all his time in Cheyenne and Arapaho country, so he headed into Kiowa lands. Then another winter snuck up on Bent, arriving as if he had not been paying attention. Still, it had been a good season, and he was loaded down with pelts when he returned to the fort. He never did find Gray Thunder's village before the winter locked him into the fort again.

Bent was mighty relieved when early in the spring Gray Thunder's band moved into the trees along the Arkansas River near the fort. Still, he had to wait awhile, since there was so much work to be done to get the caravans ready for bringing their catch east. Finally Charles pulled out, though, with fifteen wagons creaking under the weight of hides and furs. William watched as they left, mule skinners cracking their whips and cursing mightily.

Once they were out of sight over the horizon, Bent turned to St. Vrain. "You feel up to keepin' watch over things a few days, Ceran?"

"I suppose so. Why?"

"I've got a couple things to do in Gray Thunder's village." He paused, knowing he would be as embarrassed as hell if the true reason got out. He worried that St. Vrain might be able to read it on his face.

"And what is zis business?" St. Vrain asked, his face joyful, as it almost always was.

"I'd ruther not say, Ceran," Bent confessed sheepishly.

"Is it related to ze company?" His face hardened just a bit.

"Well, yes and no."

"Eh?" St. Vrain was confused. He was used to dickering and dealing with sharp-witted businessmen, but Bent was suddenly confounding him. He had no idea what Bent was getting at.

Bent sighed. "I can't explain it just yet," he said uncomfortably. He paused. "But if'n it works, it'll help the company considerably."

St. Vrain cocked an eye at him, then smiled. *"Bien,"* he said with a nod. "How long will you need for zis business?"

"I ain't sure, Ceran." His tone suddenly got an edge. "And I'd be obliged if you weren't to question me no more on it."

That baffled look spread over St. Vrain's face again, then he nodded. *"Oui.* I will not ask ze questions. What is left to be done zen, eh?" Suddenly he was all business again.

"Let's get out of this sun," Bent suggested.

"A good idea, *mon ami.*"

Inside St. Vrain's apartment, which sat in its lonely solitude above the kitchen and dining area, Bent went through the work that was yet to be done. Twice while they spoke Charlotte clumped up the stairs, bringing the two men coffee and food. The second time, the men were almost done. Bent reached for a cookie from the plate Charlotte had just set on the table. He took a good bite. "Damn," he said, "if she don't make the best *bizcochitos* this chil's ever ate."

St. Vrain, eating one of the cookies, nodded. *"Oui. Très bon."*

When Bent finished explaining the work to be done, it was still only late afternoon. He rose, ready to leave. "Don't forget, you got George, Robert, and Marcellin to help you," Bent added.

"How have zey been doing?"

Bent shrugged, uncomfortable again. "Fair, I reckon."

St. Vrain squinted at him. "Tell me ze truth, *mon ami,*" he said quietly but firmly.

Bent took a deep breath and blew it out. "Marcellin's probably the best of the three, as far as business goes, but that ain't sayin' a hell of a lot." He hesitated. "Georgie's mind ain't on his work, and Bob's still a mite young. I don't know, but maybe it's 'cause they didn't come out here in the old days, the days when you and Charlie and me were out workin' the mountains. Like that time Sylvestre Pratte was put under, up there in North Park, and you had to take over. Or the time me and Charlie held off them goddamn Snakes up on the Cache le Poudre."

St. Vrain nodded in full understanding. *"Oui,"* he said almost sadly. "Zese young pups, zey come out 'ere when all ze troubles are behind, after we have conquered ze savages, and zey know not'ing about our business."

"Well, I suppose we can't be too hard on 'em. It ain't their doin's that they just come out here."

"It's true," St. Vrain said with a nod and another

bite. He sighed and slurped down coffee. "But zey 'ave potential, eh?"

"I think they do. But it might take some doin'."

"We must be patient, zen."

Bent nodded. A half hour later he left, three packhorses and a pack mule trailing him.

Gray Thunder's lodge was easy to pick out. It sat in solitary splendor in the center of the small village. It was also larger and more ornately decorated than any of the others. If that was not enough to indicate Gray Thunder's status in the village, the tripod rack of weapons would. It held a bull-hide shield adorned with the picture of an eagle flying through storm clouds. The rack also held Gray Thunder's bow in a mountain lion case with a matching quiver of arrows. A long, thin lance with a metal point leaned comfortably against the rack, as did an old flintlock trade gun with a powder horn and shot bag.

Bent stopped in front of the tipi and dismounted. He knew that every eye in the village was on him, not so much that he was a stranger here, but because he had never come like this, with horses laden with booty. Bent called for entrance to Gray Thunder's lodge. When it was granted, he stepped inside.

It took some moments for his eyes to adjust to the dimness, but then he spotted Gray Thunder. The People still revered him, despite the wrinkles creasing his leathery skin, or the small infirmities of advancing age, or the gray streaking his plaited hair. "*Hola*, Gray Thunder," Bent said as he sat cross-legged across the fire from the Cheyenne.

"*Hola*, Little White Man." Gray Thunder grinned, showing several gaps in his teeth. It was irritating to him that his teeth were falling out, his joints ached, and his old scars seemed troublesome. The only thing he was somewhat glad about was the fact that he was not losing his hair. He had seen too many white men who had gone bald. It was a weird thing, Gray Thunder thought.

The two men sat silently as one of Gray Thunder's wives—Bent thought her name was Falling Star, but he was not sure—brought each man a bowl of food. The men ate, and then passed a pipe between them.

Finally Gray Thunder asked, "What brings Little White Man to my lodge?"

Bent hesitated. He had thought of this all winter, but now that he was here, he suddenly felt a reluctance growing inside him.

"You can speak in front of me, old friend," Gray Thunder said softly.

Bent nodded. "It's time I took a wife," he said in halting Cheyenne. He had learned that language, but he was still unused to it.

"So?" Gray Thunder said. His eyes widened, trying to show a surprise he did not feel. "And why do you come to my lodge?"

"I have seen your daughter, Owl Woman, and I have watched her for some time. She cooks well, is a good worker. The hides she has prepared are among the best I've seen. And she is pleasing to the eyes."

"All these things are true," Gray Thunder acknowledged. He knew Bent wanted his daughter; now all the old warrior had to do was see how much he could squeeze out of the trader. Not that he disliked Bent. To the contrary, he liked Bent a lot. Still, one must be practical in these matters. "But she has many suitors." A gleam of greed touched his eyes.

Bent saw the glint, and was certain the young woman would be his. He wanted, however, to get away as cheaply as possible. Not that he wanted to gouge Gray Thunder, but he too had to be practical. "I wouldn't expect otherwise," Bent said. "But I have brought many things—presents for Gray Thunder, so that he might look favorably on me."

Gray Thunder tried to look nonchalant, but Bent

still could see avarice in the old man's eyes. "Perhaps I should see some of these gifts," he said. "Then we will talk."

Bent went back to his own brand of English, knowing Gray Thunder spoke it some and understood it. "Let's cut the crap, Gray Thunder," Bent said boldly. "You and I both know I can outbid any man in the village. Or any of the other villages, for that matter. I ain't got the time, and I'm too goddamn old to be playing games over this. I've got three goddamn horses and a mule packed with gifts for you. I—"

"And you will leave the horses?" Gray Thunder asked, no shame creasing his face.

Bent shrugged. "If you want 'em, they're yours."

Gray Thunder could see the roan, since the flap of the lodge was open. "And the spotted horse?"

"No," Bent said quietly, but his clipped intonation was clear.

"It is a good horse."

"Goddamn right it is. But you ain't gonna have it. Besides, what in hell you need another horse for? Christ, you got so many goddamn horses you can't count 'em all even if you spent a week at it."

Gray Thunder grinned. He had pushed as far as he could, and he knew it. He also knew that Little White Man would have many good presents. Gray Thunder was getting a good deal here. Not only the presents, but more favorable trade terms, since Bent would be his son-in-law. "It is good," Gray Thunder said with finality. He reached for his pipe to sanctify the deal.

❧{ 21 }❧

Bent and Gray Thunder finished their negotiations in a quiet, friendly atmosphere. There was no need for either to try to impress the other. Both knew the esteem in which the other was held by his people.

Bent made many trips to the pack animals and back inside the lodge, carrying the things he had brought to give to Gray Thunder. He knew the village was watching intently, even as the Cheyennes tried to pretend they were not. Gray Thunder nodded as the gifts were laid before him—knives; packets of beads; iron kettles and spoons; sheets of thin iron for arrowheads; a fancy, spangled chief's coat with gold buttons and epaulets; brass tacks; tobacco; bolts of cloth; a clay pipe; several small mirrors; blankets; needles and awls; and vermilion.

Once that was done, and the two men had smoked again, Bent asked, "Then how're we gonna do this?"

Gray Thunder puffed on his new clay pipe—this was for enjoying, not for ceremonial purposes—while he thought. He knew that Bent had neither the time nor inclination to court Owl Woman. Bent was an important man in the big mud lodge on the Arkansas. Still, Gray Thunder hoped to have something resembling a Cheyenne marriage rite performed, if only for his daughter's sake.

Finally the old warrior talked, explaining what he had in mind. It didn't take long. At the end of it Bent nodded, accepting the plan. Then they went outside, where Gray Thunder looked over his new horses.

"You can have the damn mule too, if you're of a mind." It wasn't the one Winter Hawk had given him. That mule was a willing animal, strong and sturdy. Bent did not want to part with it, so had brought along another, one that was known to be particularly cantankerous.

Gray Thunder nodded. He did not care much for mules, but with all his new goods, brought by Bent, he could use the mule and save at least one of his ponies. One of Gray Thunder's grandsons came and took the animals away. Then Gray Thunder brought Bent to a lodge owned by a nephew of Gray Thunder. The old warrior invited the nephew and his wife to stay the next few nights with his family. The nephew acquiesced.

Bent entered the lodge, feeling a little uncomfortable about having been the one who got the family evicted. But he soothed his conscience by reminding himself that the nephew was probably honored at having such an esteemed guest staying in his lodge, while he and his wife went to live in the comfort of Gray Thunder's tipi.

He went outside, and noticed that people were watching the lodge. He was angry at that, but he also knew he could not change it, so he relaxed. Darkness was creeping over the village, and Bent headed for his horse. He unsaddled the animal and curried it. Gray Thunder's grandson came and took the horse, planning to put it with the many others of the village. Bent went back to "his" lodge.

Soon after, Owl Woman arrived, bearing a bowl of stew for Bent. She was escorted by her sister, Yellow Woman. Owl Woman was dressed in her finest—a cream-colored elk-skin dress that reached to her knees. It was trimmed in blue cloth and adorned with shells and beads. On her lower legs she wore leggings and soft, finely beaded moccasins. Her hair hung in two long braids down her back. The center part in her hair and her cheeks were brushed with vermilion.

Bent didn't know what to say to her, so he simply took the bowl and nodded in thanks. Owl Woman and Yellow Woman turned and left. Bent sat there watching the flap of the lodge for some time. He was confused, what with being engaged now, so to speak. It was an odd sensation. But certainly no stranger than Gray Thunder's offer of Yellow Woman too. Bent knew the Cheyennes allowed—even encouraged—a man to marry sisters. Bent didn't think he was that free just yet. He might be persuaded someday, though, since Yellow Woman was as comely as her sister, looking almost the same. Yellow Woman was a little shorter, and perhaps a bit fuller, but other than that, they were nearly identical in appearance.

From his surreptitious watching of the sisters over the past few years, though, Bent saw many differences in them. Owl Woman was outgoing and vivacious; she was friendly and full of chatter. But Yellow Woman was quiet and unassuming. She went about her work with a minimum of fuss, not taking much part in the singing and gabbing most of the women engaged in while working. She gave the impression of being thoughtful and deliberate. Not that Owl Woman's behavior was unseemly in comparison. Bent figured Yellow Woman's subdued behavior was a matter of her position as the younger sister.

Bent ate the stew slowly, enjoying it. Then he smoked a pipe down as he made entries in his journal. From outside he could hear the plaintive notes of a flute. He smiled a little, and wished the young man luck in his pursuit of love.

For himself, Bent was nervous, which made him irritable. That, in turn, annoyed him. He was no love-struck boy to be worried about taking a woman. He had had his share of women in his twenty-eight years. Finally he growled at himself and went to sleep.

The morning brought constant reminders of his impending nuptials. He ate in Gray Thunder's lodge and spent much of the day talking with the old man. But in the afternoon he excused himself, stopped in "his" lodge, and then wandered down to the river. Behind a screen of brush and trees, he stripped and jumped into the water. He grabbed his cake of soap and lathered himself up. The Cheyennes, he had found, bathed daily, hot or cold, and he did not want to offend his bride on their first night together. Finished washing, he lay on the grass near the riverbank to let the warm air dry him. Then he dressed in a set of fancy buckskins and went to the lodge and waited expectantly.

Just after the sun disappeared, spreading dark shadows, he heard people approaching. He sat at his fire, looking like he had not a care in the world. Suddenly Winter Hawk, Black Feather, and Rain Beating Down entered the lodge, carrying Owl Woman. They set her down, made a bawdy remark or two, and then left.

Bent did not know what to say. Everything of the past day was focused on this moment, in which he was sitting with a woman who was his wife; a woman he did not know at all. The situation was awkward.

It was no better for Owl Woman. She had thought many times of the day she would become a full woman. She had always expected that she would marry with the band, or at most, into one of the other Cheyenne bands. Now she was here with a man—a white man, no less—who was as strange to her as the big mud lodge in which Bent lived. Now she was married to him. She supposed that was a good thing; everyone said so. She could see some benefits to marrying such a man. He controlled the big fort, where the Cheyennes got many of the things that had made life easier. Still, she had heard tales of how these bearded white men treated women. This man—her husband, she reminded herself sternly—had a mean, angry face. But she could recall no instance where he had lost his temper or did anything that showed him to be nasty. Indeed, many of the warriors she knew of were far more vicious than Bent appeared to be.

"Are you hungry?" he asked, not knowing what else to say.

Owl Woman looked blankly at him, and Bent realized he had spoken in English, which she knew little of. He repeated the question in Cheyenne, feeling more foolish with every second.

"Yes." It was a timid voice, but sweet and melodious.

Bent stood and took Owl Woman's arm. She looked up at him, a bit of fear in her eyes. She did not know how to react. "Come, sit," Bent said softly in Cheyenne.

Owl Woman stared at Bent a moment. He was so strange, she thought; the hard, weather-beaten face of a warrior, the soft, caring tones of a lover. She smiled tentatively. In relief, Bent followed suit.

They sat and ate from the buffalo stew that Gray Thunder's ancient wife had made earlier in the day. Afterward, they still sat in awkward silence, sipping coffee. Bent smoked a pipe, which relaxed him some. He took the time to look at Owl Woman.

She was almost as tall as he, but seemed much tinier. She had delicate wrists and ankles. Her skin was a coppery tan, her cheekbones high and prominent. Her face was wide but came to a softly rounded chin; full lips enticed him; dark eyes encouraged him. The soft folds of her elk-skin dress could not hide the rounded curves of her body.

Bent got out his journal, ink, and quill. He began writing the day's entry, much of it reflecting on the oddity of his situation. After a few moments Owl Woman edged closer and closer, until she was looking over his shoulder. Her hot breath brushed his freshly shaven cheek.

Because of Owl Woman's nearness, Bent found himself unable to fully concentrate on the words. He kept at it, though, until he was finished. He snapped the leather-bound journal closed.

He stood and put his materials away. When he turned back, Owl Woman had stood. He watched, excited, as she wriggled out of her dress. With pounding heart she sat on the pile of blankets and buffalo robes that served as a bed and pulled off her moccasins and leggings. Owl Woman looked at Bent. She wasn't sure of herself, but she knew it was time for them to couple.

Bent swallowed hard. He was twenty-eight and had been out here for more than a decade. He had had his share of Indian women too, so lovemaking was nothing new to him. But this was somehow different. He supposed it was because Owl Woman was his new wife. He planned on being with her for some time, not just a quick roll in the robes.

Owl Woman was still waiting, and Bent edged forward, beginning to pull off his shirt. In another step he could feel his confidence—and his body—growing, rising to the occasion.

They spent two more days—and nights—in their lodge, hardly venturing out except to relieve themselves or to wash in the stream. After their first night together, they found themselves able to talk to each other. He was fascinated by Owl Woman's tales of Cheyenne life and lore; she was captivated by Bent's scribbling.

Bent had a pretty good command of the Cheyenne language, but Owl Woman knew almost nothing of English. He set about trying to teach her English, as well as Spanish.

Finally, though, Bent knew he had to get back to the fort. He wasn't thrilled with the idea, since he was enjoying his life with Owl Woman. Still, he could not impose on St. Vrain's good nature too much. With regret, he told Owl Woman to pack whatever she wanted to take.

She looked worried, but did not want to say anything.

Bent could see it in her eyes, though. He smiled at her and cupped her soft, rounded chin in one of his callused hands. "If you're going to be my woman, my wife, I want you living with me, when we can."

Questions filled her dark eyes.

"You'll come back here often enough," he reassured her. He knew that she would be worried about such a thing. After all, he was dragging her away from her family, taking her into an unknown and probably frightening world. She had every right to be concerned.

"Oh?" she asked, not quite sure how to take his statement.

"There'll be times when I'm off trading or something. At those times, you can come back here. One thing, though, you'll have to make us a lodge where you can stay at those times. Can you do that?"

Her womanly pride perked up and she nodded. "Yes."

"Good." He grinned. It softened the roughness of his face a little. "Of course, we don't have to leave right now."

She looked at him, not sure she took his meaning. One look and she knew. She felt a flush of desire, mixed with pride. She was proud that she had been a good enough wife in these few short days that he actually desired her. She smiled and nodded. Taking one of his hands in hers, she tugged him toward the robes.

Half a mile from the fort, Bent began to wonder just how much of a ribbing he would take at the fort. If Carson was there, and Charlie, he could expect a couple hours' worth. He didn't think St. Vrain would tease him much, but one could never tell with the jolly Frenchman. Seth Walsh and Ramsay MacGregor and even Solomon would be unmerciful on him, if given half a chance. He squirmed in the saddle, suddenly thinking he had made a major mistake in marrying Owl Woman.

He shrugged. It made no difference. They would only ride him for not being married at his age. He also counted on his stubbornness. He was something of a rebel. Always had been. Charles and St. Vrain had become Mexican citizens and taken Mexican wives; even Carson was leaning in that direction, though he had an Arapaho wife. William, though, felt himself drawn to the Cheyennes. If anybody didn't like that, he was more than willing to face any challenge they might fling at him.

Bent was aware that some of the men working outside the fort stopped what they were doing and stared at him. He ignored them, keeping his eyes straight ahead, a solemn look plastered on his face.

It was a little harder to ignore everyone once he rode into the *placita*, but still he would not acknowledge any of the stares or the quiet ribald comments directed his way. He stopped his horse in front of his apartment and dismounted. He helped Owl Woman down off her pony. "Juan," he called loudly. "Juan! Get your ass over here."

A Mexican boy ran up. *"Sí, señor?"* he asked, a little worried.

"Unload those two mules there, and put all the things in my room," Bent said gruffly. "Then take my horse to the corral and tend him. Get someone to help you, if you need it."

"Sí," he said enthusiastically. *"Sí, señor."*

Bent stiffly walked Owl Woman into his apartment. A few moments later St. Vrain arrived, his jovial face beaming brightly. Bent glared at him. "Not a word, Ceran," he said harshly. "Not a goddamn word."

"But *mon ami*," St. Vrain said happily, "this is a joyous time, *non?*" He answered his own question: *"Oui. Mais oui."* He laughed, partly because he liked to laugh, partly for the sour look on Bent's face. "And who is zis lovely mademoiselle?" he asked.

St. Vrain had no particular liking for Indian women. He had partaken of their pleasures often enough, but for a wife? Never would he even consider that. He wanted a woman of refinement and breeding, like the daughters of the *ricos* down in Taos and Santa Fe. Still, Bent was his friend and business partner, and if Bent wanted an Indian woman, who was Ceran St. Vrain to say no?

"Her name's Owl Woman," Bent said sourly. "Since I can't handle her Cheyenne name, I'm callin' her Sally."

St. Vrain nodded and took Owl Woman's right hand in his. He bent slightly and kissed it. "*Bonjour, mademoiselle*. Or should I say *madame*? No matter. You are welcome 'ere."

Owl Woman nodded shyly, not sure what this black-bearded man was saying. But he smiled and looked nice. She tentatively smiled back.

Within a day Owl Woman was accepted around the fort, and the teasing of her husband dwindled to an occasional lewd remark—made only by the men who knew Bent most closely, of course. New arrivals at the fort might grin and make a lascivious comment or two pertaining to Bent's talents in the robes, but for the most part Bent was left in peace.

Owl Woman quickly began learning Spanish from Bent and from the three wives of Mexican laborers, and English from Bent and Charlotte. It was almost comical to see the rotund, smiling Charlotte giving the Cheyenne woman elocution lessons. For that matter, it was the same with Bent, considering that his brand of English was nearly as fractured as was Charlotte's, just in slightly different ways.

Bent went back to work, feeling guilty for having taken a week off and leaving St. Vrain to run the fort. St. Vrain never said anything critical, and seemed not to mind at all. Still, Bent felt guilty.

However, four days after Bent had returned to the fort, St. Vrain announced his intention to leave. Sitting in the cool, dim quietness of his apartment, St. Vrain said, "There is still to come that shipment of paper and ink for the *alcalde*. Charles sent word by messenger zat it was being sent here from Sain' Louie in a different caravan."

"Charlie ain't bringin' it himself?" Bent was a little

surprised. His brother was so well thought of that he frequently was elected captain of the biggest caravans on the Santa Fe Trail. It was unusual for him to send something he had agreed to carry with another train of wagons.

"No. Ze message said zose t'ings are not arrive in Sain' Louie. When zey do, one wagon will bring zem here. We are to send zem to Taos. Charles says he'll be here soon. He could not wait for zose t'ings in Sain' Louie. As soon as he unloads supplies here, he will go on."

Bent nodded. "You got any ideas on who to send it with?"

St. Vrain ran his short, stubby fingers through the lush tangle of facial hair. The Indians even named him after it—Black Beard. "You were right," he finally said, his fingers continuing to work through the beard. "Marcellin is ze best of ze three. Maybe you could have him take ze wagons to Taos?" His voice trailed away. He was concerned that Bent might think him favoring his brother over the two younger Bents.

"I reckon if we had to use one of 'em, Marcellin's the right choice. If'n I can, I'll send a couple older boys with him, just to keep an eye on him." After saying it, Bent was concerned that St. Vrain might think he didn't trust the Frenchman's brother.

"*Bon.*" St. Vrain bobbed his head in agreement.

"Remember, though," Bent added, "I ain't sure who'll be around here then. We might have to send him along with some of the other greenhorns. I don't think I could afford to lose Seth or Solomon. And certainly not Ramsay."

"I understand," St. Vrain said evenly. "It will be a good test of Marcellin." His thoughts drifted back a few years, to his brother Felix, killed in the Black Hawk War. It chilled him to think that he might be sending another brother to his death. But it had to be done, he knew. The youth could not be coddled forever.

"Anything else, Ceran?" Bent asked.

"*Oui*. Ze message Charles sent says we are to proceed with the new place up near ze South Platte."

"You sure you don't want Marcellin to take on that task?"

St. Vrain thought a moment, then shook his head. "No. George would be ze better."

St. Vrain pulled out the next morning, escorted by six armed men. It was always that way. No one traveled alone out here, except through necessity. It was hotter than blazes already, though it was only May. Bent figured they were in for a long summer. He would not enjoy being out on the trail with such withering heat. He shrugged. Nothing could change the weather, and fretting over it did no good.

Two and a half weeks later the paper and ink arrived. Four small wagons rolled into the fort. A tall, foul-featured man of uncertain parentage, warped, blackened teeth, and lice- and flea-infested rotting clothes supervised the unloading of the items.

Bent could not stand the man—Claude Pugh—never had and never would. He didn't even like being in the same fort with Pugh, and when he was forced into it, he always tried to stand upwind of the walking compost heap.

"Your brudder say I'm to take what furs you got here and brung dem to Innypendence onct we was unload all dis shit," Pugh mumbled. The wad of tobacco in his cheek made his horrid speech even worse.

"Ain't too many," Bent said, wanting to hold his nose, but being a shade too polite to do so. "I'll have a couple boys help you load 'em."

"Sure," Pugh said. He turned a fraction of an inch to the side, closed one nostril with a filthy, crusted index finger and blew out a glob of red and green snot. He repeated the ritual with the other nostril. "Goddamn if that ain't a heap fuckin' better," he said with a disgusting grin. "You got any fuckin' grub innis shithole here?'' he asked. "Me anna boys gotta have some grub afore we leave.''

Bent nodded. "You'll leave right after you've ate and the furs're loaded,'' he suggested.

"You in a goddamn fuckin' hurry to see us gone?'' Pugh asked nastily. His scabby face wrinkled in anger.

"Yep,'' Bent said bluntly.

Pugh thought about pounding the small fort owner, but just before raising his fist, he took a look around. Several men were on the second floor walkway, leisurely holding rifles and watching intently. Pugh decided restraint was wise just now. Later, though, he might punch this little man's face in for him.

"I don't want you and your boys in my dinin' room,'' Bent said flatly. "Y'all set your putrefyin' carcasses over there''—he pointed to the area in front of the blacksmith shop—"and I'll have some eats brought to you.'' He spun and walked away, disgusted.

He went into the kitchen, found Charlotte and explained to her what she would need. "And don't give 'em nothin' more than some *atole*—all they can eat— and corn bread, if you got some made up. If not, *pika* bread'll do for that bunch.''

Charlotte nodded. "Don' you worry none about dat, Mistah Bent. I knows how to treats folk like dem.''

Bent nodded, and then grinned. "But first, I'd like some *arroz dulce*—that is what I'm smellin', ain't it?''

"Yassir,'' Charlotte said with a huge smile. Charlotte Green was a good cook, and took pride in it. It always pleased her when she received a compliment like that. She grew a little serious. "But was I you, Mistah Bent, I'd let me feed dem folk out dere first.''

"Why?''

"De faster dey gets dere food, de faster dey's gonna eat. De faster dey eat, de faster dey's gonna get outta dis here fo't.''

"Makes sense to me,'' Bent agreed. "But could you bring me some coffee first, at least?''

"Sho' can."

Bent sipped at his coffee, watching as Charlotte, her husband, and Inez Soto—one of the laborers' wives and one of the few women at Bent's Fort—carried a large kettle of thin corn gruel, several wooden bowls, spoons, a bunch of tin mugs, and a huge coffeepot outside.

Soon Charlotte and Dick were back, and Charlotte served Bent a heaping portion of the rice pudding. Bent dug into the delicacy, enjoying its rich, sugary taste. He was about halfway through when Charlotte entered the dining room. After feeding Bent, she went back outside to see if Inez needed help with feeding the visitors. As she came in, Bent could see a worried, perplexed look on Charlotte's face.

"What is it?" he asked, a spoonful of pudding frozen halfway to his mouth.

"I cain't find Inez nowhere," she said, worried.

"She go back and see Pedro?" Bent asked.

"Naw, sir. Pedro be out with de horses tidday."

Bent set his spoon down, stood, and walked out the open door. He stood there, looking all around. Something tugged at his brain, and he tried to give it a little room to grow as his eyes swept the *placita*. In a few moments he realized what it was—two of the freighters were not there. He figured they had gone to use the outhouse or something, but he couldn't be sure. He stepped from under the portico into the thick heat of the sun and walked across the bare, dusty earth, eyes constantly on the move. He ignored the curious looks from the teamsters.

He thought he heard something out of the ordinary, but with all the noise of the fort, he could not be sure. Still, it seemed to have come from back near the powder magazine. He strolled that way, alert.

He found the two missing freighters—and Inez. The men had her down and had stuffed a filthy rag in her mouth.

One of the men was kneeling on her arms and was bent over to hold her legs apart. He was kneeling near her head, and the way he was bent placed his revolting crotch inches from Inez's face.

The other man had shoved up her dress and pulled down her thin cotton undergarment. He had also dropped his pants and was kneeling between Inez's legs.

Bent came up on that man and without a thought slammed him in the right temple with the butt of his flintlock pistol. The wood of the pistol cracked and the man fell to the left, landing on Inez's right leg. He was not unconscious, but Bent knew the man would not be bothering anyone for a while.

The other man looked up, fear, anger, and consternation stamped on his brutal face. He released the woman and stood. "Whatcha do dat fer?" he asked. He was of medium height and build, but Bent supposed he was stronger than he looked. Most of the teamsters were.

Bent kept his eyes on the man, but said, "You all right, señora?"

"*Si,*" she answered, her voice shaky.

"Can you get up?"

"I think so." She was mortified with embarrassment at lying in the dirt with her dress shoved up, her undergarments down, and her privates on view for all to see. She wriggled mightily against the dead weight of the man on her leg, finally extricating herself. She rose quickly, awash in relief as her faded cotton dress fell back down, covering her.

"They debase you, señora?" Bent asked, eyes locked on the man.

"No," Inez said, sobbing softly.

"All right, Inez," Bent said with a nod. "Go on back to the kitchen. Charlotte'll take care of you."

"What are you going to do, Señor Bent?" she asked.

Bent looked at Inez for the first time since he had

clubbed the one man. He had kept his eyes on the man standing, not only to make sure he did not do anything, but also because he wanted to avoid embarrassing Inez even more. "I'm going to make sure these two don't never bother another woman," he said with finality.

She nodded and started to walk away.

"You ain't gonna do no shit," the man said sharply. He had sized Bent up while the fort owner had been playing nice fellow to the woman. He figured he could take Bent easily.

Bent ran a hand through his hair, feeling the warm moistness of sweat. "What's your name, boy?" he asked icily.

"Jethro Carpis," the man said, suddenly confused. "Why?"

"Him?" Bent asked, pointing at the man groaning in the dust.

"Buford Crump," Carpis said. "Why?" he asked again.

"Need to know for the grave markers," Bent said matter-of-factly.

Carpis laughed, the sound wheezy. "You think you're some kinda big chief just cuz you own 'is fort, do yuh? Well, 'at don't mean a goddamn fuckin' thing to me."

Bent shrugged. "It don't mean shit to me what you think—if you even can think."

Without another word Carpis pulled his knife and charged. When he was only a step away, Bent thrust his left arm up, deflecting Carpis's knife arm. At the same time, he pivoted on the ball of his left foot, shoving Carpis to the side.

Bent spun and moved three steps. He smashed a balled fist into Carpis's face, breaking the man's nose. As Carpis was reeling from that blow, Bent jerked his knee up, crushing the man's testes.

Carpis gasped, eyes wide with shock. He dropped his

knife and brought both hands down to his crotch, try-ing somehow to ease the pain that radiated from his privates. The move left the rest of him open. And with the shock, he could not focus on Bent anyway.

Bent stepped up, pulling his knife at the same time. One swift motion and Carpis fell to the dirt, blood spurting from the gaping slash just above his Adam's apple.

Bent turned and saw that Crump had managed to get to his feet. The side of his head was smeared with a little blood and already swelling. His eyes were dazed.

Bent did not care. He simply crossed the few steps separating him from Crump and then buried the knife to the hilt in Crump's chest.

23

Bent strolled through the small passageway between the *placita* and the powder magazine. He stopped in front of Pugh and dropped something in Pugh's lap, barely missing Pugh's fourth bowl of *atole*.

Pugh looked up in surprise, then down at the bloody scalps lying in his lap. "What da hell id dis here?" he asked.

Bent ignored the question. He pulled out his pocket watch. "You got a quarter hour to get your stinkin' carcass out of here," he said, biting back the rage. "You'll find what's left of Crump and Carpis back there." Bent pointed. "You want to bury them, cart 'em out with you. You don't, we'll toss 'em out with the trash and manure."

"Whadda hell is dis all about? You kilt two a my best men." Pugh looked aggrieved.

Bent shrugged. "They shouldn't try takin' liberties that're best reserved for a husband."

"What?" Pugh asked, eyes widening in surprise and wonder. "That bean-eatin' bitch?" Bent's look was answer enough. "Hell, she's a fuckin' Mexican is all. Jesus, it ain't like she's a white woman or sumpin' like 'at."

"She's a woman," Bent said in clipped tones. "That's enough for scum like you to understand. But more than that, she was under my protection. This is my goddamn fort, and I make the goddamn rules." He looked at his watch again. "You got twelve minutes left."

Bent turned, took three steps, and then spun back. "And if you mess with our furs you'll be takin' back to St. Louis, I'll have your puny little balls decoratin' my lodge."

"Shit," Pugh breathed. "You cain't do shit to us." He suddenly felt unsure of himself, though, as hard-faced, well-armed men suddenly appeared around the fort.

"I've got a heap of friends in Missouri, and in Mexico, and damn near wherever scum like you'll turn up. I get word you've messed with my property, and you'll pay hard. You got eleven minutes."

Bent went back into the dining room, all his pleasure at the pudding dish he had been eating gone. He sat in the same spot. Charlotte came out of the kitchen and filled his mug with fresh coffee.

"Thank you, Mistah Bent," Charlotte said as she finished pouring.

"For what?" Bent asked, a little surprised.

"Fo' standin' up to them bad men like you jus' done. Ain't too many men's gonna go against another'n for the sake of a woman who ain't white folk."

Bent smiled wanly. "I only done what was right," he said softly.

"Dat you did, Mistah Bent. We be obliged, though, me'n Inez. You wants anything else right now?"

"No, thank you, Charlotte."

Bent had set his pocket watch on the table when he sat down. He looked at it frequently. It seemed that since he was watching it too closely and because he wanted the time to get past, that the second hand took an hour or so to make each small circuit.

Finally, though, it was time. Watch in hand, Bent walked outside. Pugh's men and fort workers were just about done. One of Pugh's men had spotted Bent and fear grew between his legs and in his stomach. He called softly to Pugh and jerked his head in Bent's direction.

"Hell wid 'im," Pugh said, hoping the others couldn't hear his fear.

"Shit. You saw what he did to Bufe an' Jethro. Done 'em both in wit' a knife. I ain't ever seed nobody was as good wit' a knife as Bufe."

Pugh's fear was beginning to get the better of him. "Jus' shut that flappin' goddamn hole in your face and get them ropes tied down, dammit. I wanna get outta this fuckin' hole."

Skunk Waller—who was quite aptly nicknamed—shut up and hurried to get done.

Just as Bent called out, "Time's up, boys," Pugh, standing next to the lead wagon, cracked his whip and the entourage was on its way. As soon as Pugh and his small caravan were gone, Bent called Seth Walsh. "Pick four men, good ones, saddle up and trail those bastards."

Walsh nodded. "How far?"

"All the way to Independence, if it seems needed. I want to make sure our furs—all of 'em—get there."

Walsh grinned. "Should we take them boys down?" he asked.

"Only if they try something foolish."

Walsh nodded again.

Before he could leave, Bent said. "First, though, send me a couple of the Mexican kids."

A few minutes later two boys marched stiffly up to where Bent was sitting in the dining room. They had their hats in their hands. "You wanted to see us, Señor Bent?" one asked.

"*Sí*, Miguel." Bent smiled at the boys, both of whom were twelve. "Arturo, I want you to go over by the powder magazine. See if the bodies of those two bastards are still there. If they are, gather up a few of your *compadres* and drag the bodies over by the heap of manure. Then tell ol' Crutsinger to haul 'em off soon's he can."

Arturo nodded solemnly, knowing he had been chosen for important work by the *jefe*.

Bent placed a silver dollar on the table and pushed it across toward Arturo. The boy's eyes bugged and his heart pounded. It seems, he thought, that he is giving me that money! "For your troubles," Bent said, leaving the dollar right in front of Arturo.

The boy swept it up, still not believing his good fortune. After all, this was what the hunters were paid for a day's work. "*Gracias*, Señor Bent," he said fervently. "*Muchos, muchos gracias.*" He ran outside, clutching the dollar tightly in a sweaty palm.

"And I have a chore for you too, Miguel," Bent said after a sip of coffee. "Go saddle that mouse-colored mule of mine. You tell old Juan it's on my say-so. Then you ride out to where the *vaqueros* have the herd. You know where that is?"

"*Si,*" Miguel said proudly.

"*Bueno.* You ride on out there, and tell Pedro to get his ass back here pronto. You stay there and take his place."

Miguel's blood was racing through his veins. He, little Miguel Perez, was about to be allowed to watch the horses. For so long he had dreamed of such a thing. Now it was really going to happen. He was sure that if he showed the *jefe* that he could do the job, maybe he would get it permanently. He tried to bring his focus back to what Bent was saying, hoping he had not missed anything important.

He hadn't. Bent simply had asked, "Think you could do that, boy?"

"*Si,*" Miguel answered, still overwhelmed by all this. In such a state was he that he could not figure out what he wanted to say to Bent. Or ask. He knew there was something, but his mind was still on the opportunity being given him, and his eyes were on the two—two!—silver dollars Bent was pushing toward him.

Miguel picked up the money, thinking he was

dreaming to have such riches in his small brown hand. He mumbled his thanks and started for the door. Suddenly it hit him, what he had to ask. He hurried back to the table, hoping he was not disturbing the boss.

"Yes, Miguel?" Bent said.

"Which Pedro do you want me to send back here?"

Bent looked at him blankly a moment, then nodded. "Of course. We have two Pedros, don't we? How foolish of me. Pedro Soto is the one. And don't say nothin' to him. Just tell him I want to see him pronto."

Miguel nodded, spun, and ran out of the building.

Bent smiled softly. He disliked violence, but could dish it out fiercely when the need arose. It had about ruined his day, but he decided to put it out of his mind. Help arrived in the form of Charlotte Green and the heaping bowl of *arroz dulce* she carried. Bent nodded thanks and dug in, once more enjoying the rich pudding.

An hour later Bent stood at the gate saying good-bye to Walsh's small group. They had been in no hurry to leave, considering how slowly Pugh's wagons would be moving. Walsh did not want to be right on Pugh's trail. Just close enough to get to them quickly if they tried ditching the furs or if they were in imminent danger of being attacked by Indians. In the latter case, Walsh would be out to save the furs, not Pugh and his men. There wasn't a man in the fort this day who wouldn't have gladly cut Pugh's heart out and served it to him.

Bent turned and walked back into the *placita*—and barely got out of the way as Pedro Soto galloped through the gates. A couple of chickens almost got trampled as they fled in squawking protest. Soto stopped his horse and tumbled off, fear clutching at his heart. Señor Bent would not have sent Miguel for him without reason, and all the reasons Soto could think of were bad.

He ran toward Bent, who was walking in his direction. "What is it, Señor Bent?" Soto asked. "What's wrong?"

"Inez had a bit of trouble," Bent said quietly in Spanish. "She is all right. She was not hurt. But I think it's good that you be with her now."

"Trouble, *Jefe?*" Soto's mouth dried up. "What kind of trouble?"

"She will tell you."

"Where is she?" Soto asked anxiously.

"In a moment. First let me say that she will need your kindness of spirit, your affection, and most of all, your sympathy. She had no choice in what happened. Do you understand?"

"*Sí,*" Soto said, not really understanding. It was hard for him to speak, since he was unable to work up any saliva. His groin tightened in fear and worry, until he hardly felt like a man at all down there.

Bent was certain Soto didn't really hear him, but there was nothing he could do now. If Soto caused trouble later, if he cast Inez off, Bent would deal with it. Right now, though, it was Soto's problem. Bent had enough of his own to concern himself with.

"She's in Charlotte and Dick's room," Bent said quietly.

"*Gracias,*" Soto mumbled before racing toward the kitchen.

Bent saw Soto and Inez leaving the dining room, Soto's arm protectively around Inez's shoulders. His face was grim but determined; she had her head down, embarrassed and fearful. They headed for the room they shared with several other families of laborers. The room was small and crowded usually, when everyone was in it. But it was better than living in a tent outside the walls, where one had to fear Indian attacks.

The couple disappeared inside the room. Nothing was heard of them during the day, and when the other laborers went into the quarters after the day's work was done, they found the Sotos angry but determined to overcome their private travails.

Bent nodded when he got the information at supper. He was relieved. Since Pedro Soto had taken on the task of informing the Cheyennes and Arapahos of the smallpox epidemic, he had become one of Bent's most valued laborers. Bent would have hated for such troubles to crush the man and his wife.

Bent, his two younger brothers, and Marcellin St. Vrain were eating supper together in the dining room that night, as was their custom.

After they had polished off a large meal, and Charlotte had cleared the dishes, Bent lit his pipe. He puffed away, eyes half closed. Every once in a while he would rock forward, pull his pipe out, take a sip of coffee, shove the pipe between his teeth again, and lean back.

The other three wondered what he was up to. They had never seen Bent so pensive before. They were afraid to talk, though, being unsure of what his reaction would be.

Finally Bent pulled the pipe out of his mouth. He leaned forward, resting his forearms on the table. "Go get us a small jug of Lightnin', Bob," he said.

The three waited silently until Robert Bent returned with a jug.

"I'll get us some cups," George said, starting to rise.

"The hell with cups, boy," William half growled. "It's about time you boys learned to drink like men." He pulled the cork from the jug and tossed it on the table. He hefted the jug, finger crooked through the small handle, the fat part of the jug resting on the back of his forearm. He took a fairly good sip. "Aaaaah," he breathed. "That shines with this ol' hoss," he said, smiling. His mood had taken a sharp turn for the better. He took another long swallow and then set the jug on the table.

The three young men looked from William to the bottle and back.

"Hell, boys," William growled in mock anger, "you gonna set there all night just starin' or are you gonna take yourself a snort?"

George, being the most impetuous of the three younger men, grabbed the bottle. He tried to emulate his older brother's technique. He wound up spilling some over his chin and shirt, but he got the knack pretty quickly. He took a drink, eyes watering, then handed it to Robert. "Good," he croaked, throat not working properly.

Robert laughed and reached for the jug.

24

"I need a load of goods taken down to Taos," William Bent said. He and his three young companions were still sitting in the fort's dining room, nipping at the whiskey. William puffed his pipe, and George Bent had made up a cigarillo with harsh trade tobacco rolled in a corn husk.

"What is it?" Robert asked.

"Mostly that paper and ink brought in today by those festerin' piles of buffler shit."

"Where's it goin?" George asked.

"Taos, as far as I know. Charlie might be sendin' it on to Santa Fe. I ain't certain. All I know is to ship it down to Taos."

"We got to make a trip all the way to Taos for some paper and ink?" George asked.

"There's other things—robes and such that we couldn't fit in Pugh's wagons. And," he added with a chuckle, "church missals."

"Hell, ain't they got enough religious statues and such?" George snorted.

William shrugged. "It ain't my place to ask such questions." He slugged back another drink. "I'd be obliged, Marcellin, if'n you'd take the load down there into Mexico. Think you could handle that?"

The twenty-two-year-old was overjoyed. *"Oui, oui,"* he said excitedly. It was the most trust anyone had placed in his hands, and he liked it. William smiled at the young man. Marcellin looked and acted very much like his brother Ceran. He had an amazing knack for making friends, and doing so quickly, no matter where. He had his older brother's twinkling, humorous eyes, and thick black beard.

George and Robert did not look half so thrilled. George, being the oldest of the three, thought that such an important job should be given to him. "That ain't fair, dammit," George complained. "I'm older'n Marcellin, and I've been out here a year longer too. Why is it I get all the shit jobs, and others get the good ones?"

"Whinin' don't become you, boy," William said harshly. "It's time you became a man. You keep actin' like this and there ain't a man from here to Missouri who'll give you a job callin' for some responsibility."

"But I . . . Dammit." George shut up.

"Besides, if you'd of kept your trap shut a minute, you would've learned I had another job for you."

"What's that?" George asked suspiciously. He figured William was going to simply throw him a bone, some unimportant, unadventurous job that none of the others at the fort wanted.

"Bent, St. Vrain and Company is plannin' to expand, boy," William said after another slug of whiskey. His pipe was out and he knocked the ashes out of it on the heel of his hand, then he set it softly on the table. "That means we need another tradin' post."

"And?" George asked, trying to hide the sudden excitement that flushed through his body.

"And, I want you to supervise the buildin' of it."

"Waaaaah-hooooo!" George whooped. He jumped up and did an impromptu little dance around the table.

The others laughed, before William grew serious again.

"Such doin's don't inspire confidence in me, boy," William said more harshly than he had meant. Still, he would not back away from it. This was important business, and George had to understand that.

"This is crucial for the company. You foul this up and we might be facin' starvin' times," William warned. It wasn't that bad, really. However, if Bent, St. Vrain & Company was to compete with the American Fur Company to the north, they would have to have a strong presence on the South Platte. The partners had discussed it over the winter and made their decision.

George stopped his dancing and looked worriedly at William. Like his older brother, he was impetuous; unlike William, he had not found a control to override his impetuousity. He sat, wide-eyed and solemn.

William looked at his brother, five years his junior. George was the dapper one in the Bent family, full of fire and dash. He was often rash and reckless, but usually managed to extricate himself from trouble.

"What about me?" Robert asked. He felt terribly put out, as if he didn't count because he was the youngest. William looked at him, wondering where the youngest of the Bents had gotten his looks. Robert was the handsomest of the Bent brothers. And, while not as wild as George, he was impetuous in many ways.

"I need you here to run the fort," William said. Robert brightened straight off. "You'll be in charge whilst I'm off tradin'."

"You think it's wise to leave him in charge?" George said, suddenly jealous of the authority given his younger brother.

"Why not?"

"He ain't gonna have nobody here to help him. Charles is off God knows where, and Ceran's in Taos. You'll be gone. Even Seth ain't here."

William shrugged. "Ramsay's here. He can handle anything Bob can't." He turned toward Robert. "And you're to listen to him, boy. He's a good friend and a good employee. He's been with the company a lot longer'n you have. You're to trust in his judgment. You got that?''

Robert nodded.

"Good," William said. He took another sip of whiskey, grimaced and set the jug back down. He decided he had had enough of the Taos Lightning for one night. Its lingering aftertaste still lay thick on his tongue. "Hey, Charlotte," he yelled.

Charlotte strolled out. "Yassir?" she asked, unworried. There had been no anger, no reprimand in Bent's voice.

"You got any of them *bizcochitos* made up?"

"Yassir. You be wantin' some?"

"Yes'm. And some of that hot chocolate you conjure up of a time."

"Will dere be anything else, Mistah Bent?"

"I reckon that'll do."

The men talked of generalities until the cookies and a large pot of hot chocolate were set in front of them. The men ate and drank silently. Finally, William leaned back, patting his slim stomach. "Damn, that ol' Charlotte plumb shines when it comes to cookin'."

The others could not argue with that.

"Well, it's about robe time for this ol' hoss," William said, standing. He arched his back with his hands on the small of his back, stretching. "I'll be settin' out in a couple days. Marcellin, you should be able to leave come mornin'. Georgie, you can depart anytime you're of a mind to. I'll tell you which workers to take. When Marcellin gets to Taos, he can tell Ceran what you're up to. Ceran'll hire the extra men you'll need and either bring 'em up to you there or have someone else do it."

George and Marcellin nodded, still a little overwhelmed at their new and growing responsibilities.

William slept a little late the next day. That was unusual for him, but he had felt the need for Owl Woman more than was usual too. Not only had he needed her physically, but also to listen to him. He was a man who had never taken to killing, as so many others out here had done. He did it out of necessity, and was not shy about it when called upon. Still, there was something disturbing in the way he had dispatched Carpis and Crump. It seemed somehow so cold-blooded to him, though he knew that was not true. The two men deserved to die, every bit as much as had that Blackfoot war party that had jumped him and Charles up along the Snake that one time. Still, these were white men—no matter how foul and cowardly they might be—not Indians.

Owl Woman had proven to be a good listener. Bent found he could talk and talk to her, and she would always be sympathetic. He wondered sometimes just how much she understood. Her English and Spanish were greatly improved, but still, he was sure a large portion of what he said was not understood.

No matter, though, he had told himself more than once. He knew he just needed a sounding board. Owl Woman would nod knowingly, and comfort him or soothe him, always patient, always kind.

He had realized just after bringing her to the fort that he was falling in love with her. He had not thought such a thing possible. Like many of the other white men who were out here in the vast loneliness, he had picked out a woman who seemed strong, healthy, who did her chores with dispatch and without complaint. Being comely didn't hurt much either. Still, it had been for him a marriage of convenience. Now he realized that his feelings had grown much deeper in the past few weeks. He only hoped she felt the same. He could not question her about it, feeling that to do so was unmanly. Still, he watched her closely, and it did seem that she was more solicitous of him.

By the time he awoke and stepped outside his quarters, Marcellin was ready to leave. Bent walked up and down the line of a dozen mules, checking to make sure everything was packed so that it would not hurt the mules. He shook hands with Marcellin. Then the young St. Vrain pulled himself up onto his horse.

"Have a safe journey, Marcellin," Bent said. His two brothers also wished St. Vrain well. The three watched as Marcellin led the way out of the fort, swung around toward the west and moved on.

Bent went back into his quarters—and to Owl Woman.

Marcellin rode into the fort seven days after he had left. With him were only five of the six men who had left with him. Their horses were flecked with foam, showing they had been ridden hard in the blazing sun. It must've been something bad, Bent figured, if the men had used their horses that hard.

Bent had been in the trade room when he heard one of the lookouts shout, and he had rushed outside. Moments later Marcellin and the others roared in, stopping in a swirl of dust and horse sweat. Bent grabbed Marcellin's bridle. "What the hell's gone on?"

"Pawnees," Marcellin said shakily. "Goddamn Pawnees. Zey come out of nowhere." He seemed dazed, disoriented.

Bent waved an arm and several men came running. "Let's get these boys over to the dinin' room. Make sure Charlotte has some coffee—laced with whiskey—for them. And somebody get my medical kit. Some of these boys're wounded. Move!"

Coffee was waiting by the time the travelers had been helped into the dining room. While the men began gulping their bolstered coffee, Bent took a look at the three wounded men, trying to see which one was worse. None was wounded badly, which was a relief. Bent was the closest thing to a doctor they had at the fort, and he only knew what he had been able to pick up in the wild, mostly because of expediency.

When the wounded were bandaged, Bent said, "Tell it."

The life seemed to have come back in Marcellin's eyes. Having the coffee had helped, but an even bigger aid was the knowledge that the men who had been under his care were now safe and taken care of. He nodded. "We were up near Timpas Creek, heading for Raton Pass. Zen ze damned Pawnees came at us."

"You sure they was Pawnee?" Bent asked. "It ain't like them to be raidin' so far from home."

"It was Pawnees, all right," Roberto Gomez said. He had been a Bent-St. Vrain employee for several years, and had never been known for lying, or even much exaggeration.

Bent nodded. "They get all the mules?"

"*Oui*," St. Vrain said bitterly. "And some of ze horses."

"You had six men with you. The other one been rubbed out?"

St. Vrain nodded. "Carlos Ruiz."

Bent took a deep breath. "He comport himself well?"

"*Oui*. I t'ink he went ahead of us just to give us time to get away."

"That sure is what happened," Gomez added. He was a friend of Ruiz's, and felt his loss deeply.

Bent nodded. "Well, shit, his widow's got to be told."

"I'll do it," Gomez said, grief thickening his accent.

Bent nodded. "She needs anything, you come see me."

{25}

William Bent was perplexed. He needed to be out trading, but so many problems confronted him. If the Pawnees were angry enough to be raiding this far from home, they could be troublesome. It also might mean the Comanches, Kiowas, Arapahos, and Cheyennes were touchy too. Another problem was that George would be looking for more laborers to arrive to help build the new fort. And Ceran St. Vrain was sitting down in Taos wondering just where the hell everyone was.

"The mules and supplies are lost, Bill," Ramsay Mac-Gregor told him as they held a small council of war—the two, plus Robert Bent and Marcellin St. Vrain, both of whom knew enough to keep their mouths shut. "Isn't a thing can be done aboot them."

"I know," Bent said wearily. He had hardly slept in the day and a half since Marcellin returned.

"And your first loyalty should be to the company. Business must come first, or there will be nothing left to worry aboot."

"I know that too, dammit," Bent snapped. "The trouble comes in trying to figure out what I should do that would best help the company—as well as keep our workers alive."

"Well, you canna delay going too much longer, or all the Indians we usually deal with'll be moved off."

Bent nodded. He sat in thought, clouds from his

pipe lying over him like morning fog on the river. Finally he nodded. "First thing we got to do," he said, feeling his way along, "is to get word to Ceran."

"Who's going to do that?"

Bent shrugged. "Ain't sure."

"I'll do it," Marcellin said firmly. He felt awful about having fouled up his first big assignment, and he wanted a way to make amends.

Bent looked at him. Marcellin appeared to have grown up in the past few days. He certainly was not the youth he had been when he left on the ill-fated journey. "That suits," Bent said. "See if'n you can get six volunteers. If you can't, start picking men as you'd like to ride with."

"Ain't that gonna be dangerous?" Robert Bent asked.

"Everything's dangerous out here," William answered. "I reckon this one'll be a little less dangerous than the last."

"Why?" Marcellin and Robert asked in unison.

"Main reason is you won't be taking pack mules. Taking all them animals, loaded down like they was, slows you down considerable. Just six or seven of you, carryin' some staples on your horse and relyin' on huntin' for your meat, you'll be able to move fast."

The two young men nodded.

"I expect I can travel northwest and hit the Cheyenne and Arapaho camps up near the South Platte," William said.

MacGregor nodded. "Aye, laddie. And you'll stop by to tell yon brother George of what's occurred."

"Yep." Bent was not thrilled with the plan, but it was the only way he could think of accomplishing everything that needed to be done.

"When will ye be leavin' us, laddie?" MacGregor asked.

"Day after tomorrow," William said. "Now that everything's settled down, I can get some sleep. We'll pack everything tomorrow, and I'll head out the next day.'' He paused. ''Bob, you'll be in charge, like we spoke of last time. But Ramsay here'll have my authority to countermand any order you give.''

Robert started to protest, but his brother cut him off. ''It's the way it is, Bob, like it or not. It sticks in your craw too much, you can opt to be relieved of your duties.'' His voice was flat and harsh.

Robert wanted to object some more, but the look in his brother's eyes disabused him of that idea. He simply nodded.

''That's better,'' William said. ''And don't worry, Bob,'' he added placatingly, ''Ramsay ain't the kind to try and wrest the reins of control for no good reason. You'll be in charge of the everyday shit. You have a momentous decision to make, you consult Ramsay.''

Robert still was not happy, but he nodded again. He thought he might test his authority as soon as William was gone. His mind dwelled on that awhile, until he realized that doing so would be foolish. MacGregor was the type of man who lived for challenges. Robert figured that if he pulled such a stunt, there was a good chance that MacGregor would knock the tar out of him. Or he might up and quit, and then there would be hell to pay when Bill got back. He decided to swallow his pride and do what he was supposed to.

Bent finally got to bed. Owl Woman sat behind him, his head in her lap. She rubbed his head, practiced fingers making small, firm circles on his forehead and temples. He drifted into a half sleep, relaxing for the first time in weeks.

''You sure know how to treat a man, Sally.'' He suddenly opened his eyes, looking upside down at her. ''You mind that name?'' he asked.

''No,'' Owl Woman said. ''It's a nice name.''

Bent closed his eyes again, wondering what she was really thinking. He could tell nothing on her face when she wanted nothing revealed. She could be so distant while being so close physically.

He again began to drift off into the odd world of half sleep. Then he heard himself say, "I love you, Sally —Owl Woman." He was not sure if he actually said it or had just thought it.

Nor was he sure she had replied, "And I love you, Little White Man." He hoped he had heard it. Then he fell asleep.

He felt considerably better when he awoke. A good night's sleep could do that for you. He splashed water over his face and head, then dressed. He and Owl Woman went to the dining room.

While eating, he watched Owl Woman. She ate without much joy, and Bent realized that much of what she ate at the fort was alien to her.

How lonely she must be, he thought. She had few real friends here, although Owl Woman and Charlotte got on well. Still, Owl Woman had been raised in an atmosphere of cooperation. It was the one thing that set apart the races. Whites, and even Mexicans, were independent, or so they liked to act. The Indians—all of them that Bent had seen—usually acted in concert. The women helped each other in butchering, fleshing and tanning hides, making pemmican and jerky, picking berries, making clothing. Virtually everything an Indian woman did was with friends. As they worked, they would sing or chatter incessantly.

Owl Woman had none of that here. The closest she came was when a trapper or buffalo hunter who had an Indian wife came along. Then it seemed like a reunion, even if they did not speak a common tongue.

"You want to come along with me, Sally?" he asked, so suddenly that he shocked himself as well as her.

Owl Woman regained her composure and nodded, lowering her eyes so he could not see her desire to be away from this mud lodge.

He was thinking furiously. Now that he had made

her the offer, he had to come up with a way to make it work. "Gray Thunder's village gonna be over toward the Big Sandy?"

Owl Woman nodded, nibbling at her breakfast. She had come to like some of the strange foods she had eaten since coming to the fort, but she missed her own delicacies—roasted dog, buffalo entrails, chokecherries, many things. She thought about being in the village again. That would be nice, she knew. Still, she didn't want to get her hopes up too high.

"I'm figurin' on heading up toward the South Platte," he said, mouth suddenly dry. He wanted to do something nice for Owl Woman, but in the process there was a chance he might lose her. "It wouldn't put me out none to stop by Gray Thunder's village and let you visit while I was traipsin' around. That suit you?" He showed none of the nervousness he felt.

She looked at him obliquely. Looking at a man straight on was a bad thing, she had been taught. She nodded, her heart lightened.

"You won't go findin' yourself another man in the village whilst I'm gone, will you?" Bent asked. His voice was even despite his worry.

"No," she said.

Something in the tone or timbre made him believe her. He stared at her, almost sure now that she had pledged her love to him last night. Bent went back to eating with renewed energy.

In two weeks they were at the village. Bent lingered a little while to trade. But he could not stay too long. He made arrangements with Gray Thunder to meet at the fort. And then, with a heavy heart and a knot of worry in his guts, Bent and his men pulled out.

They found George up near the confluence of a small stream and the South Platte. William explained what had happened.

"I was beginnin' to wonder if we was left up here to

die of neglect," George said in relief. He was worried about Marcellin, but he was relieved at knowing what had happened, at least.

"If Marcellin don't get set upon again, you should be seein' them workers ride in soon."

"You got any more cheerful news?" George asked sarcastically.

"Don't let the Company scare you off, Georgie." William warned.

"They bein' troublesome?" He was a little worried.

"Some, from what I hear. They've got a post not far from here, and I expect they're gonna have their men swarmin' all over the place."

"You think they'll give us trouble?"

"Not war, if that's what you're thinkin'."

George acknowledged that was what he had wondered about. "How can you be sure, though?"

"They pulled some shit like that and word got out, there ain't a man in the mountains that'd deal with 'em. I wouldn't put it past them cutthroat bastards to do everything short of an outright attack, though."

"That's a relief, I guess," George said. "We ain't got a whole lot of boys here used to handlin' guns."

The next morning Bent—with three wagons, a dozen mules, and eight men, two of them camp helpers—moved onward. Three months later they had made a wide circle through territory claimed by Cheyennes, Arapahos, Sioux, Pawnees, Kiowas, and Comanches.

"Damn," Bent muttered as he pulled into the fort. He didn't know whether to be angry or worried. Despite the many Cheyenne lodges, those of Gray Thunder's band were not among them. He was cheered only a little by Ceran St. Vrain's presence in the fort. He had been there a few weeks already.

"You get some workers up to Georgie?" Bent asked as he and St. Vrain went into the dining room. Charlotte served coffee and tamales.

"*Oui*. Nearly a hundred. Zey left Taos long ago and arrived safely. Messengers still bring word occasionally zat all is well zere."

Bent knew St. Vrain had something else to tell him, and it could not be good news, considering that the usually jovial Frenchman was rather downcast. "What's wrong?" he asked as he grabbed a tamale.

"Zere is trouble in nort'ern Mexico."

"What kind of trouble?" Bent asked, his words garbled by the wad of tamale in his mouth.

"Some of ze Indians at ze pueblos, zey are unhappy. . . ."

"Those bastards're always unhappy with somethin'. If it ain't the goddamn Taosaños, it's the goddamn Zias, or the Jemezes."

"Ze new governor—Perez—is making zem nervous. He 'as imposed new taxes on zem. High taxes. And he is ousting all ze local officials and replacing zem wit' his own men."

"That ain't unusual neither," Bent said, but he knew there was more to the story.

"I agree. But Armijo—you remember him, don't you?"

"Yep. Used to be the governor down there a few years back. He got dumped and became the customs man."

"*Oui*. Well, some t'ink he has given help to ze Indians."

"That's to be expected from the likes of Armijo. He'd do about anything to get elected—or appointed —governor again."

"Yes. Well, after he aided them, if he really did, he was not made governor. One of the pueblo chiefs is governor."

"Jesus," Bent breathed. "That's poor doin's if I ever heard any. Armijo might be a cowardly bastard, but he won't take such shit easily."

"*Mais non*. And I t'ink he is about to do somet'ing about it."

Bent squinted at St. Vrain. "I don't think I like where this's goin'." The food was all but forgotten.

St. Vrain shook his head. "A messenger came and told us Armijo has an army in Santa Fe ready to head north, cleaning out pueblos."

There was nothing Bent could say about it, but it would be trouble.

"I worry about Americans zere. Even ones with Mexican citizenship."

"Like Charles."

"*Oui*. Charles is zere. He came back a few weeks ago."

"There anything we can do?"

"Wait, *mon ami*. Just wait."

Bent nodded, but the tamales sat in his stomach like rocks.

⟪26⟫

Bent was in sour humor both from St. Vrain's news as well as the fact that Gray Thunder's band still hadn't arrived. He growled and grumped around the fort, until not even thick-skinned Ramsay MacGregor or the generally jovial Ceran St. Vrain wanted to be near him.

Five days after he had returned, a lone rider galloped into the fort. His horse was nearly spent, as was the man himself. He was alone, which either meant his companions, if he had any, had been killed, or the news was so bad that the man had taken the risk of riding alone through miles and miles of territory that several tribes considered their own.

The man practically fell off the horse. Bent and St. Vrain, who had been in one of the storerooms, heard the commotion and ran outside. Seth Walsh managed to catch the man, and eased him down into the dust. Walsh had been back for a month and a half, had reported that Pugh and his men had gotten the furs to Independence with only a little "encouragement." It was the only good news Bent had gotten at the fort.

"One of you boys get some water over here," Walsh bellowed. A worker raced over with a bucket hastily filled from the fort's well. The bucket also had a dipper in it. The young laborer held the dipper for the man, who sucked greedily at the liquid.

"You know him, Ceran?" Bent asked.

"*Oui*. Not well, but I know who he is. His name is

John Knox. He owns a tin-making shop in Taos I t'ink.''

Bent nodded and knelt beside the man. "Mr. Knox," he said quietly but urgently. "Mr. Knox, can you hear me?"

Knox blinked a few times. "More water," Bent ordered. When that was done, Bent repeated his question.

The light of comprehension lit in Knox's eyes. He nodded weakly.

"Good." Now that Bent knew the man still had his wits, Bent felt some of his urgency drain away. "What brings you here, Mr. Knox?"

He got no answer, so Bent asked, "Do you know where you are?"

Knox's head moved a little, indicating no. "Wanted Bent's Fort," he said, his voice a faint whisper.

"That's where you are." Bent paused, then plunged ahead. These questions had to be answered. "What's brought you out here all this way from Taos by yourself?"

Knox tried to speak, or at least seemed to, but no words came out; only some strangulated sounds.

"Give him some more water," Bent ordered.

"Hell and tarnation, Bill," a trapper said hoarsely, "that chil' needs somethin' a mite stronger'n water." He thrust out a battered tin flask.

Bent almost smiled, but he nodded. Walsh took the flask and poured some of the rotgut into Knox, who sputtered as the whiskey eased its way down into his gullet. A little color came back to his face.

"Now, Mr. Knox," Bent asked, some of the urgency returning, "what's brought you here?"

"Armijo. He's . . . he's . . ."

"Dose him again, Seth," Bent said. Walsh obliged by pouring more whiskey into Knox.

"What about Armijo?" Bent demanded.

"He came to Taos." It was a struggle for Knox to get

the words out. "Shooting . . . arrests . . . Americans." He stopped, knowing he was making little sense. He took a deep, ragged breath, and then tried again. "Armijo came and started arresting people—Americans."

"Son of a bitch," someone muttered.

"It's better than being shot down, like the Indians were."

Bent gulped, knowing he had to ask, but not wanting to get the answer he feared. "What about Charlie? Charlie Bent? What about him?"

"He was arrested," Knox said. "He's still in the jail. I hurried to get here. . . ." His voice faded.

Bent stood, his face knotted in fury. He glanced at St. Vrain, who nodded once. No words needed to be spoken between the two men. "Bob, you and a couple of the boys get Knox into one of the rooms," Bent said to his brother. "Give him whatever he needs."

"What about you?" Robert asked.

"I'm headin' for Taos. Me and Ceran."

"I ain't stayin' here while you're off savin' Charlie," Robert said.

"Yes, you are," William said harshly. "You don't know shit about such doin's. You can be of the most service here. Ramsay, you stay with him, help him out as he needs."

Walsh had set Knox's head gently down. Then the big blacksmith rose. "You ain't leavin' me here, goddammit," he said hoarsely.

"Nor me," Solomon said. He spun and headed for his small room in the back of the blacksmith shop.

"I'm goin' too," Marcellin St. Vrain said.

"Mais non," Ceran snapped.

"But—"

Ceran ripped off a few bursts of French that were too angry for Bent to understand, but Marcellin certainly did. The younger St. Vrain finally nodded, his face pinked over.

"What'd you tell him?" Bent asked.

"I told him to go to ze new fort and tell George what's happened. If George wishes to join us, he may do so, while Marcellin stays zere."

Bent nodded. He sucked in a long breath and then blew it out, cheeks puffing. "We best get a move on. Ain't no tellin' what them crazy bastards down there'll do."

"*Oui.*"

Less than half an hour later a group of angry, well-armed men rode out of Bent's Fort heading southwest, following the Arkansas River.

They returned in little more than a week, with Charles Bent.

"What happened?" Robert asked. He was still annoyed at having been left behind, missing all the glory.

William shrugged as he dismounted. "It weren't pretty," he growled. "Go'n tell Charlotte we can use some grub, Bob."

"But I want—"

"Ain't a one of us boys gives a flyin' shit what you want," Charles snapped. "Just go and do like Bill told you."

Robert looked hurt. He walked off, hoping he could keep his head up, but he seemed slumpish more than anything else.

Before long ten men—nine of the twelve who had ridden south with William Bent, plus Charles—were sitting at tables in the dining room, tossing back a variety of foods, coffee, and whiskey. Robert Bent sat stiffly off by himself. Other men from the fort crammed in, waiting to hear what had gone on there in Taos.

Finally the men sat back, bellies full. Out came pipes and cigars, more coffee was poured.

"Well tell it, goddammit," one man finally snapped.

Ten mountain men rode out of the fort less than a half hour after John Knox had told his story. They were a hard-looking bunch, grim-faced and well-armed. Each man carried two pistols in his belt and two in saddle pouches. Most were single-shot percussion pistols, but a few of the men had double-barreled ones, giving them a little more firepower. Each also carried a plains rifle, a fair percentage of them made by the Hawkin brothers in St. Louis. And all toted along an extra musket or two. The men—most of them were mountain men, or had been—wore buckskin pants with fringe down the outside of the seams. Some also wore buckskin shirts, though almost half wore shirts of simple material.

All in all they were a dirty, high-smelling, cantankerous, leather-tough, foul-tempered lot.

They also moved fast, having no supply mules or anything else to slow them down. They made camp quickly and with no fuss. Supper was a few hunks of deer haunch and a hard biscuit washed down with water. The only reason they stopped at night was to make sure their horses got some rest. Before first light they gobbled down a bit of bacon and then were on the trail again.

They pulled up in a copse two miles east of the Taos plaza just after dark, three nights after leaving the fort. It was a quiet, tense camp.

Shortly after midnight, the men rolled out of their robes and into the shadows until they knew what—or who—had woke them. It turned out to be George Bent and Red Water, who had been sent from Bent's Fort to let George know what was happening.

The brothers' reunion was short and gruff. Then William asked, "You come by way of the fort, Georgie?"

George shook his head as he gobbled down some meat. "Just come straight from up on the Platte. Why?"

"Gray Thunder's band ain't come to the fort yet.

Owl Woman's with them, and I'm gettin' a might itchy to know what's come of her.''

"She'll be all right," George said with more certainty than he felt.

Within minutes the men were asleep again. Before dawn, William Bent sent Red Water and Ollie Clark into Taos to reconnoiter. Clark had shown up at the fort several months ago, looking and acting contrite. Bent was suspicious, considering their parting several years earlier. But Clark gave him no trouble. He had worked steadily and without complaint. Bent was surprised when Clark volunteered to go along on this expedition, but he had accepted it. Now he figured he would see just how much Clark had changed. Bent knew that Red Water would kill Clark in an instant if Clark tried anything bad.

They returned just after dark. The small army huddled over a fire. "What'd you boys learn?" Bent asked quietly.

"Armijo ain't here," Clark said. "He's gone off with most of his army, down toward the pueblos near Santa Fe."

"Only two dozen soldiers're left," Red Water grunted. He seemed to find that darkly humorous.

"Charlie?" Bent asked. "What about Charlie?"

"He's in the *calabozo*, like Knox said," Clark growled. "Couple other Americans're in there too." He paused. "Charlie's alive, Bill."

"You sure?" Bent tried not to reveal his anxiety.

"Pretty much. I called for him to answer, and he did. I don't figure no one could conjure up his voice so close."

Bent nodded. "Where're the soldiers?"

"Mostly near the jail house. Or what they're usin' for a jail these days. They took ol' Dunne's place for their barracks and his shed behind it for the jail."

"What happened to Dunne?" St. Vrain asked.

Clark shrugged. "Don't know for sure, but I heard

he was killed straight off." He paused for a long sigh and a short drink of coffee. "Anyway, it seems them soldier boys ain't too happy about bein' left behind in this hotbed of Indian intrigue," he added wryly. "Because of that, they're not moving around much."

Bent nodded. "Good. That'll make our job a heap easier." He swiftly sketched out a brief plan.

Like many plans, this one did not work nearly as well as William Bent had wished. Most of the men rode boldly into town just after first light. Despite the early hour, the city was, for the most part, awake. Cocks crowed, vendors set up their carts, shop owners opened for business, cattle roamed about, herded by boys out to the pasture.

Almost everyone stopped to stare at the procession of flinty-eyed Americans. And soon many of the people were following the mountain men—at a safe distance. Behind them, unseen, were Kit Carson, Red Water, and Clark. The three slipped into small courtyards, then climbed to the flat roofs of the adobe houses. They stretched out flat on the roofs, rifles ready.

Bent and St. Vrain, leading the other men, stopped near the makeshift jail. "Charlie!" Bent bellowed. "Charlie, you in there?"

A faint, "I sure as hell am, dammit," floated out of the house. "Now come and get me out of here. Pronto."

"That's why we're here." He looked around, wondering where all the soldiers were. In moments he had the sick feeling that he had walked his men straight into a trap. "*Cache*, boys! *Cache*!" Bent roared.

Less than a second later gunfire erupted from the windows of several houses. As Carson, Red Water, and Clark tried to lay down a covering fire, Bent and his men swung low on their horses and raced off in any direction they could.

Bent and Seth Walsh tore off to their left as fire raked toward them across the courtyard. Just beyond the courtyard to their left was a house from which gun-fire also was pouring. The two slid to a stop at the side of the house and slipped out of their saddles. Right behind them was Emiliano Flores.

"These goddamn doin's don't shine with this god-damn chil' no how," Walsh growled.

"Shit," Bent said simply. He knew they had been set up, but he wasn't sure how. There were many im-ponderables. Bent sighed. How it happened was moot at the moment. What he had to do now was get his men out—and save Charles—before they were mas-sacred. "Take a look 'round back, Seth," he said. "See if there's a way in."

Bent scanned the land out ahead of him. One man and two horses lay, apparently dead. Bent wasn't sure, but he thought it was a man named Brantley Collier. He could see Carson, Clark, and Red Water, still firing occasionally.

Walsh slipped back up. "One window on the far side of the door," he said. "Nobody's at the window. And," he added with a determined, harsh smile, "the door ain't locked."

Bent nodded. "You two boys ready?" he asked as he checked his pistols and rifle.

"Goddamn right I am," Walsh snapped.

"*Sí,*" Flores said. He was scared but trying not to show it.

Without another word Bent turned and moved toward the back of the house. He paused at the corner and peeked around. Everything still seemed serene. He moved on. He stopped for a quick breath to settle his nerves, then eased up the door latch. It pulled free soundlessly. He rested his rifle against the wall next to the door, and his two companions did the same. All three pulled their pistols.

Suddenly Bent kicked the door open and jumped inside, moving to his left, firing one pistol straight off. Flores hit the room an instant after Bent and moved to the right. Walsh was last in, his big, bulky body blocking out much of the light in the doorway.

Shots rang out, and through the haze of smoke and dimness, Bent could see four soldiers. All four spun at the sound of Bent's first shot, and within moments all four had fallen.

The three companions reloaded their pistols after checking to make sure all the soldiers were dead, and then retrieved their rifles.

Bent stuck his head out one of the windows facing the courtyard, straight across from which sat the jail. It was quiet now, with everyone waiting for something to happen, for someone to show himself.

"Shit," Bent muttered.

"What's wrong, Cap'n?" Walsh asked.

"I expect we're gonna have to ferret each and every one of those sons of bitches out of the houses." He spit on the dirt floor. "And I don't expect we can do so without getting cut to pieces ourselves."

"We're in a fix for sure, Cap'n," Walsh commented. He did not seem concerned. He figured that Bent would get them out of this somehow; he always had before.

27

Bent paced the room while Flores and Walsh watched out the windows. Gunfire, sounding muffled, drew Bent to a window just in time to see Red Water and Kit Carson jumping off the roofs of the houses they were on. All the while, puffs of dust broke out along the roofs.

"Bastard's are shootin' up through the roofs at our boys, goddamn 'em all to hell and back," Walsh growled. He threw his rifle to his shoulder, aimed quickly and fired. They heard a screech from one of the houses, and the three figured Walsh had at least hit someone.

Suddenly Red Water and St. Vrain raced around the front corners of the building Red Water had jumped from moments before. Pistols in hand, they jammed to a stop before the windows, one on each side of the door. They each fired their pistols through the windows, none of which had glass. Then Red Water jammed his big, hard shoulder against the door, slamming it off its poorly made hinges. Tomahawk in one hand and war club in the other, Red Water disappeared inside the house. St. Vrain, similarly armed, went right after him.

Screams and a few gunshots came from the house. Bent watched, worried perspiration streaking in small trails down his face. All he needed now was to have Ceran St. Vrain get put under.

Moments later Red Water and St. Vrain stuck their heads a little through the windows.

"How many'd you get?" Bent bellowed.

"Seven," St. Vrain answered.

"We got three. And maybe one more inside one of the houses. Still a dozen or so left," Bent added. "Shit." While standing there looking across the courtyard, trying to figure out his next move, Bent suddenly spotted a soldier in one of the windows of the house across from him—the one on which Carson had originally stationed himself.

"I'll show you, you son of a bitch," Bent said. He brought his rifle up, but the soldier moved away from the window a little. Bent could still see him, though not clearly. He didn't care. He fired. The man and a portion of the house's front wall disintegrated with a healthy explosion.

"What the hell . . . ?" Bent muttered.

"You hit his powder horn, *Jefe!*" Flores shouted excitedly.

"Lordy, that was some doin's, Cap'n!" Walsh said with a laugh.

Carson, George Bent, Solomon, and Art Honnicker swept around the building. Two barged through the door, the other two through the new hole in the wall. In no time at all George Bent stuck his head out and roared, "Six more gone under. And a goddamn mess it is too."

Silence fell again as all the men tried to figure out the next move. After a few minutes Solomon and Honnicker slipped out of the damaged house, went along the side and then around the back. Only ten yards separated them from the house on which Clark still lay. There were no windows on that side. Solomon looked up. "Hey, Ollie," he called. "Best get yo' ass down from there."

"Why?"

"You'll see. Now jist get yo' ass down right fast."

Solomon gave Clark no more thought. He just took a deep breath, and then he and Honnicker trotted across the land. At least two rifle balls kicked up dirt near them, but they did not stop until they were at the corner.

"You ready, Art?" Solomon asked.

"Ready as I'll get, I suppose." He stood at the corner, his two pistols in his hands as Solomon slinked along the ground.

Solomon went under the window and stopped at the door. Gently, he set down the five full powder horns he had. Then he slipped backward, under Honnicker's watch. In moments they trotted back to the damaged house.

George Bent stuck his head out the window just a tad. "Think you can do it again, Bill?" he roared.

William Bent said nothing; he just fired. At the sound of the explosion, George Bent, Solomon, Honnicker, and Carson raced from their building to the newly damaged one. St. Vrain and Red Water came from the other side.

"Six more," St. Vrain announced.

"That means only two left," William Bent shouted. "And they got to be in the place on our left here."

"You soldiers over there!" George Bent bellowed, cupping his hands around his mouth to get more volume. "You best give yourselves up, you want to live." He waited almost a full minute.

When there was no response, Flores said, "Let me try, *Jefe*."

Bent nodded.

Flores stepped outside and faced the other building. He was nervous, standing there as an easy target. He shouted the message in Spanish, and then added, still in Spanish, "You have one more minute and then we will storm the house. And you will die."

That produced a response. "They say they are afraid," Flores shouted for anyone who understood little Spanish. "They are afraid that if they come out, we will shoot them down."

St. Vrain stepped out of the house across the courtyard. "You soldiers know me, eh?" he said in as good a Spanish as he could muster. "I tell you we will not hurt you, if you come out now and release our friends from the jail."

Silence hung heavy, but then the door of the house creaked open. A white piece of cloth on a rifle appeared through the door, followed by a soldier, and then another one. The latter held his left hand on the big bloodstain on his left side.

"Red Water," St. Vrain said. "You and Art check out that house."

The two charged off. Moments later they were back. "It's empty," Honnicker said.

"*Bon,*" St. Vrain said gravely.

"All right, boys," William Bent said harshly, "give over the key to the *calabozo.*"

"Sergeant Esquivel has it," the unwounded soldier said. "He was in that house." He pointed to the second one to be damaged.

George Bent hurried to the house. A few minutes later he returned with a key in hand. He and William quickly unlocked the door of the house. It had been haphazardly turned into a jail by the installation of metal-barred doors, at all the rooms but the front one. The Bents unlocked Charles's "cell" and then all the others.

An hour later—after a stop to replenish their supplies at the Bent-St. Vrain store—they rode out of town. The bodies of Brantley Collier and Sam Butler were across the backs of mules. The Bents figured to bury them somewhere out in the mountains on the way back to the fort.

They stopped at the place they had camped overnight. They were tired, hungry, and still angry. They needed time to calm down, soothe the minor wounds some had received and let the festering sourness in them ease out.

After eating, most of the men pulled out their pipes and laid back with pipes or cigarillos. William Bent sat between his two brothers, facing one of the two fires in the camp. St. Vrain sat to Charles's right, and Carson on St. Vrain's right. Next to George Bent were Seth Walsh and Emiliano Flores.

"Seth," William Bent said quietly, "please ask Mr. Clark to join us." Walsh looked at him in question. "And keep an eye on him."

Walsh was still surprised, but he shrugged and left. Clark was at the other fire with Solomon, Luis Saltillo, Art Honnicker, and Red Water. Walsh walked back with Clark and then stationed himself just behind him. The others at Clark's fire watched, interested but baffled.

"Sit, Mr. Clark," William Bent said.

With a puzzled look, Clark did. "Somethin' wrong?" he asked.

"Why?" William asked.

"Why what?"

William tapped the mouthpiece of his pipe on a knee. Then he spit into the fire. "I'm in no humor for goddamn games, boy," he finally said. "We was set up in Taos, nice as you please. And you're the only son of a bitch that could've set it up. I ask you again, boy: Why?"

"I got no idear what you're talkin' about," Clark said evenly.

"No one but us knew we were comin'," William said with a sigh.

"Hell, could've been some Mexican farmer or somethin' saw us on the trail and gone on into Taos to spill the beans."

Clark's mess mates moved up until they were sitting across the fire from the Bents, listening intently.

"You think a dozen old mountaineers is gonna miss

some stupid farmer?'' William asked harshly. ''Besides, how many goddamn peons'd take it on himself to help the goddamn soldiers?''

''Hell if I know,'' Clark insisted. ''These stupid goddamn Mexicans don't make sense at the best of times.''

''Then there's the little problem of where you stationed yourself,'' William said, almost as if to himself. The silence of the night was broken only by the snapping of the flames and one man's quickly stifled belch.

''What about it?''

''How come you was the only one not fired on from inside the house? Them soldiers did so with Kit and Red Water, but not you. Why?''

''I already tol' you I don't know what those bastards think.'' He was sweating more than could be accounted for by his nearness to the fire.

William took some moments to check his anger. Then he said, ''We can do this easy, or we can do it hard, you want it that way.'' He pulled a pistol and held it loosely in his hand. ''This'll be the last time I'll ask you, boy: Why?''

''They was holdin' my wife and my little girl,'' Clark said, eyes suddenly downcast.

Suddenly William and Charles Bent fired their pistols. One ball cracked into the center of Clark's chest, the other went in just under his left cheekbone. The impact knocked him backward.

''What the hell'd you two go and do that for?'' George Bent asked. He was stunned that his two brothers would do such a thing.

Charles Bent looked at his brother with hard, unforgiving eyes. ''He's a lyin' sack of shit,'' he said harshly. ''He ain't got a wife. Nor a child. Leastways not in Taos or anywhere near it.''

''You sure?'' George asked, still surprised.

''I am.''

''Besides,'' William Bent added, ''when him and Red Water split up to check different parts of town, Red

Water followed him. The son of a bitch went straight to the house they're usin' as a barracks. Red Water waited the whole time he was in there. He come out counting gold.''

"That right, Red Water?'' George asked.

"Sure as hell. Your brothers never fully believed Clark regretted his past foolishment. They devised this little plan to see just how truthful Clark was. It appears,'' he added dryly, "that Clark wasn't truthful a-tall. Trouble is, we didn't know exactly what he was up to.''

The other men were quiet, saddened not by Clark's death but by his betrayal of them.

The group moved on in the morning, leaving Clark unburied. None figured he deserved a decent burial.

"You figure any likely reason for what Clark did, Charlie?'' William asked his older brother at their fire that night.

"Well, the son of a bitch wasn't none to happy with us all this time.'' He paused. "Besides, I hear he lost a bundle to Don Hernandez and didn't have the specie to make it good. Don Hernandez gave him a couple days to raise the cash. I don't figure Clark could. I heard he appealed to Armijo and General Gallegos. Since Don Hernandez didn't raise Clark's hair, I suppose a deal was struck. What with the war, Clark probably told 'em he could work with us or some of the other boys and pick up news about what the Americans were fixin' to do. That'd give him revenge for that time we made him run the gantlet, and put him in Armjio's good graces.''

William nodded. "Seems likely,'' he offered. "It's a damn shame, though.'' He paused. "You think all this's gonna mean trouble for us?''

Charles shrugged. "Armijo's always been a rotten puke. You know that well's I do. But he knows his way around politically. I reckon he's got enough sense to know that if he starts to mess with me or any of the others in Taos, he'll be in deep shit. Besides, I figure he's gonna be kept busy for a spell. By the time he gets back—if he gets back—he'll most likely have more important things to worry about than the loss of a couple dozen soldiers and the escape of a couple Americanos."

"Still," St. Vrain interjected, "he's ze kind of dumb bastard to hold a grudge. We'll have to watch our steps maybe a little, eh, Charles?"

"We always do," Charles said with a small grin. "Sometimes it don't work too well, though."

Back at the fort, after the tale was told, the men began drifting off. William walked outside with his brothers. He stopped just outside the dining room and looked somewhat longingly toward his apartment. His jaw dropped when Owl Woman stepped shyly out.

Robert Bent burst into laughter. "A couple of Gray Thunder's bucks come 'round a few days ago, said ol' Gray Thunder had set up camp near Big Timbers. I rode on out and brung her back with me."

"Well, I am obliged," William said, meaning it.

"Well, go on and go to her," St. Vrain said with a chuckle.

William needed no other encouragement.

The next days were a fevered rush of work. It was fall, and Charles had to get back on the trail soon if he was to avoid the worst that the coming winter could throw at them. Hundreds of furs had to be baled, wagons checked to make sure they were ready, hunters and trappers heading out for their season needed to be outfitted; horses, mules, and oxen needed to be shod; Indians arrived in droves, looking for supplies to last them through the winter.

About the same time, George Bent said with the pride of possession, "Well, I'd best get on back to my fort."

"Hell with that," Charles said. "I need you to help me get all this"—he waved an arm to encompass the huge amount of furs—"to the States."

"Get someone else to help you," George said petulantly. "I built Fort Lookout and by God I'm gonna run it."

"Like shit," Charles said bluntly. "You ain't a partner in the company. You might get to be one someday if you stop sassin' me."

"But—"

"But," Charles roared, "Marcellin's there. He can handle it for the winter. Nothin' much'll be goin' on there once winter really sets in." He softened his voice a little. "You can go on back up there come spring."

George nodded. He wasn't happy with it, but short of riding out on his own and risking his brother's wrath, there was nothing he could do.

Finally, after some Herculean efforts, everything was done, and Charles made his final preparations for leaving. He, William, and St. Vrain met in the dining room to make their decisions.

"You think we did the right thing, leavin' Marcellin up there at Fort Lookout all on his own?" Charles asked.

Both William and St. Vrain nodded. "I've said it before," William noted, "that Marcellin has the best chance of makin' a go of the business. Georgie's showin' real promise, though. I didn't think he'd have gotten the fort done like he did, but he managed."

"And Bob?" Charles asked, chewing on a piece of cookie.

William shrugged. "Sometimes I think he'll do just fine. Other times, hell, I just don't know. He's awful young, you know."

"He's older'n you were when you come out here," Charles said.

"I know, but things're different now."

Charles nodded. "I reckon we can give him another

year or two to see if he comes around." Charles poured himself more coffee. "Now that we're all settled on the younger ones," he said, setting the pot down, "we can turn to you, Bill."

"What about me?" William asked, startled.

"When're you comin' down to Taos to find you a wife?"

"I got a wife," William said quietly. But his hackles began to rise.

"Hell, that ain't a real wife. You can keep her up here, and a real wife, church sanctified and all, down there. The best of both."

"I ain't ever gone against you, Charlie. Not full out anyway. But if that's what's needed to get you off my back on this, then so be it. I'll meet you anywhere, any time, and any way you care to choose."

Charles was taken aback. "You serious about this, Bill?" he asked.

"I am."

"You don't want yourself a fancified Mexican wife? One that don't smell of grease and blood? One whose pa owns half of northern Mexico?" He was surprised.

"I got the woman I want."

"You been out in that sun too long on your tradin' expeditions?" Charles asked, still trying to figure it out. He and St. Vrain were looking oddly at William, who figured they deserved some kind of explanation.

"I don't know what it is, Charlie," he said slowly, trying to sort out the ideas and words that bounced around inside his head. "I just ain't as fond of the Mexican people as you and Ceran are. It ain't that I got anything against 'em, mind you. I just feel more comfortable with the Cheyennes than I do with the Mexicans."

"That don't make no sense," Charles said.

"To me it does." William drained his mug. He sighed, knowing he did not have the words to explain himself to his brother. "Maybe it ain't even the people so much as it is the place," he said, trying again.

"The place? What'n hell's wrong with Taos?"

"Nothin', really. It's just too crowded for this chil'. I know it's odd, but I like being out there." His right hand made a vague motion, indicating all and nothing. "I like being out on the plains, or in the mountains. I feel cooped up here in the fort. That's why I take tradin' expeditions every year. Hell, I could assign it to Seth or any of a dozen other men. But I like it."

"Taos makes you feel hemmed in too, huh?" Charles asked, staring over the rim of his coffee mug at his brother.

William nodded, looking glum. He and Charles were so close—had been for years—that William didn't want to disappoint his brother.

Suddenly Charles began laughing softly. "Hell's bells, boy," he said with a newborn jocularity, "you always was the black sheep of the family. Always contrary, even when you was a sucklin' babe. And a bodacious troublemaker soon's you grew some."

William smiled. "Then you don't hold none of this against me?" he asked hopefully.

"Hell no, brother. Most of the boys come out this way couldn't find anyplace back in the settlements where they'd like to stick. All of 'em footloose and goddamn fractiously independent. If your stick floats with Owl Woman and the Cheyennes, then I give you my blessing." He laughed some more. "If'n you want it."

William nodded, a small smile across his lips. "Besides," he added, the smile growing, "she's with child."

That led to a long round of ribald revelry, commentary, and more than one toast with a mug of Taos Lightning.

❦{ 28 }❦

Bent rode toward Gray Thunder's village in a punishing downpour. He had almost delayed the trip because the storm showed no signs of abating any time soon. But he had put it off several times already because he was overwhelmed with work. When he finally got a lull in his duties, he was determined to go. He took a few goods to distribute for goodwill. Owl Woman rode behind him, towing the pack mule.

Owl Woman was showing real signs of her pregnancy, and was flushed with happiness—when she wasn't dealing with morning sickness, new and unusual pains, likes and dislikes. For no good reason, she could not bear to be near coffee, though she had always enjoyed it. Nor could she abide pemmican. She had found, though, that she could not get enough of Charlotte's hot chocolate drink.

Bent had felt the first hints that winter was not far off, and he wanted to visit Gray Thunder and catch up on any news involving his people before the Cheyennes began moving off on the fall buffalo hunt.

What he found was a village of angry, grim-faced warriors and surprisingly quiet women and children. Bent dismounted in front of Gray Thunder's lodge and allowed his and Owl Woman's horses to be led away. The mule was tied to a stake pounded into the ground.

Bent and Owl Woman went inside the lodge, shaking the water from their blanket coats. As he slapped raindrops from his hat, Bent wondered what had happened. It was unlike Gray Thunder not to come out in greeting; nor was it like him to be unsmiling. Bent sat, while Owl Woman went off to visit with her sister. Gray Thunder's youngest wife, Smooth Water, disinterestedly handed Bent a bowl of boiled buffalo. Bent ate it swiftly. Only his soft slurping and the crackle of the fire broke the silence. When he finished, Bent set the bowl down.

Bent was normally an impatient man, though outwardly he seemed patient when dealing with the Indians, who took their own sweet time in doing anything. The more important the task, the longer they took to act, it seemed. This time, though, Bent had no desire to play the game. "What the hell's gone on here, Gray Thunder?" he asked bluntly.

Gray Thunder shrugged.

Bent was furious at the snub. "Listen, dammit. You and me been dealin' together a long time. I've married into not only this band of the People, but also into your own family. What touches you, touches me too. Now, what's got into you and your band?"

Gray Thunder sighed. It was a lonely, discouraged sound. He felt every one of his sixty-two winters. His teeth were falling out, and his hair was iron-gray instead of glossy black. His knees ached if he was on his feet more than a few minutes, and he seemed to be filled with gas most of the time. His eyesight was failing, and old scars, once worn proudly as a mark of heroism, were puckered with the fleshy folds of his sagging, leathery skin.

"After the spring hunt," he said, speaking as if every word cut his tongue, "Buffalo Spirit called for all Bow Strings to go to war with him, against the Comanches."

Bent didn't like where this was heading. The Bow Strings were a Cheyenne warrior society. As far as he could tell, the Bow Strings were the bravest of the societies except for the Dog Soldiers, the most elite.

"Forty-one men rode with him," Gray Thunder said, his voice sounding far off and pained. "Most of them were from Yellow Wolf's band, but many of the other bands sent a few men. Rain Beating Down was one." For a moment Gray Thunder's voice was tinged with pride.

Bent was really worried now. Rain Beating Down was Gray Thunder's adopted son, the progeny of Gray Thunder's brother, Eagle Wing, who had died when Rain Beating Down was just a boy.

"None came back," Gray Thunder said, voice cracking.

Bent felt an icy chill run down his back. He could see Owl Woman sitting at the rear of the tipi. "Why didn't you tell me this?" he asked, not taking his gaze from hers.

Owl Woman shook her head, sick at heart. "I didn't know," she answered quietly.

Bent thought that strange. He looked at Gray Thunder. "When did you learn about this?"

Gray Thunder calculated a minute. "Eight suns ago," he said. "Yes, several Arapahos had also gone to make war on the Comanches and Kiowas. One last raid before they would go with us for the fall hunt. They found all of our people." His eyes brimmed over with tears of frustration and rage. If only he were younger, he had thought many times since receiving the news, he would show those Comanches something. As it was, he still would try, though he was not nearly as spry as he would have liked to be.

Bent nodded. No wonder Owl Woman had not told him. She had been back at the fort almost a month now. She would have had no inkling. "You plannin' to do anything about it?" he asked.

Gray Thunder shrugged. "Who can say. We have held councils on it, but have not made any decision yet."

Bent stared at him, eyes narrowed. "You're goin' af-

ter them, ain't you? No matter what the council de-
cides." Silence mounted. "Answer me, dammit!"

Gray Thunder nodded once.

"When?"

"Sometime," Gray Thunder said vaguely. "Nothing
can be done now," he said wearily. "Winter comes
soon. We must make meat for the cold moons; find a
sheltered place to put up our lodges."

Bent nodded. He figured the Cheyennes wouldn't
make a vengeance raid until at least early spring, probably not until after the spring hunt. He hoped that by
then the Cheyennes, particularly Gray Thunder because of his age, would have reconciled themselves to
the defeat and forget the idea of revenge. In his heart,
though, he knew the chances of that were mighty slim.

He brought his gifts in and placed them in front of
Gray Thunder. There was no more to say, so he and
Owl Woman headed for the lodge she had made for
herself—and for him when he was around. It was still
raining heavily, and a decidedly cold wind whistled
over them, catching up the smoke from the tipis and
spreading it like a pall over the village.

Bent had planned on staying in the village a few
days, but he could see no point to it now. They stayed
in the lodge the rest of the day, making love to the
music of the rain drumming on the tipi, the snapping
of the flames, and the roaring wind.

It was still raining quite hard when Bent saddled
their horses the next morning. They mounted up and
rode out without saying good-bye to anyone. Bent did
not want to intrude on the Cheyennes' grief any more
than he already had.

The winter probably was no worse than any other,
though for some reason it felt as if it was. The only
bright spot came in late January. It was a fine day, with
a bright blue sky, a few wisps of clouds and the temper-

ature hovering near zero. Bent was working in his quarters when Owl Woman hollered from the bedroom.

Bent poked his head into the bedroom. "It time?" he asked nervously.

"Yes," Owl Woman gasped.

Worried and coatless, Bent hurried outside. Though it was only a few yards to the dining room and kitchen, Bent was freezing by the time he got inside. "Charlotte!" he bellowed. "Charlotte! It's Sally's time."

"I's comin'," Charlotte said. She bustled out of the kitchen, her rawhide bag of medicines and such clutched in her hand. Trailing her was her husband. "Now you go on and fetch Miz Inez," she ordered him. Then she was out the door.

Bent, knowing he was not needed or wanted, got some coffee from the kitchen. He sat in the dining room battling his worry. Finished with the coffee, he paced. Then he sat, then he paced some more.

Finally, after a lifetime of waiting—though only two and a half hours by his watch—a smiling Charlotte and a beaming Inez Soto walked into the dining room. "You be a papa, Mistah Bent," Charlotte said with a throaty chuckle. "It be a girl baby."

Bent rushed out, not feeling the cold so much this time. Owl Woman was propped up against the headboard, a tiny bit of humanity in her arms. Owl Woman pulled the blanket back some. "Your daughter," she announced, a little worried that Bent would not be pleased that his first child was a daughter instead of a son.

Bent touched the infant's puckered face flesh. "She's a beauty, ain't she?" he muttered.

"Yes." A pause. "You are pleased?"

"Hell, yes," Bent said with a big smile. "You mind if I name her Mary? That's one of my sisters' names."

"It's a good name."

* * *

Winter passed, though, as it always did, and with it came a renewal of life in the fort. St. Vrain arrived to see what was needed and how many furs had been collected. Charles Bent had already headed to Independence, taking a load of furs and other Mexican goods. On the return, he would take the Cimarron Cutoff and go on to Santa Fe and Taos. There he would drop a fair portion of supplies at the company's stores. Then he would head toward the fort, where he would leave the rest of the supplies and pick up the haul of furs. Finally he would head east again for Missouri, completing the circle.

Bent sent his brother George northwest, with orders to take command of Fort Lookout and to send Marcellin St. Vrain back to the fort with whatever furs he had.

William began preparing for his yearly trading trek. At the same time, other Bent, St. Vrain & Company employees were doing so too.

Then the Cheyennes began arriving. As their lodges went up, Bent and St. Vrain were astonished. "I ain't ever seen the like," Bent said. It seemed that with every hour, more tipis blossomed. Three days after the Cheyennes began arriving, Bent rode out. After a half day's ride east along the Arkansas, he was still passing Cheyenne lodges. The next day he did likewise in the other direction, with the same findings. A little worried, Bent ordered the guard doubled. Armed men walked the second floor twenty-four hours a day.

The Cheyennes began coming into the fort. The Indian trade room formed the left wall of the "tunnel" that led into the fort. The room had been built small on purpose: No trader worth his salt would allow more than a half-dozen Indians, no matter how friendly they had been, into a trade room at one time. The counter was wide, and the goods piled behind the trader so the Indians could not reach them and pilfer.

The Cheyennes had all done this many times before, so they knew the procedure. The warriors would arrive at the fort with their furs. Bent, Walsh, and sometimes St. Vrain would be outside with wagons. They would check over each Indian's catch and issue him a marker. The warriors would leave their horses and mules in the care of boys, who would take them away from the fort to where there was forage. Then the Cheyennes and Arapahos would line up. Six were allowed into the trade room at one time. When they finished their business with Ramsay MacGregor, the chief trader, the Indians filed out, and six more entered the trade room.

After that, the Indians were allowed to stop by a barrel off to the side, where Solomon doled out whiskey. Solomon would pour from a large dipper into whatever the Indians brought—bottle, cup, jug, whatever—with a limit of one pint each. The Cheyennes and Arapahos, as well as other tribes, had learned that if they dealt with Bent, St. Vrain & Company, they would not be cheated out of their furs because they had gotten drunk. The company also thought that by limiting the whiskey given the Indians, they made life safer for themselves and for the Indians. Some of the Indians got around the one-pint limit by buying a friend's portion, but nothing could be done about that.

Halfway through the first day, MacGregor noticed something. He turned to Bob Bent, who was helping him in the trade room. "Go 'n' fetch Bill and bring him here, laddie. Tell him it's important."

"What about Ceran?" Robert asked.

"Bill can tell him whatever he wishes—after I've told Bill." Ramsay MacGregor had nothing against Ceran St. Vrain, it was just that he felt he was a Bent employee, not a St. Vrain one. "Now go on, laddie. And make haste."

Robert Bent returned with William, and the two brothers crammed themselves in behind the counter with MacGregor. "What's wrong?" William asked.

MacGregor finished the transaction he had been

making and then turned. "Bob, take over a spell here."

Bob nodded, squeezed past MacGregor and began doling out goods. MacGregor took William's arm and urged him toward the storeroom next door. Once they were away from the Indians, MacGregor said, "There's been a run on some few items, laddie."

"We runnin' low?" Bent asked, sure they had plenty of everything.

"Not too bad, though if it keeps up, it might come to that."

"Well, dammit," Bent snapped, "what are they?" He had been irritable for days because of overwork.

"Powder, lead, sheet iron, and trade guns," Mac-Gregor said flatly.

Bent's eyes narrowed in worry. "How many have asked?"

"Damn near every warrior has asked for some if not all of them. You know what's behind this, don't you?"

"I reckon so. But I can't be sure until I talk to a few of them."

"You want me to keep dolin' those things out?"

"Might as well," Bent said. His stomach was knotted in irritation. "But you might try puttin' 'em off some. Tell 'em we're runnin' low on such things, and that if they want everyone to have some, they'll have to take a mite less. That might help."

"You're going to talk with some of them?"

"If'n I can. Best one'll be Gray Thunder." He left mumbling angrily.

It took a little while to find Gray Thunder. The old warrior had been the first to go into the trade room that morning. Bent talked with a few of the warriors on the line that snaked from the trade room, through the tunnel and outside, curving down toward the river. Bent found that Gray Thunder had completed his business and gone back to his village.

Bent rode out. He stalked to Gray Thunder's lodge,

called for entrance, and then stomped inside without waiting for permission. It was an unthinkable thing to do, but Bent didn't much give a damn.

Gray Thunder was more than a little startled by the action, but he kept his composure and indicated that Bent should sit. Little White Man did so, anger stamped on his face and in his movements.

29

"I know what you're up to, Gray Thunder," Bent said, trying to keep some of the anger out of his voice.

Gray Thunder shrugged. He was too old to worry about the rantings of the young.

"You're bein' a damn fool," Bent told his father-in-law bluntly. "All this fightin's going to hurt the People sooner or later."

Gray Thunder heard but would not listen. "It is out of my hands," he offered as a reason, if not an excuse.

"What do you mean it ain't in your hands?"

"The council has decided. Every warrior spoke in favor of it. We cannot let the Kiowas and Comanches get away with such things."

"Dammit, Gray Thunder," Bent snapped. He paused, wanting to think of what to say, so it would come out coherently. "All this war ain't gonna help the People. Nor the Arapahos, the Comanches, or Kiowas." He pulled off his hat, dropped it and ran a hand through his hair. "You take your men down there, Gray Thunder, it'll hasten the end of the People."

Gray Thunder shook his head. He almost believed what Bent had to say, but he would not—could not—listen. Gray Thunder had made medicine in preparation for this venture. His medicine was strong, but unknowingly his oldest wife, Falling Star, had violated one of the taboos that made his medicine strong. He knew he would die, and he was glad, so he would not blame his Falling Star, whom he had married many years ago. Age had taken its harsh, unyielding toll on Gray Thunder. In his mind's eye he still saw the young man he had been.

Gray Thunder was among the most mighty warriors his tribe had ever produced. He had been strong and fearless, and he always had strong medicine. Many were the raids he made on the Comanches and the Crows, Shoshonis and Kiowas, Pawnees and Utes. Enemies trembled when they heard his name. He had grown to manhood with an arrogance bestowed only on those beyond the norm in some way.

Now he knew he was going to die, though he had told no one, not even Falling Star. He did not fear the end; indeed, he looked forward to being young, healthy, and whole again in the Afterworld, free of pain or want. And, perhaps best of all, he would be dying like a true Cheyenne warrior—in battle, instead of rotting to death from age and infirmities.

Bent stared at Gray Thunder, and soon his anger began to ebb. He rose, hat in hand. There was no more he could say or do. He still thought the impending attack foolish, but he could understand its importance —even necessity—for Gray Thunder. Without another word, Bent slapped his hat on and left. The ride back to the fort was a little fuzzy as his mind dwelled on Gray Thunder. He wondered whether he should tell Owl Woman, but he decided it was best not to.

At the fort, Bent went back to checking furs and offering markers, though part of his mind remained on Gray Thunder. It was still eating at him four days later when the Cheyenne forces gathered a mile west of the fort. One of the *vaqueros* had learned about it and told Bent, who rode out to watch.

It was some spectacle, he thought, as he watched the warriors, led by Gray Thunder, ease into the Arkansas. Gray Thunder rode with a straight back. He was proud and strong, a young man again. He wore a feather headdress, the tail of which he had to pull up onto the horse with him, lest the last several feet drag in the water. Other warriors wore war bonnets, but none, not a single one, was as grandiose as Gray Thunder's. It showed the many honors he had claimed in his lifetime.

"Shit," Bent muttered. He could watch no longer. He turned his roan and headed back to the fort.

Bent was just about ready to leave on his trading trip when Marcellin St. Vrain came in. Bent and Ceran waited for him inside the gate. When Marcellin and his men entered, they had no pack mules with them.

Ceran looked at the young man with wide eyes. "But where are ze furs and hides, eh?"

Marcellin grinned. "I sold zem."

"Sold zem?" Ceran asked, his brow creased with confusion and budding anger. "To whom?"

"Pete Sarpy and Henry Fraeb." He was quite proud of himself.

"Ze American Fur Company?" Ceran asked harshly. Bent, St. Vrain & Company had been fighting the American Fur Company for a couple of years, and had managed to hold off any of that company's efforts to make inroads on Bent-St. Vrain territory south of the Platte. It was the main reason the company had built Fort Lookout, which was in spitting distance of an American Fur fort.

"*Oui.*" He dismounted, grinning widely.

"How many furs you sell zem?"

"Just over two t'ousand buffalo robes—two t'ousand forty-nine, to be exact. And forty-four beavair plews."

"And just how much did you get for all ze furs?" Ceran was tense.

Marcellin pulled a buckskin pouch out of his possible sack and tossed it to his brother. Ceran ignored the sack, which hit his chest and fell to the ground. The whole while, he kept his eyes on his little brother. "How much?" he asked again.

"*Mon Dieu,* Ceran," Marcellin said with a grin, "you have nevair acted zis way about money before."

"How much?" The voice was rough and ragged, containing not an iota of the humor it usually contained.

"All together, five t'ousand one hundred eighty-eight dollars and seventy-two cents." His smile dropped when he saw the anger that had grown on his brother's countenance. He had been happy, thinking that he had done right. By selling the furs, he had removed the danger and work of having to haul them here and then on to Missouri. Suddenly, though, he wondered. His brother's reaction confused and surprised him.

Ceran nodded. He bent and picked up the pouch of money. He almost smiled at his brother, but could not bring himself to do so.

"What's wrong, Ceran?" Marcellin asked, his worry not lessened any by his brother's fractional warming toward him.

"You were taken, *mon frere,*" Ceran said quietly. Some of his anger had faded, but not all of it.

Marcellin looked crushed. "How is zat true?" he asked.

"You sold zem for too little money," Ceran said harshly. Every time he thought about it, the real anger showed up again.

"How much should I have gotten?"

"At least t'ree dollars for ze buffalo, maybe even four. Ze bevair, it don't shine no more. Maybe you should've held out for two dollars zere too." He sighed. "Ze best t'ing would have been to give zem ze beavair plews free, if zey would give you more for ze buffalo."

"*Mon Dieu,*" Marcellin said, sickened that he had let his brother—and Bent, St. Vrain & Company—down.

"*Mon Dieu,* indeed," Ceran snapped. He started in on his brother in French, wanting the others to understand as little as possible.

Bent listened, watching as Marcellin turned beet-red under the berating. Then he had had enough. "Stop it, Ceran!" he ordered harshly.

St. Vrain turned angry eyes and a scowling face on Bent. "Stay out of zis," he ordered. "Zis is family affairs, and of no concern to you."

"Buffler shit," Bent snapped, his own anger starting to rise.

"Eh?" Ceran asked angrily.

"You heard me, goddamn it. What he did was to sell the company's plunder. It weren't yours nor his. That makes it company business."

"Stay out of zis," Ceran warned.

"Why're you bein' so hard on him? He ain't done anything so bad."

St. Vrain hefted the pouch of gold coins. "It is not so much zis," he said after a few moments of wrestling with his anger. He sighed. "I had higher hopes for him, but he makes ze errors all ze time."

"Like what?" Bent asked.

"Like last year when he was attack by the Pawnees and lost all ze goods. And like zis." Again he flipped the pouch a few times.

"Hell, Ceran, we've all been attacked like that."

"*Mais non,*" Ceran said sharply. "Yes, we have all been attack by Indians, but unless we were not alert, we always saved our plews or trade goods. He was not attentive, and so he lost all ze company's t'ings, and one of his men is kill."

Bent shrugged. He still was not convinced. "On the other 'un, he was just inexperienced in dickerin' is all."

"*Oui. Très* inexperience. But he should not have been so. He should have paid attention to what we were doing. He has been under our tutoring for more zan two years, and has not learned anyt'ing.''

Bent shrugged again. It was not his problem, and he had done what he could to reason with his partner.

It took two more days before Bent was ready to leave, but he finally pulled out with his wagons and mules loaded with trade goods. He left Owl Woman at the fort, though remnants of Gray Thunder's band were still camped near it. He had lied to her, telling her that he wanted her in the protection of the fort, for Mary's sake.

He headed south, across the river himself. He had had some success in trading with the Comanches, and wanted to expand it. In addition, he figured most of the Cheyennes were south of the Arkansas in the war party, that there would not be enough of them left to trade with. Besides, the Cheyennes had done most, if not all, of their trading at the fort. He just hoped that the Cheyennes had not gotten the Comanches and Kiowas too riled up with their thirst for vengeance.

A month or so later he was leading his small caravan across the dusty Llano Estacado. The heat was staggering, beating down on the small group of men with a malicious fierceness. The six men were covered with dust streaked with sweat. All were bearded, their eyes rimmed with red from riding through the dust.

Finding some respite on the shaded banks of the Washita River, they made camp, figuring to stay a few days to let the animals and themselves recuperate a little, since the mules and two wagons were piled with buffalo hides.

"When you aimin' to head back, Cap'n?" Walsh asked.

" 'Nother month or so, I reckon. Why?"

"Them mules're worn out," Walsh said, tossing away a buffalo rib bone he had picked clean. "And we ain't got no place left to put furs."

"I reckon that's so. But there's only a couple more

bands of Kwahadis to see. We should be able to handle that much."

Walsh said nothing, but he apparently believed Bent.

The decision was made for them, in a sort of way, when Black Feather, Winter Hawk, and several other warriors rode into the camp.

"What're you doin' here?" Bent asked as the Indians dismounted.

"Looking for Comanches to count coup on," Winter Hawk said, heading to the fire. Without asking, he and his companions poured themselves coffee, using the white men's tin mugs.

"Didn't you get enough of that last time?"

Winter Hawk's face hardened. "We're here because of that time."

Bent did not like the sound of that. "What happened?" he asked, mouth as dry as the Big Sandy usually was.

Winter Hawk sliced off a hunk of buffalo meat. He tore off pieces of the half-seared meat, dripping blood and grease down his chin. "We found a small party of Comanches and killed them all." He sounded proud. "Then we came on the main camp." He scowled and ate silently for a few moments. He swallowed and shook his head. "Gray Thunder went down in the first charge against the village."

"The medicine arrows?" Bent asked, holding his breath. Bent did not know the significance of the arrows. All he knew was, they were considered big medicine by the Cheyennes and that it took a special man —one like Gray Thunder—to be their keeper. Bent figured that if the four arrows were lost, the Cheyennes would be in deep trouble. He did not want to contemplate that.

"He had them, as was his responsibility. His youngest wife, Smooth Water, retrieved them. With an escort, she took them back to the village, near your big lodge."

"You keep on fightin'?" Walsh asked.

Winter Hawk nodded sadly. "Yes, but many others did not."

"Heart wasn't in it anymore, eh?"

"No."

Bent and his men pulled out the next morning, heading north for home. The Cheyennes went the other way, angry and bent on revenge.

When Bent got back to the fort, he found that Owl Woman had learned what had happened to her father already. And so she had grieved as her people had grieved since time immemorial. She had whacked off her hair and slashed at her arms with a knife. With relief he found that St. Vrain—who did not hold their little tiff against him—had prevented Owl Woman from doing any more damage to herself.

30

The massed attack on the Comanche village by a surprisingly cohesive and large force of Cheyennes and Arapahos had confused the Comanches. They had never seen the likes of such a thing before. And they started to look upon their enemies in a slightly different light.

William Bent heard that talk as he took his trading caravan out in the spring. He left earlier than usual, wanting to get a jump on any trouble that might be brewing. But no matter where he traveled that spring and early summer, he heard Indians discussing the bloody fighting that had gone on in the past several years. And as he listened to the talk, Bent also spoke, urging the four major tribes to seek some sort of conciliation amongst them.

Despite the Indians' talk, though, they were not convinced to seek peace. Too many years of hatred existed between them. It bred suspicion and fear, though few would admit to the latter. The raids persisted, back and forth across the Arkansas. Some were merely horse-stealing expeditions; others were decidedly more deadly.

Bent tired quickly of talking himself blue for no good reason. All the Indians simply shut their ears to any talk of peace. They were too riled up to listen to common sense. Disheartened, Bent turned for home.

No sooner had he arrived at the fort and unloaded

the spring's take of furs and hides, than Kit Carson, Bill Williams, and a few other friends showed up. Except for Williams, they were haggard, beaten.

"What the hell happened to you boys?" Bent asked. He was back in control of the fort again. Charles was, as usual, somewhere between Missouri and northern Mexico, and St. Vrain was in Taos, watching over the store. George Bent was in Fort Lookout. Marcellin St. Vrain was given a chance to redeem himself by working as a trader out of that new fort.

"Damn if I know," Carson snapped angrily. Since he was normally a feisty man, the anger in Carson made Bent think of the spring mechanism on a beaver trap. Carson yanked the saddle off his horse. He nodded at the Mexican boy who came to take the horse away.

Bent knew enough not to prod Carson, since he himself would have acted the same if something was stuck in his craw.

"Grab that possibles bag, Bill," Carson said.

Bent understood it was a request and not an order. He picked it up, and the two men moved upstairs.

Bent noticed that Bill Williams had unsaddled his horse and dumped his gear next to the blacksmith's shop. He was already entering the bar-pool hall on the second floor of the south side of the fort.

Bent almost grinned. Nobody in his right mind would mess with Ol' Solitaire's gear, no matter where he placed it. Every time Bent saw the tall, lanky, laconic trapper, he thought what a queersome fellow the redhead was. He was older than most of the others in the mountains, and had a heap of odd ideas. He didn't often have dealings with others, and almost never trapped with anyone. Mostly he went his own way through life, and the rest of humanity be damned. Williams would never speak of where he trapped, and most years he set out into the mountains alone. He would show up at Bent's Fort or Taos or rendezvous come the summer, and more often than not he had

more and better plews than any other man. He was a
wild one too, especially when he was in his cups, which
he frequently was when not on duty, as he saw his job.
He also was given over to occasional bursts of sermon-
izing and berating the damned. He had started out as a
Methodist preacher who had come west to convert the
heathen Osage. Trouble was, they converted him instead. He also was known for his frequent bursts of
lunacy.

"This 'un, Kit," Bent said, stopping in front of one
of the rooms he kept as trappers' quarters. They were
simple rooms, sparsely furnished. About all they contained were a round-front fireplace, a rickety wood table and a couple of matching chairs, some rope strung
up for the men to hang wet clothes on, and two or
sometimes three simple wood cots with rope ham-
mocks on which a man could throw his bedroll. Many
of them slept on the floor, feeling more comfortable
there, since they were used to sleeping on the ground.

Carson kicked open the door and stomped inside.
The room was empty. He was relieved, since he didn't
want to be around folks much these days. He dropped
his saddle next to one of the cots and leaned his
Hawken rifle against the wall.

Bent set the possibles bag on the bed. "Obliged,"
Carson said.

"Now, how's about you tell this ol' hoss just what the
hell's got you lower'n a snake's belly."

"None of your goddamn business, Bill. You just keep
your nose out of my affairs, dammit."

Bent took the insults in stride. He knew Carson
didn't mean them. He had a little bit of trouble controlling his temper, but he managed. "If that's where
your stick floats, I'll respect it. Charlotte'll have supper
ready in about an hour." He turned for the door.

"Ah hell, Bill, come on back here and set your ass
down. I'm of a need to jaw at an ol' friend who ain't

likely to get troublesome at the foolish things I might say.''

Bent grinned. ''Tell you what, ol' hoss, you set and cool your heels a few minutes, whilst I go get us somethin' to oil your tongue.''

Carson smiled wanly. ''Reckon that'd shine with this chil','' he said, then mumbled, ''It'll be the only goddamn thing that shines for this critter these days.''

Bent returned with a bottle of halfway decent whiskey and a huge hunk of half-cooked hump meat. Carson was just getting the fire going. Bent set the bottle down, pierced the piece of meat with a pointed iron bar and hung it over the fire. He and Carson sat in front of the flames, the bottle between them. Neither felt the urge to get drunk, but the bottle would do to cut the travel dust in Carson's throat.

''Almost like the old days, ain't it?'' Bent said.

Carson smiled crookedly. ''Sure as hell is. Two ol' critters settin' at a fire, without a damn thing but their hides to call their own.''

''That what's stuck in your craw?''

Carson nodded and took a sip of whiskey. Holding the fat part of the bottle, he jabbed the neck in Bent's direction to emphasize his points. ''I know you tol' me a couple years ago that the beaver wasn't gonna shine no more. But goddamn, I never thought it was gonna be this goddamn bad.'' His eyes looked pained. ''Christ, Bill, we couldn't raise two packs between us in both the fall and the spring hunt. Even Ol' Solitaire could make no beaver come. I ain't ever seen the day where Ol' Solitaire couldn't raise enough beaver for a couple decent packs.''

''You got any specie put up?''

''A couple hundred dollars settin' down in Taos. It ain't much, what with havin' to pay you back for the year's supplies and such.''

''Don't fret about that, Kit. I ain't worried over it. Neither will Charlie or Ceran. Hell, we've all of us been in the same straits before. You pay us back when you got the wherewithal." He paused for a sip. "We can find you some work, if you're of a mind."

"Like what?" Carson asked. He might be down on his luck, but he was still a proud man. He wasn't about to take some job hauling manure with old Crutsinger.

"Huntin'. We got more'n a hundred folk workin' here now. Such a thing calls for a heap of meat."

Carson figured hunting wasn't so bad. "How much you payin'?"

"Dollar a day," Bent said without embarrassment.

"That ain't a hell of a lot."

"It's a hell of a lot better'n we're payin' most of the Mexicans."

Carson thought about it. A dollar a day wasn't much to a man who often made a couple thousand in a good year of trapping. On the other hand, it was a lot better than having no cash in your possibles bag.

Bent leaned forward and stabbed a knife into the meat, then sliced off a piece with another. Holding the skewered meat up in the air, he chewed off chunks. He also watched Carson, knowing what the man was wrestling with. Carson was a friend, and he wanted to help a friend. On the other hand, he was a businessman, with responsibilities to his partners. Still, he figured there must be some way he could help his good friend a little more than any old mountaineer who showed up.

Bent nodded. "Tell you what, Kit," he said. "You get a dollar a day, plus room and board. And you can keep what hides you get. I'll buy 'em off you for whatever the goin' price is."

It took Carson only a moment to decide. It wasn't so much that he didn't have a choice. He could get by on his savings, living off the land as he had been these past ten, twelve years. Mostly what made the decision for him was the knowledge that Bent was going out of his way to help. Only true friends would do such. He nodded.

The two men shook hands, and solidified the deal with a snort of whiskey each. They sat back then, both relieved at the accord. They gnawed at the seared, dripping meat, sipped from the bottle, smoked their pipes, and talked of the old days, when beaver were so plentiful that almost all a man had to do was come up on a beaver crick, grab the critters and toss their soft, sleek fur in his pack.

Both fell asleep, half drunk, in front of the fire. Their hangovers in the morning weren't too bad, but they would've appreciated more shut-eye. Bent stepped outside to see what was causing the ruckus that had woke him. He spit some of the foulness out of his mouth and down on the *placita*.

"What the hell's goin' on out there?" Carson called from inside.

"Ol' Solitaire's raisin' hell again."

A moment later Carson was standing next to Bent, watching the antics below.

Williams was in the *placita*, chasing a plump chicken. The bird was squawking wildly as it skittered here and about, always a half step out of Williams's reach. Meanwhile, Charlotte was trying to protect her favorite egg-laying hen. She was running about, screeching louder than Williams and the chicken combined, and trying to whack Williams with an iron frying pan. Charlotte was not a woman of small girth, and the tableau was quite like one of the mirages men would see out on the plains.

Suddenly Williams dove and managed to get his hands on the chicken. Holding the squawking fowl in his left hand, he started to push himself up with the right. Charlotte was waiting and slammed Williams a good shot on the back of his head. He went down like he was poleaxed.

"Teach you to mess wif' my chickens," Charlotte

gloated. She flapped her apron at it, shooing it toward its coop behind the kitchen.

Williams sat and held his head in his hands. "Wagh! Damn chicken," he mumbled. He spouted off again, sometimes in Osage, sometimes in Ute, a few words in English, but even those made no sense to the watchers.

Finally he stood, looking dazedly around. It was as if he suddenly found himself in a foreign land, transported by some magic. He shook his head. "Wagh!" he said brightly. "It's time this chil's set to the table."

"This ol' hoss has got to see this," Carson said, heading for the steps, his hangover almost forgotten.

Bent chuckled and hurried after his friend.

They managed to get inside the dining room before Williams did, and were seated in anticipation. It was rather anticlimactic, since Williams seemed to have no remembrance of what had transpired. He simply sat and scratched absentmindedly at the knot on his head. When Charlotte headed toward him, he smiled and said, "Mornin', ma'am. I'm of a mind for some of them shinin' flapjacks you make."

Charlotte stared at him as if he had gone mad. Williams looked around the room, wondering what everyone was laughing about. Charlotte headed back to her kitchen muttering as unintelligibly as Williams had done a few minutes ago.

Carson and Bent shook their heads, wondering about this oddity of a human.

As they ate, Carson asked, "When you want me to start?"

"Today."

Carson nodded.

After eating, Bent headed off to the trade room; Carson went and saddled his horse. A few minutes later he rode out of the fort, accompanied by a helper driving a mule-drawn wagon.

Life settled in at the fort to the monotonous regime

that was normal. Making that possible was the departure of Williams. Bent was almost sorry to see the man go. Williams was an almost constant source of amusement and entertainment.

31

At every opportunity, Bent would implore the Indians with whom he dealt to seek a peace among themselves. He spent as much time as he could in Sun Dog's lodge and village. Now that Gray Thunder was dead, Sun Dog became the keeper of the sacred arrows. He could not be considered the main chief of the Cheyennes, since no Indians had such a thing. That was one of the problems with officials dealing with Indians—they could not grasp the idea that the Indians were completely independent as individuals. The military and their minions, who were beginning to arrive in Indian lands, always had to designate someone as the chief of all that tribe. Such a thing was guaranteed to cause trouble, even if the whites could not see it.

While Bent spoke to all the tribes, the majority of his efforts were directed at the Cheyennes, since he was closest to them, and so thought them the most reasonable of the four major tribes in the region. He also worried the most for them; he would hate to see them destroyed. He could see that more and more whites were coming along the Santa Fe Trail. It was only a matter of time before some of them started settling in. Bent knew there would be a heap of trouble then.

Sun Dog, as well as all the other Cheyennes and Arapahos, would not heed Bent. They simply refused to see that their constant warfare would be their destruction. The Cheyennes were still a major power on the central plains. Because of that, they were arrogant, as were the Kiowas and Comanches south of the river.

Sometime during the winter of 1839–40, Sun Dog showed up at the fort, looking to trade some buffalo robes for supplies. Like most of the other tribes—including intractable bands like the Kwahadi Comanches —the Cheyennes had unwittingly come to be dependent on the white traders for many items they could not make or find: kettles, pots, cloth, sheet iron for arrowheads, guns, powder, lead, steel knives.

Bent took the opportunity to harangue Sun Dog and the small contingent of warriors who had accompanied him. They all went into the council room and sat crosslegged on the floor. Charlotte brought them a big pot of coffee, enough mugs for all, and two platters of *bizcochitos*. The Indians loved the sweet cookies.

"You lost forty-two Bow Strings a couple years ago," Bent said, voice growing heated with frustration. Nothing he was saying to them was new. He had been over it all already. "Last year you lost Gray Thunder. Christ, Sun Dog, how many warriors can you afford to lose?"

Sun Dog shrugged. "After the spring hunt, we will crush the Comanches," he said arrogantly, holding out his right hand, palm up, then closing the fist. "The Kiowas too."

"Dammit, Sun Dog, that's what the People said the last two times, and look where that got you."

"This time will be different. Gray Thunder had lost his medicine. He lost much of the sacred arrows' medicine too. I will make strong medicine." His chest puffed out with haughty self-importance.

"I never knowed you to be this damn stupid," Bent said bluntly.

Sun Dog's eyes narrowed at the insult. He would kill most any man who said such a thing to him, especially a white man. But Little White Man had been a good friend of the Cheyennes for some years. Unlike most white-eyes, Bent had not come among the Cheyenne people, taken what he wanted from them, including a wife, and then left. He still visited the camps regularly. He allowed the Cheyennes to camp near the fort anytime they wanted. He gave the People a considerable amount of freedom to wander in the trading post. He was a man admired by many of the warriors for his honesty, integrity, and valor.

"We will not become weak like the timid deer that runs from everything. We are Tsistsistas!"

"What you're gonna be is goddamn dead," Bent snapped. He wanted to pound some sense into Sun Dog.

"All must die," Sun Dog said, as if it would defeat all arguments.

"I don't mean just you, you damn fool. I mean the People—the others too—will be no more if'n you don't stop killin' each other."

"We have fought the Comanches since time began," Sun Dog said simply. That the statement was not true made no difference to Sun Dog. "We will not show any sign of weakness to our enemies."

Bent sighed. This was like talking to the walls surrounding them. "You've seen the freight trains—the many mules and wagons?"

Sun Dog nodded once, regally.

"You noticed anything about them of late?"

Sun Dog shrugged and reached for another cookie. He was bored, and wished he was in his own lodge. He had to admit, though, that it was warm inside this mud lodge, and the cookies were sweet.

"There's more of 'em comin' every year."

Sun Dog shrugged once more. Such things did not concern him. "They do not stop," he said, spitting out cookie crumbs as he spoke.

"Someday they will," Bent said. His frustration had ebbed, replaced by a dull fatalism.

"What has this to do with us?"

"You and the Comanches keep killin' each other,

and there won't be many of you left to fight the white man once he stops on your land and puts down roots."

"Then we will deal with them," Sun Dog responded.

It was hopeless, Bent decided.

The Cheyennes left four days later, after sitting out a blizzard that beat on the fort like a relentless giant seeking admittance.

Bent made a similar appeal to Little Mountain, one of the foremost Kiowa leaders. And later to the well-known—and widely feared—Comanche war chief Old Wolf. Bent and his traders had made progress in developing trade with the Comanches and Kiowas in the past few years. Traders did not have the well-established connections with those two tribes as they had with the Cheyennes and Arapahos, but it was enough to allow the whites to push the idea of an Indian peace, and get away with it, as long as they did not insult the warriors too much.

As spring began edging into the region, word filtered into the fort that smallpox had paid the Kiowas a deadly visit over the winter. Soon after, Little Mountain and Old Wolf sent word that the Kiowas and Comanches might be willing to listen to words of peace with their old enemies, the Cheyennes and Arapahos.

Feeling cautiously hopeful, Bent quickly sent some Plains Apaches, who were connected to the Arapahos by way of marriage, to the Cheyennes and Arapahos. They returned with the good news that the two tribes would also be willing to come to a council, since the Comanches and Kiowas had made the first overture.

His hopes growing, Bent sent the Plains Apaches out again, this time across the river. They returned, explained what had occurred, and then went to talk to the Cheyennes and Arapahos again. Finally they reported to Bent that a date and place had been selected for the council.

For their tireless efforts, Bent gave each of the Plains Apaches a trade gun, powder horn, tin of powder, bar of lead, and a bullet mold. They went away happy to show off their newfound wealth.

Bent sent traders to the Kiowas and the Comanches, though it was much earlier than usual. As soon as those men were on the way, he explained what was going on to a newly arrived St. Vrain, and Charles Bent. Then he hastily made up a small caravan of goods and, with five men, left to visit the Cheyenne camps.

He found each camp filled with excitement. All the Cheyennes and Arapahos were preparing for the great council. Because of that, the Indians were distracted, and so of little mind for trading. Finally Sun Dog said to Bent, "We will come to your stone lodge before the council."

Bent accepted his word as the truth. All the while Bent had been in the village, Sun Dog made no reference to his own earlier efforts to bring about such a grand meeting as this. Bent did not see any reason to remind Sun Dog. He figured the Cheyenne chief was too proud to admit that he had been right all along. Bent could understand that.

As Bent and his men turned for the fort, a sense of excitement rose in him with each passing mile. If this worked, it would help him in a couple of ways. For one thing, his Cheyenne and Arapaho friends would be safer, and so could turn their attentions to other pursuits. For another, Bent, St. Vrain & Company should do well with the four major tribes here at peace. The possibilities for the company were immense.

Eager expectation also gripped the fort. Nearly all the men who worked there or visited regularly wanted this council to be successful, since most believed that if there was peace between the various tribes, their own lives would be safer.

Word must have gotten around, since many old-timers stopped by—Kit Carson, Old Bill Williams, Uncle Dick Wootton, Peg-Leg Smith, even the ill-tempered and lie-telling Jim Beckwourth. The latter left right af-

ter arriving, since Bent told the mulatto that he would
turn him over to the Cheyennes if he didn't. Beckwourth, who had been made something of a chief by
the Crows, boasted of what he would do to the Cheyennes, but then quickly saddled his horse and headed
for parts unknown.

The Cheyennes and Arapahos were the first to arrive, coming by the hundreds. Their lodges began
sprouting on the north bank of the Arkansas, about
three miles from the fort's gates. The number of color-
fully painted tipis and horses was impressive.

Traders and all went out to look the sprawling camps
over. Kit Carson returned one evening and joined
Bent, who was eating a hasty supper.

"Lord almighty," Carson said, "I ain't ever seen the
like. Jesus, there's Cheyennes and Arapahos from here
to Independence, the way it looks. Hand games're
bein' played in front of every goddamn lodge."

Bent looked at him skeptically.

"I'm tellin' true, dammit. Go on over there your
own self and see."

"Ain't got time, Kit." Bent's eyes were rimmed with
black, and his eyeballs were bloodshot. He looked—
and felt—like hell.

"Them Injuns keepin' you hoppin'?"

Bent finished the mouthful of chicken spiced with
chili peppers. "I ain't had time to piss since they
started arrivin'." He sighed. "This is a good thing for
everybody, I'm thinkin', but Jesus Christ, I wish it was
done and over with."

"Good for business, though, ain't it?"

Bent smiled wanly. "Hell yes. Each and every Cheyenne and Arapaho've been in here, it seems, buyin' all
kinds of foofaraw for themselves, their women, their
young 'uns, hell, even their goddamn ponies. Plus
they're buyin' presents for the Comanches and Kiowas." He paused. "I just hope those sons of bitches
show up. They don't and there's gonna be one hell of

a lot of angry Injuns on this side of the river." After a deep breath he added, "Hell, I even sent Owl Woman and Mary out to Sun Dog's village since I got no time for 'em."

He scooped up the last bite of chicken and swallowed some coffee. "Adios, amigo," he said before rushing for the Indian trade room again.

His fears about the Comanches and Kiowas not showing up were unfounded. The Kiowas arrived the next afternoon and began setting up their lodges on the south side of the river.

With the arrival of the Kiowas, Bent found business falling off to almost nothing. The Cheyennes and Arapahos wanted to be near their women and children in case the southern tribes planned some deviltry.

Bent took the opportunity the next morning to ride out with Carson to the Cheyenne and Arapaho camp down the river. Little Mountain of the Kiowas sent a messenger for Bent, asking him to come to the Kiowa camp. Bent shrugged at Carson, indicating he had no idea what was going on, but he mounted his horse and followed the young warrior across the river. Carson and hundreds of Cheyenne and Arapaho warriors lined the north bank, worried but hopeful as they saw Bent enter Little Mountain's lodge.

Bent returned half an hour later, bearing a carefully folded blanket. He handed it to Carson and dismounted. "We got to talk, Sun Dog," he said to the chief, then retrieved the blanket from Carson. "Just you and me, Kit, if that's where his stick floats."

Carson nodded. He hated being left out when there were secrets to be told. The three entered Sun Dog's lodge, and Bent set the blanket down. "Little Mountain and the Kiowas send this as a token of their peaceful hearts to the Cheyennes."

Sun Dog watched as Bent began unfolding the thick blanket. His eyes widened when he saw the contents.

He looked sharply at Bent, then again to the pile of neatly cured scalps.

"All forty-two of 'em's here," Bent said.

"What the hell's this all about?" Carson asked, surprised.

Bent quickly explained the Bow Strings' raid three years ago. "They've given back the scalps to show they mean their talk of peace."

Carson nodded, but Sun Dog shook his head. "No," the Cheyenne leader said. "We cannot take them."

"Why not?" Bent asked, a little surprised. Forty-two Bow String warriors were floating around somewhere, unable to get to the Afterworld since their spirits were not free.

"Showing them to the People might be a disaster. The families of those warriors might get violent if their grief is renewed seeing these."

Bent nodded. He folded the blanket again. Walking outside, he handed the blanket to Carson, mounted his horse and took the blanket back. He rode slowly, almost regally, across the river and explained Sun Dog's refusal to accept the gift.

Little Mountain nodded, accepting it. "Sun Dog is wise," Little Mountain said. "He sees well. I would have done the same."

32

Bent was still in the Cheyenne camp that afternoon when an Arapaho warrior shouted and pointed to a huge dust cloud sweeping slowly, magnificently, toward them. Everyone waited expectantly, lining the north bank of the river in anticipation.

Before long a faint rumble began, growing louder and louder, until it seemed there was no other sound in the world. Finally Old Wolf rode into view on a beautiful cream-colored mare. He thrust his spear point into the dirt, as if claiming the land as his own. Then the rest of his people started to move into view, as did the Comanche horse herds.

Bent, Carson, and Sun Dog stood on a small ridge, giving them a slightly better vantage point than most of the other Cheyennes and Arapahos. What they saw, they had trouble believing.

"Jesus Christ almighty," Carson whispered, voice reflecting his awe. "You ever see so many horses?"

Bent was dumbfounded. "There's got to be a thousand of them."

"Many more," Sun Dog said, his usual calm demeanor shaken.

"I got to go with Sun Dog on this one, Bill," Carson said. "Maybe more like five thousand."

Horses were still pouring over the sand hills on the south side of the river. It seemed there was no end to them, and Bent began to figure that he was seeing one of those weird mirages.

"Best I can figure it," Bent said when the horses did finally stop coming over the sand hills, "is eight thousand. Give or take a thousand," he added a little sarcastically. They watched for a little while as the Comanches began setting up their tipis.

Finally Bent headed for his horse. "I best be gettin' back to the fort, in case the Comanches overrun us."

Carson nodded. "I'm gonna set here and see what happens."

Bent nodded and rode off.

Carson pulled into the fort just before dark fell. He found Bent in his quarters. Bent had a two-room apartment. One room was his office, the other his bedroom.

"You ever hear of some ol' boy by the name of Jim Hobbs?"

Bent thought about it while he filled his pipe and lit it from a candle. Then he nodded. "Sure. He was with one of Charlie's caravans, must be three, four years ago. Him and another 'un . . . what the hell was his name . . . ?" Bent mused loudly.

"Hobbs mentioned someone else," Carson said. "John somebody. Baptiste I think?" He was not sure.

"Yeah, John Baptiste. They were with Charlie, and took off after a buffler. They was caught up by Comanches. You say you seen 'em?"

Carson nodded. "Hobbs said him and this Baptiste feller are livin' with Old Wolf. Hobbs said he's doin' fairly well, and even got himself hitched Injun style to one of Old Wolf's daughters. Baptiste, I figure, ain't fared as well."

"What's he want?"

"Freedom. Said he wanted me to get word to you—and Charlie, if he was around. He ain't happy livin' with the Comanches," he said dryly. "Think you'll be able to help him?"

"Depends on Old Wolf. He wants to be a pain in the

ass, maybe not." He paused. "They got any other captives, do you know?"

"Hobbs said there was two young white women married to a couple of Old Wolf's sons. I don't expect they're being well-treated. He didn't think Old Wolf'll even let you parley on the subject."

"Hell, never hurts to try. You know their names?"

"All Hobbs knew was that their last name was Brown. They was took some time back, from down around San Antonio."

Bent nodded. "I'll see what I can do about all of 'em. You see Hobbs again, you tell him that. But also tell him I ain't makin' no promises. As you well know, them damned Comanches can be cantankerous bastards."

"I'll tell him."

"You headin' back out there?"

"Might's well. Makin' Out Road misses me," he said of his new wife. "And for damn good reason too." He and Bent laughed.

The expected flood of Kiowas and Comanches had not come, so at first light Bent rode out to the meeting area. Every Cheyenne and Arapaho—from an aged, wrinkled warrior to the littlest suckling babe—was dressed in his or her finest clothes and was sitting along the south bank facing a people with whom they had been at war for all their lifetimes. Bent was astonished at the sight, though he realized in a moment that he shouldn't be. After all, this was why they were here.

He sat on his roan and watched as the Comanches and Kiowas brought horses out of the sand hills and presented one to every Cheyenne and Arapaho. The northerners waded back across the river with their gifts. It took all morning before it was done.

Then the Comanches and their allies crossed the river and sat down to a feast presented by their former enemies. They enjoyed foods they had never even seen before, strange white man's delicacies bought from

Bent's Fort. After the eating was finished, the Cheyennes brought out other presents—cloth, knives, pots, and more. Then they began to mingle between both villages. Warriors swapped stories of their prowess—always careful to make no mention of battles between each other, lest they ruin the festive atmosphere. Men also gambled, raced horses, and more. Women chatted with their former enemies, and men and women alike danced to the pounding of drums and piercing wail of voices.

Bent quickly tired of the noise and excitement, so he told Carson he was going back to the fort. An hour after he arrived, one of his traders—a maniacal, vicious man named Blackfoot John Smith—pulled in and dismounted in front of Bent's apartment.

Bent came outside. "What can I do for you, John?"

"How's about sendin' some Lightnin' out for us folks," he growled, trying to grin. Not having had much experience at it, he failed.

"No," Bent said flatly.

"Hell, I'll even buy." It was not something Smith did very often. In fact, no one could even remember him saying such a thing.

"No," Bent said, a sharper tone to his voice. "You got maybe two thousand warriors out there were mortal enemies yesterday. Sendin' in some whiskey wouldn't just be risky, it'd be goddamn downright foolish, and almost certainly fatal."

"Well," Smith said slyly, "ain't nothin' stoppin' me from buyin' a barrel or two on my own. Then I can do with it what I please." There was a threatening tone in his voice.

"I'll stop you," Bent said, not intimidated.

"Hell," Smith said with a raspy laugh, "you ain't gonna do shit."

"You might have the goddamn Mexicans cowed, but you sure as hell don't scare me."

"You think you could take me, you little son of a bitch?" Smith said, puffing himself up.

"Don't make no difference," Bent said with a shrug. "All you need to know is that if you come against me, you're gonna go under."

Smith laughed again. "Damn, you think a lot of yourself, don't ya? Think that cuz you're the damn *bourgeois* here that everybody's gonna kiss your scrawny little ass. I'm of a mind to kick the shit out of you."

"I wouldn't do that was I you," Solomon said from behind Smith.

Smith turned around, taking in the well-muscled man, who held a blacksmith's hammer in his right hand. Solomon tapped the hammer lightly against his left palm.

"This ain't none of your affair, you black son of a bitch."

"Mistah Bent be one of de few men who's ever looked on me as jus' another man. Somebody be threatenin' him, I make it my affair."

Smith looked from one to the other. He knew that if he caused any more trouble here, he would die. Besides, he liked working for the Bents, or at least as much as he liked working anywhere. "Bah," he scowled. He jumped on his horse and galloped away.

"Thank you, Solomon," Bent said.

Solomon shrugged, but he smiled a little.

A clamor drew Bent out of his office. "What's goin' on, Ramón?"

A disturbed Ramón Lopez looked down from the blockhouse over the gates. "Comanches're coming," he said with virtually no accent.

"Many of 'em?"

Lopez's head bounced up and down.

"How many?" Bent asked, a little exasperated. He could barely hear Lopez, what with all the racket going on outside.

"All of 'em."

"All of them who?"

"All the Comanches God ever made."

"This ain't the time for exaggeratin', Mr. Lopez."

"I'm not, Señor Bent. Come see."

Bent trotted up the stairs and looked over the wall. "Jesus," he breathed. "I'm sorry I doubted you, Ramón." He estimated that nearly a thousand Comanches were on their way toward the fort, led by Smith and Carson. And every one of them howling. It created quite a din. Bent didn't like this one little bit. He was relieved when the Comanches stopped just outside the gate.

"Come on down here, Bill," Carson shouted, cupping his hands around his mouth. The din was deafening.

Bent headed down the stairs, shaking his head at this foolish move. Then he was outside, standing next to Smith and Carson. Smith seemed to have completely forgotten their small confrontation before.

"I told some of the chiefs you'd show 'em around the fort," Smith said, shouting to be heard over the cacophony. Smith had a Cheyenne wife, but he had spent enough time trading with the Comanches to get close to a few chiefs and warriors. Now he was trying to show off his newfound importance with the Comanches.

Bent answered the same way. "A few chiefs I don't mind. This howlin' army is another matter."

Smith nodded and strolled off. Bent and Carson stared at each other, rather stunned by all this. They exchanged more knowing glances when Smith walked up with an old warrior and said, "Boys, this here is Old Wolf, a great war chief of the Comanche nation."

Bent nodded toward him. Then he moved up right beside Smith and shouted in his ear, "Any way you can stop all this damn howlin'?"

Smith nodded. He yelled at Old Wolf, and the two of

them went moving through the Comanches. Soon the roaring began to dwindle, until it was at a reasonable level.

Smith and Old Wolf returned with fourteen other war chiefs. "This way, gentlemen," Bent said. They all walked inside the fort, and the Comanches stopped. They had never been inside Bent's Fort, though they had seen it from the outside.

"Wait here a minute," Bent said to all his guests. He headed for the trade room and talked with Ramsay MacGregor. Then he rejoined the group and began showing them each and every room. He took care to show the Comanches the fort's two small cannon, the weapons hanging on the walls, the loopholes in the adobe walls, even the cactus growing atop the walls of the corral. He wanted to make sure the Comanches knew how impregnable the fort was.

Just after the tour started, MacGregor went outside with several workers and started trading. Smith saw it, broke off from Bent and the Comanches, and wandered out that way. He returned soon after.

Bent was just showing the Comanche war leaders the big fur press and trying to describe how it worked when they heard a commotion outside. They all ran for the gates.

Two Comanches, of different bands, were rolling in the dirt trying to kill each other. Two war leaders with Bent—Yellow Eagle and Bear Foot—ran over and pried the men apart. The four shouted in Comanche. Finally Yellow Eagle turned to Bent. "Whiskey," he said.

"No," Bent said in English, while signing it at the same time.

Yellow Eagle shook his head. "No, whiskey," he said in heavily accented English. He shook the warrior he was holding and slapped the chest of the other combatant.

Bent shrugged, indicating that he could not understand. "What's he tryin' to tell me, Blackfoot?"

Smith chatted in Comanche with the chief, then turned back to Bent. "He says whiskey made them fight."

"Where the hell'd they get whiskey?" Bent asked. He was angrier maybe than he had ever been. That was all he needed was a thousand or so Comanche warriors goaded into war by alcohol.

Smith shrugged.

Bent's eyes narrowed and blazed hotly at Smith. "Where the hell'd you go when you left us a while back?" he demanded.

"Out here," he said without apology. "But I didn't bring no whiskey."

"You lyin' son of a bitch," Bent snapped. "I'll—"

He stopped when one of his Mexican workers who had gone outside to help MacGregor with the trading tugged at his shirtsleeve. He kept imploring, "Please, Señor Bent. *Por favor* . . ."

"What do you want, Tomás?" Bent said, irked at the interruption.

"I gave them the whiskey, Señor Bent." He looked like he expected to be struck by lightning at any moment.

Bent fought to control his temper. He finally managed, and asked, "You got any more?"

"Some," Tomás Avilla said in a strangled voice.

"Bring it," Bent commanded. When Avilla brought the small keg of whiskey, Bent said, "I'll deal with you tomorrow." Then he took the keg under his arm, carried it into the fort, and locked it in his office. He turned back to continue the tour.

With an effort, he maintained his control, and soon even some joviality began to shine through.

Old Wolf was fascinated by everything inside the fort. Never had he seen a place so captivating. He constantly touched the walls, the beams, gear, trade goods, anything he could place a hand on.

The other Comanche chiefs were not as entranced, and as the afternoon waned, so did their interest. They chatted with Blackfoot John, who finally said to Bent, "These boys are about half froze to get the hell outta here, Bill. You mind if I was to take 'em outside?"

Bent shook his head. He was getting tired too, but wanted to make overtures to Old Wolf for the release of his two captured employees and the two girls he had heard of. "You want to stay awhile yet, Old Wolf?" he asked innocently.

The old chief nodded.

Bent pulled Smith aside. "It's gettin' dark, and I ain't real happy with havin' a goddamn thousand Comanche bucks outside."

"A reasonable thought," Smith said dryly.

"Indeed. You know the ritual when the sun goes down."

"Sure. All the Injuns outside and the gates closed and barred."

"The time's come for this night. I'll make an exception with Old Wolf, though."

Smith nodded.

"You gonna stay out there with the Cheyennes?" Bent remembered that Smith had a Cheyenne wife.

"Nope," Smith said with a hearty laugh. "I got me some little Comanche squaw all lined up for a good humpin'." He laughed some more, the crusty sound ricocheting around the adobe-ringed *placita*.

Bent shook his head in disgust. He knew Smith and his proclivities. More than likely, the squaw he had lined up had barely achieved puberty. Well, it was not his business. "There any of my other people outside that you know of?"

"A couple of 'em. Ol' MacGregor pulled in his trade goods and closed up shop an hour or so ago. Him and Lopez are inside. But there's still a few down the way. I reckon all them fellers'll be stayin' the night down there." He laughed once more. "Not all of us is so high and mighty as to have a fancy place to take the squaws we was about to hump."

Smith's ingratiating grin was all that kept Bent from jumping him and pounding his brains out. That, and knowing that Smith didn't really mean it. It was simply a case of a man having a mouth that worked separately from his brain on too many occasions.

"Just get your ratty ass out there. And be sure you want to stay out there too, 'cause I'm barrin' the gates."

"Don't make me no never mind," Smith said with a shrug. He was arrogant, but it was an arrogance built on the fear he sparked in others. Not long ago Mexico offered a five hundred dollar reward for his head. That was a fortune to the peasants, but not a one tried to collect it.

He turned and strolled away, all the Comanche chiefs except Old Wolf and his two sons in his wake.

Once Smith was gone, Bent said, "What do you boys want to see now?" He repeated it in Spanish, and with signs.

"I speak English—and Spanish," one of Old Wolf's

sons said. "I'm Bull Nose." He was taller than the aver-
age Comanche, with a handsome face marred by a
seemingly perpetual scowl.

Bent nodded. "Then you're gonna translate for us?"

Bull Nose shrugged, as if he didn't care.

"You're a big goddamn help," Bent said scornfully.
"Your brother speak English?"

"No."

"What's his name?"

"Medicine Wolf."

Old Wolf had strolled regally toward Bent's apartment, followed by his sons. Bent and Carson exchanged shrugs and trailed along. Old Wolf stopped at
the door and turned to face Bent. "Whiskey me?" he
asked, jamming a thumb at his chest.

Bent looked at Carson and flashed a grin. He was
solemn, though, when he faced the Comanche chief.
"Sure, Old Wolf," he said with a nod. "Wait here." He
unlocked the door and went inside. When he returned, he had three small jugs. He handed one to
each of the Comanches.

Old Wolf looked at his jug suspiciously. "Bigger
me," he intoned, holding out the jug.

"There's plenty more where that come from,
Chief," he said. He signed the message too.

Old Wolf nodded and tilted the jug up. He seemed
to swallow half the whiskey in one long gulp.

Bent moved up to stand next to Carson. "You think
he don't know no English?" he said *sotto voce*. "Or is he
stringin' us along?"

Carson shrugged. "I don't reckon he's joshin'," he
answered in kind. "We give him enough whiskey, we
should find out, though." He turned his head and
looked at Bent with a small smile on his lips. "You *are*
plannin' to fill that ol' fart up, ain't you?"

Bent nodded. "Sonny boy too." He indicated Bull
Nose.

Carson smiled, knowing Bent and he were thinking alike.

The two escorted the three Comanches around the fort, all of which the Comanches had seen, but Old Wolf seemed unable to take everything in with just one look. So Bent and Carson took the chief and his two sons around to see everything again. On occasion Carson would amble off with Indians' jugs and refill them.

By the fifth such incident, the Comanches were staggering a little but still seemed in fairly good control of themselves. However, the Comanches outside were howling and yelling again. Bent and Carson didn't know too much of the Comanche language, but they finally got the drift that the Comanches outside were afraid that Bent had done something to Old Wolf.

"You got to calm them boys of yours down, Chief," Bent said in sign, as well as poor Comanche. He hoped Old Wolf understood. With as much whiskey as the old man had consumed, it was an iffy proposition.

"Tell 'em me," Old Wolf said proudly, thrusting his thumb at his chest and almost missing.

"Jesus Christ," Bent muttered, rolling his eyes.

Carson hid a snigger behind a cupped hand.

"This way, Chief," Bent said, gently taking Old Wolf's arm and directing him toward the stairs at the fort's northeast corner. "You two set here," Bent ordered Old Wolf's sons. He pointed to a bench near the stairs. The two sat, laughing at something only they could see or hear. It was a real job getting the staggering Comanche war chief up the stairs, but Bent and Carson finally managed it.

"Damn," Carson puffed as they got to the second floor walkway, "you don't figure we got this son of a bitch *too* drunk, do you?"

"Maybe," Bent conceded, "but it's too late for worryin' about it now. All we got to do is let the screaming bastards outside see that Old Wolf's alive, and sort of well."

They "escorted" Old Wolf toward the wall. The old chief was singing some Comanche song in a high-pitched, reedy voice. Neither Bent nor Carson could understand it, and Old Wolf's incredibly poor performance did not make deciphering it any easier.

The two whites bellowed and roared, trying to get the Comanches' attention, to no avail. The crowd, which had shrunk by only a few people in the past several hours, was too loud. And since it was dark, they could not see the men on the wall, despite the many torches burning.

Both were getting hoarse when they huddled to try to decide what to do. "The cannon," Carson yelled.

Bent nodded. "You keep an eye on the chief there." He headed off to the round adobe bastion nearby. It, like its counterpart in the diagonal corner of the fort, had a small cannon. Bent made sure the cannon had no shot in it, then he packed it pretty well with powder and used a rag as wadding. He tilted it upward and pointed it in the vague direction of the river. He set off the fuse with a torch.

The resultant blast had the desired effect. The Comanches stopped their howling, and many seemed about ready to flee. Bent grinned into the night. Not only had the cannon blast gotten the Comanches' attention, it also served as a warning for the future. They would not want to try attacking such a forcibly armed fort.

Bent strolled toward Carson and Old Wolf. Standing near the edge of the wall, where he could be seen, he held the torch high. In halting Spanish he shouted, "Old Wolf is here and unharmed." He waved an arm behind him, indicating Old Wolf should stand next to him.

Carson gently took the jug from Old Wolf's hand and set it aside. Then he managed to maneuver the lurching chief up to the wall next to Bent. He stopped to take a little breather as Old Wolf began orating to his people, flapping his arms the whole while. Then, for some reason, he decided that in his present care-free condition he could walk on air.

Carson almost broke his neck when Old Wolf suddenly lurched forward, and he grabbed a handful of Comanche blanket. Then Carson managed to latch the right hand on Old Wolf's arm.

Bent was a mite slower in reacting, seeing as how he was standing next to Old Wolf and not really looking at him. He grabbed Old Wolf's other arm and they dragged him gently back from the wall a few feet.

"You go see if them Comanches are mollified out there, whilst I keep an eye on ol' hoss here," Carson said. He was puffing a little and was growing more annoyed now that Old Wolf had started his screeching song again. "Jesus Christ, Chief, cut out that goddamn wailin', would ya?" Carson said, not figuring it would do any good, but wanting to register a protest anyway.

Bent returned. He sighed. "They seem to feel things are fine. Quite a few of 'em look to be headin' back toward their camp."

"Good," Carson said flatly. "Now if we could only shut up his goddamn screechin'."

"This ought to help," Bent said as he grabbed Old Wolf's jug and handed it to the chief.

Getting Old Wolf down the stairs was an even trickier proposition than getting him up them. They managed, though, with the old chief half sliding the last few steps.

"I think you best make your pitch, Bill," Carson puffed.

"I do believe that's a fact." He turned and walked toward Old Wolf, who had staggered over to stand near his two sons. "Hey, Chief," he said, smiling nicely, "I got something to discuss with you."

Old Wolf looked at him with bleary eyes.

"You got a couple captives?"

"Many captives me," Old Wolf said, his poor English worsened considerably by the whiskey.

"The two I'm thinkin' of are Jim Hobbs and John Baptiste. Know 'em?"

Old Wolf shrugged.

"Damn," Bent muttered. He turned to Carson. "You remember their Comanche names?"

"Shit, what was them names he told me?" He pondered, wrinkling his face up with the effort. He had a good mind for sign and for tracking, for finding beaver and buffalo. But he wasn't so good at names, especially when he didn't give much of a hoot for the person. "White Shirt, I think is Hobbs. The other'n is . . . damn, I should've paid more attention . . . Flat Nose," he suddenly said. "Yeah, that's it."

Bent turned once more to Old Wolf. "You have some captives named White Shirt and Flat Nose?"

Old Wolf nodded. "White Shirt is the husband of my daughter Antelope. Flat Nose is less than a man." He spit in contempt.

"How's about you let me buy 'em from you, Chief?" Bent asked, his voice flat and level, displaying no emotion.

Old Wolf shrugged. "Whiskey me," he said.

"Sure. Kit, you want to do the honors?"

"My pleasure," Carson said sarcastically. He took the three jugs and headed toward Bent's room.

"Tell you what, Chief," Bent said, "I'll give you a bottle of whiskey and two knives for the two."

"More me."

"All right, then, I'll give you a pound of tobacco—my finest—plus some of that red cloth you admired. Hell, I'll even throw in an ounce of beads. What do you say?"

Bull Nose translated this longer passage, then spoke to Bent. "He says that is fine—for White Shirt."

Bent nodded. "What about the other 'un?"

"He's worthless," Bull Nose translated from his father.

"Then why don't you throw him in with the other?"

"Even a worthless thing like him has some value."

Carson had come back up and handed the Comanches their jugs. Coming back to stand next to Bent, he said quietly, "Offer him my ol' mule. That walking sack of shit ain't even worth swearin' at no more."

Bent grinned and made the offer, which was accepted. Bent sucked in a breath and asked, "You got two white women in your camp, Chief?"

Bull Nose answered without waiting for his father. "They are mine and Medicine Wolf's. They are our wives." He seemed intractable.

"I'll give you a good price for them," Bent said.

"No!" Bull Nose roared, taking a step forward. His hand was on his knife. Tension snapped and crackled in the air between the two men.

Bent nodded. He turned to Carson. "Why don't you escort our old friends here back to their camp?"

Carson nodded. "I'll get the horses, you get Old Wolf's presents." In a whisper he added, "I'll try'n find Hobbs and Baptiste when I'm there. It's best, I think, if we can get them out of there before that sorry bastard changes his mind." He pointed at Old Wolf.

Bent nodded. "Good idea. I'll keep watch on the wall for a while to let you in if you get back here."

⦗34⦘

Less than two hours later Carson was back—with the grateful Jim Hobbs and John Baptiste in tow. Bent, who had been standing on the second floor, leaning against the watchtower wall, saw them coming and hurried down the stairs to open the gate for the three men.

"Have any trouble?" Bent asked when the door was bolted again.

"Not much," Carson answered. "Ol' White Shirt there's squaw started raising a ruckus." He started to laugh. "He managed to quiet her up with a handful of beads, some vermilion, and a looking glass I had."

Hobbs nodded, too stunned yet by his freedom. He was afraid to laugh and almost afraid to say anything.

Baptiste cowered, as if trying to crawl in a hole or disappear into the shadows.

"You all right, boy?" Bent asked, standing in front of Baptiste.

"Yep." The voice quavered and was faint.

Bent looked at Baptiste. The young man's face was cast in odd light and shadow from the flickering torches nearby. He looked ghastly, but Bent could not see if anything was actually wrong with him. He strolled over to where Carson and Hobbs were talking quietly.

"Baptiste have it rough with them Comanches, Jim?" Bent asked.

Hobbs nodded. "I'll tell you about it, but . . ."

"But what?" Bent asked.

"Mr. Carson tol' me what you done for me'n John, to get us out of those devils' clutches. . . ."

"Wasn't much, Jim," Bent said. He wondered what Carson had told the two men. He wouldn't put it past his feisty friend to have told Hobbs that his ransom was several hundred dollars in goods.

"That ain't the way I see it, Mr. Bent." He paused. "Hell, it's my own damn fault I got caught up by those damn Comanches, and you didn't have to go'n buy us out of there."

"Hell, boy, anyone would've done the same."

"Naw, sir, I ain't so sure. I'm obliged for it too. And it don't make me no goddamn never mind whether you gave those goddamn devils a dollar's worth of goods or a thousand, by God, I'm obliged to you."

Bent nodded. "Glad to do it, boy. Now, you were about to tell us about Baptiste there."

"Oh, yeah." He paused. "Even though I'm in your debt deep now, Mr. Bent, I was wonderin' if you might have . . . let me have . . ."

Carson started laughing. "Hell, Bill, ol' Jim there needs somethin' to cut the dust in his throat."

"It'd be near about one of the first things I'd be lookin' for was I in your place," Bent said with a laugh.

"How's about we go to your office, Bill," Carson said. "I could stand a snort or two myself."

"I reckon you ain't the only one," Bent said with a grin. Turning serious, he looked at Hobbs. "You feel like helpin' John over there?"

A look of disgust passed ever so fleetingly over Hobbs's face. "Sure will," he said with a decided lack of enthusiasm.

Minutes later the four were crammed into Bent's small office. Three were sitting on old wood chairs; Carson perched precariously on the edge of a desk. The desk, like the rest of the room, was piled high with papers, loose plews, cans, bottles, jars, boxes, and whatnot. But the focus was the small keg of whiskey sitting in one corner.

Cups were passed around, and then Bent said, "Tell us, Jim . . ." He paused, tapping two fingers on a tin of Bent's Water Crackers on the table next to him. "Would you prefer that we were alone?"

Hobbs followed Bent's eyes to Baptiste. He shook his head. "Won't make no difference, I don't guess."

Baptiste was sitting in a corner, seemingly oblivious to everything and everyone around him. The only signs of life in the man were the occasional lift of the cup of whiskey and a tic over his right cheekbone.

"Ain't much to tell, Mr. Bent," Hobbs said. "Me'n John went against your brother's warnin' and we scooted out after a bufferlo. Next thing I know, there's a passel of red devils comin' down on us."

He stopped for a long swallow and a refill. "I've dealt with the Injuns a little, with your brother and all. Not too much, but enough to know them Comanche devils admire bravery and such, so I made up my mind not to scream out or nothin', no matter what they did to me."

Another swallow was taken. "They swarmed all over us, jabbin' at us with their lances and knives, cuffin' us around. It wasn't really so bad, so I kept my yap shut. But John, hell, I don't know what come over him, but he was jabberin' and blubberin'. Them Injuns finally left off hurtin' him, but they was havin' a high ol' time makin' fun of him."

Hobbs held out his cup. Bent filled it for him. "Once we got to the camp, they were tellin' everyone that I was pretty tough, or at least that's what I figure. John, there, though, kept on blubberin' and such. Old Wolf took us both into his lodge. I learned their language pretty easy. Surprised hell out of myself in the doin' too."

He stopped, kind of staring out into space, as if he was having a hard time in believing he was out of that camp. That he was free. He shook his head, coming back to his senses. "Couple months there, and I was married to one of Old Wolf's daughters. That set me up pretty good, since nobody wanted to mess with Old Wolf's family. John, though, he just never took to livin' there. Couldn't even pretend he was enjoyin' it, like I done. They was always makin' fun of him and such. They didn't really try to hurt him, but they sure ridiculed him enough. He just kind of curled up inside himself after a while, just like now." He pointed his cup to where Baptiste sat.

Bent looked at Baptiste and shook his head. He figured Baptiste would never be a real man again, just an empty, hollow shell that breathed but felt nothing but humiliation.

"That's about all there is to tell, Mr. Bent," Hobbs said.

Bent nodded. "You got plans, Jim?"

Hobbs smiled wanly. "Can't say as I do just yet. I'm still tryin' to get used to the idea that I ain't in that damned Comanche village. It'll take me a day or so to puzzle it out."

Bent nodded. "You're free to stay here at the fort until you do. Then I'll try 'n' help you get wherever it is you choose to go."

"I'm already too far in your debt, Mr. Bent," Hobbs said evenly. It was true, and there was nothing he could do about it. He wanted to make sure Bent knew it too. He hadn't sounded apologetic this time, but he did feel a heaping dose of guilt.

"Don't you mind that, boy," Bent said. "You get back on your feet one day and want to pay me a little somethin', that's fine. Same if you don't—or can't. You were a Bent-St. Vrain employee, and we try to help our own." He smiled. "Just as long as you don't try to abuse my efforts."

"Wouldn't think of it, Mr. Bent." Hobbs held his cup up in a salute and then drank.

"I'd be obliged to you if'n you was to see to Mr. Baptiste. It seems he's taken to you in your time with the Comanches, and I expect he'll feel a little more comfortable was it you he stayed with."

Hobbs grimaced, then shrugged. "I'll do it 'cause you asked, Mr. Bent. It's the least I can do after what you've done for me."

Bent nodded. "Well, I don't know about the rest of you boys, but I'm due some robe time. The cock crows early these days."

Carson grinned. "Much as I'd like to put a bigger hole in that keg, I'll be a heap better off was I to get some sleep too." He set his cup on the desk and stood. "Come on, you two," he said to Hobbs and Baptiste.

The celebrating of the peace went on for days. While most of the revelry took place in the camps three miles down the river, the fort was hectic from dawn till dusk —the hours the fort gates were open.

Hobbs more or less stayed out of sight, not wanting Old Wolf to suddenly decide he wanted his "son" back. Besides, Old Wolf's two sons had little liking for Hobbs, and less for Baptiste. That unfortunate man also stayed hidden, though not with the barely caged energy of Hobbs. Baptiste was still incapable of doing much more than eating or sitting there staring into space, whether the space was an adobe wall two feet away or the distant horizon.

Bent visited the two men whenever he had a few free minutes, which wasn't very often considering the volume of traffic through the fort. Still, once the sun went down, the men inside the fort would gather in the dining room or in the council room and jaw with each other, spinning their tales, laughing riotously at the stories, whooping at whoever was being skewered with verbal barbs, boasting of their prowess on the hunt or in the robes.

Hobbs enjoyed the sessions and felt at home in

them. He even managed to weave a tale or two of his own about life with the Comanches. And, like every other man there, he embellished his participation in these events, and was thought all the more manly for it.

Baptiste did not participate in these sessions, and he worried Hobbs. So much so that three evenings after he was freed, Hobbs knocked on the door to Bent's office.

Bent pushed aside his journal and pen when Hobbs entered. "Take a seat, boy," Bent said evenly, wondering what was up. Hobbs was usually an outgoing, friendly young man, but now he seemed nervous.

Hobbs sat, but his fingers danced, tangling and untangling.

"Well, speak up, boy," Bent said jovially. "You didn't come in here just to sit and stare at my handsome good looks."

"I . . . I . . ." Hobbs stammered.

Bent smiled. He dug in a drawer of the desk and came up with a small flask. He opened the top of it and handed it to Hobbs. "Maybe that'll loosen your tongue a bit."

Hobbs took it and swallowed. "Thanks, Mr. Bent," he said as he handed the flask back. He was not much younger than Bent was, but he felt like a child sometimes around the hard, feisty little man.

Bent nodded, took the flask, shrugged and sipped. "Now, Jim," he said as he closed the lid on the flask, "why'd you come here?"

"I'm kind of concerned about John," Hobbs said slowly, working over each word before releasing it. "He's still in some poor shape. Hell, all he does is sit there with them big, empty moon eyes of his. It's spooky. And," he paused, "well, I was wonderin' if you knew what we could do with him."

"Hadn't thought on it," Bent said truthfully. He knew he would have to do something about Baptiste, but he had been too busy to devote any time to pondering it.

"I expect you're a busy man, Mr. Bent, with a heap of other things to concern you." He stopped, uncertain about continuing, but able to pin no reason on his hesitation. "Well, I was thinkin' on it, and about what I was gonna do."

"And what have you come up with?"

Hobbs looked at Bent and figured Bent was not making fun of him, that he was interested. "Well, sir, I owe you a heap. I've said that before. And I don't know as if I could ever pay you back for what you did. But I was wonderin' if maybe you could sign me on to one of your caravans headin' back East." He looked eager, expectant.

"Had enough of this wild and harsh country?"

"Yes, sir, I can say without qualifyin' that such is a fact. I might come back one day, but for now I think I'd be better off back East."

"A wise thought."

"So can you get me on one of the caravans? I'll tell you true too, that I ain't about to go chasin' any god-damn bufferlo."

Bent laughed a little. "That's a wise thought too. I expect that could be arranged." He paused. "What about Baptiste?"

"I've been thinkin' on that too. I found out sometime back, not long after we was caught by them red devils"—his face kind of scrunched up on itself—"ya know, Mr. Bent, I still don't trust them."

"Nor do I, Jim," Bent said solemnly.

Hobbs nodded in confirmation. "Anyways, I found out from John that he's got folks back East. Kentucky. If'n you wasn't to mind too much, I'll take him home. I . . . I . . . Well, dammit, you've done well by me, Mr. Bent, and I hate to impose on you some more, but if I could be paid just a tad of wages, I could make it from Missouri to Kentucky."

"What do you mean, a tad of wages?" Bent asked. "You don't think I'd hire a man on and not pay him, do you?"

"Well, no, sir. I just figured that you'd keep most— or maybe even all—my wages to pay you back some of what you've give me. That might not be enough to pay you all back, but it'd be somethin'. And I figured I'd work for two, since John ain't capable of it. So I thought, maybe, I could have a little wages, just to get John home."

"I don't—"

"Well, if needs be, Mr. Bent, I'll sign up on another of the Bent caravans comin' back out here and work again for no wages other'n some grub. That might come close to payin' you back."

"What I was gonna say, Jim, if you'd shut that hole of yours a minute, was that I don't think all that's gonna be necessary. You don't owe me a damned thing, boy. You'll get your full wages in Missouri. What you want to do with 'em when you get 'em is up to you."

Hobbs beamed. "You won't regret it, Mr. Bent, and I'll tell you, I ain't gonna stay away from this here country for long. I just need a bit of time away, raise a little hell in some 'civilized' kind of place."

"I think we all could use that of a time," Bent said with a chuckle. "I'll make arrangements with Charlie. He should be along any day."

"I'm obliged, Mr. Bent. Again."

Bent nodded. "Go on and fill your meat bag, boy. I intend to see that Charlie works your ass off."

35

Charles arrived a week later, carrying goods for the fort and some gotten in Mexico headed for markets in the East.

"You got good timin', Charlie," William Bent said as his brother wolfed down a meal in the fort's dining room.

"Good timin' my ass," Charles said, not slowing down his eating any. "I knew what was goin' on here, and I wasn't about to bring my wagons along through here with all them damned Injuns settin' here just waitin' for somebody to wander off the trail a mite."

"The Cheyennes ain't gonna bother us none."

"Don't expect so," Charles said. The words came out garbled, since his cheek was stuffed with corn bread and chicken with chili peppers. "But you never can tell with Injuns. A couple score of them Comanches could've thought to impress their new goddamn friends and attack anybody they saw comin'."

"Not likely, but always a possibility," William allowed.

"Besides, I don't trust them goddamn Comanches as far as I could throw this fort."

"Me neither, but I'll give 'em the benefit of the doubt for a spell."

"How so?"

"Old Wolf, Bull Hump, and a couple other chiefs was over here the other day—damn, it seems like they were here all day every day for weeks. Anyway, they made it known that since they've made peace with their old enemies, they might's well include us in the deal."

"How long's it been since we traded with the Comanches?"

"Regular? Couple years. Blackfoot John's been down there in that time. So's Mexican Sol, but they ain't part of the Company, of course."

Charles nodded and shoveled in the last of the food on his plate. "Damn, that ol' Charlotte sure as hell knows her way 'round a kitchen."

William smiled and nodded.

Charles grinned. "I might have to just take her back to Taos with me, ol' brother. Let her do all my cookin'."

"Shit, you ain't in Taos long enough of a time to enjoy anything."

"Damn, that's the truth." He patted his mouth with a grimy rag pulled from his pocket. "So, what do you think?"

"About what? The Comanches? Or you stealin' Charlotte from me?" He laughed. "I already told Old Wolf and the others that we'd be happy to trade with 'em regular."

"Think that's safe?" Charles was skeptical, and with good reason.

"Depends on how cantankerous those bastards are. I ain't about to risk too many people on findin' out. I'll send Blackfoot and Sol and maybe one or two other of the boys who've got some gumption too."

"Gumption my ass. They need a cannon," he said seriously.

"Might not be a bad idea. I fired that little one-pounder here a few times during the festivities. Scared the livin' shit out of 'em. We send one with crazy Blackfoot and they start givin' him any shit, he can haul it out. Probably won't even have to load it."

Charles grinned. "It's temptin', but I expect it'd cause more trouble than it'd save." Charles finished his coffee and turned to call for Charlotte. She was there, surprising him. With a big smile she filled his cup, and William's too.

As the brothers sat puffing pipes and sipping at hot coffee, William said, "You remember Jim Hobbs?"

"Who the hell's he?" Charles responded.

"Feller on one of your caravans. Four years ago, I think. Him and another feller took off after a buffler and got grabbed by Comanches."

"Jesus, Bill, I've taken umpteen caravans on the trail both ways in the past nine years or so. I can't be expected to remember all of 'em."

"No need, I guess. Anyways, I ransomed both of 'em from Old Wolf. Hobbs is fine, but the other'n—John Baptiste—is queersome."

"He stove up?"

"Not physical. Just seems like his brain pan is empty."

Charles shrugged and blew a smoke ring, and then watched it drift toward the ceiling. "What's all this got to do with me?"

"Hobbs wants to hire on."

Charles cocked an eye at his brother. "This was a feller ran off to chase buffler and got took by the Comanches?"

"Yep," William said with a small grin. "I believe he's learned his lesson." He sighed. "Besides, he wants to take the other'n back to his folks. He needs a way to get there. I told him it'd be all right."

Charles shrugged again. "I expect it won't put me out none. He aimin' to come back?"

"Don't know. He ain't real thrilled with this land much these days. But he ain't got much give-up in him that I've been able to see. Any white man who could be captured by Comanches and not only survive but marry a daughter of a big chief has got to have some gumption.''

"He's got more than gumption," Charles laughed roughly. "That boy's got balls, and I'll be glad to have him along—if he don't go chasin' no more buffler."

"He's promised he won't," William said with a laugh. He paused. "You best make a fast trip, Charlie. After havin' all them Cheyennes, Comanches, and whatnot through here every goddamn hour of the day, we ain't got enough left here to trade for a goddamn muskrat plew."

Charles laughed. "Think you can feed yourselves till I get back?"

"Might be hard pressed, but we'll make do," William said flatly.

With the coming of the cold months, peace settled over the huge area in which Bent, St. Vrain & Company traded. Business, though, was rather sparse that fall and winter, considering that the thousands of Indians had traded most of their furs during the great peace conference.

William looked forward to the spring, figuring that with peace between the Cheyennes and Comanches, his men should be able to move unmolested in areas where others had feared to go last year. He planned to send his men out in force, hauling company trade goods from North Platte to the southern reaches of the Llano Estacado.

Even before spring had fully bloomed, though, Charles Bent pulled into the fort to pick up the winter's load of furs to haul to Missouri. He was in a foul, sour move.

"What the hell's wrong with you, Charlie?" William asked an hour after Charles had shown up. Charles had stormed around, snarling at the workers to begin loading the wagons and such.

"Nothin'," Charles snapped.

"Buffler crap," William said bluntly. "Now leave off growlin' at them men. They'll get it done in due time."

"I've got to get on the trail."

"Like hell you do. Even with all the men workin' you ain't gonna get out of here before dark." He softened his tone a little. "C'mon, Charlie, let's go get us some coffee." He tugged on his brother's sleeve. Then he grinned. "Charlotte's gone and made a heap of them *bizcochitos* you like so much."

A spark of interest flickered in Charles's eyes. "All right, dammit," he snapped, though with less bite, "if you're gonna be a damn nag . . ."

"Well," William said untruthfully, "it's either nag or I stomp your ass into the ground."

"That'll be the day, Billy," Charles said, tone unfreezing a bit more.

They went into the dining room and sat at a back-corner table. Charlotte shuffled up with two pewter mugs and a pot of coffee. She had been expecting them, though she had figured they would've come in before this. She shrugged. It didn't matter; she always had coffee on the stove, ready for anyone who came along. And when she made the *bizcochitos,* she was mindful enough to set aside a platter of them for the Bents. After two more trips, she left.

"All right, Charlie," William said after a bite of cookie, "what in hell's got you so contrary?"

Charles's eyes darkened with a sudden renewal of his anger. He said nothing for a bit. Finally he sighed and said, "It's that damn Armijo. Again." Just the mention of the man's name was almost enough to set him off on a tirade.

"What's the esteemed governor done this time?"

"The bastard's gone off on a tear. Thinks he's the goddamn emperor of the world, or at least his goddamn chunk of it. I can't abide that overgrowed skunk's ass."

"I've heard rumbles from some of the boys comin'

through that the Texians are settin' up to take over all the lands to the Rio Grande. That have anything to do with Armijo?''

"Sure as hell does." He realized that he should've sent word of all this to William long ago. He always felt better for having talked with his brother. "I don't know how the hell all this got started, but word got out that Texas was plannin' to send an army out to Taos and Santa Fe. Armijo got wind of it and started crackin' down on all us Americans.''

"You get caught up in any of it?" William asked quietly.

"Some, but we handled it this time.''

"Hell, you knew all you had to do was tell me and I would've rounded up the boys and come set things to right. Like last time.''

"You know it, I know it, and most of all, Armijo knows it. That's all he needed was a hundred mountaineers come to kick his ass while being pressed by the Texians. He wasn't none too pleased about the drubbin' you boys gave his men that time in Taos. He ain't tried to retaliate for that, but still, I figure he's kept it to mind.''

"Anything come of the Texas invasion?"

"Hell, yes," Charles said, laughing hollowly. "Ol' Armijo's a goddamn hero, practically the patron saint of Mexico, for Christ's sake, all for repelling the Texian hordes," he said bitterly.

William looked at his brother questioningly.

"The Texian hordes was less'n three hundred poor bastards who got so lost in the Llano that they split up into two groups. Both of 'em bogged down in different places, and staggered into Mexican towns barely alive. That's when Armijo and his thousand-man army crushed them. Killed some and arrested the rest.''

He bit his lip trying to quell his renewed anger. "We got word from some Mexicans we trust that Armijo had several men executed.'' There was no dampening the anger now. "Sons of bitches made a few of them Texians kneel over and then shot 'em in the back. Chicken-shit bastards."

The two sat and let their anger settle and maybe even ebb a little while William poured himself and his brother more coffee.

"Anyways, not much else came from it." Charles's anger still percolated. "But that goddamn Armijo is suspicious of this place. He's got it into his mind somehow that we're armin' the Injuns to insurrect against Mexico. He also seems to think that this here fort is the center of a goddamn plot to have a bunch of the mountaineers go down there and pick off what Mexicans is left after the Injuns are done with 'em."

"Jesus," William breathed, stunned at the Mexican governor's thinking. He shook his head. "Son of a bitch keeps such thoughts in his head, he could be dangersome to us."

❧[36]❧

William Bent stood near the guard tower over the gates of his fort, watching as the last of the Bent, St. Vrain & Company train and its escort of mule skinners, guards, and hunters pulled out. His brother Charles was already lost to sight where the horizon sank down into one of the interminable grassy dips in the rolling land.

It was, in some ways, a relief for William to see the wagon trains pull out. While they were at the fort, the place was a madhouse, with bedlam going on all around. Ox handlers and mule skinners screamed curses in several languages; whips cracked; yoke chains clanged; oxen bellowed; mules brayed. Amid all the noise, workers raced helter-skelter, none looking like he knew what he was doing. They did, though, and in surprisingly little time the caravan was ready to go.

The Bent brothers' debate continued while the wagons and mules were readied. They decided that business would be conducted as usual, though William at the fort and St. Vrain at the Taos store would be a little more vigilant than usual, and Charles would use all haste to Missouri and back.

Watching Charles leave, William thought for the umpteenth time, it seemed, of how different he and Charles were when they were so much the same. Like with the choice of living—Charles was perfectly happy with his Mexican home and Mexican wife. William was equally joyful with his Cheyenne wife and home in the lands of the Cheyenne.

Their other main difference, William had come to realize, was in their business acumen. William could not abide the wheeling and dealing that went on behind the scenes of business. Oh, he could dicker with the best of them, and he usually got a fair enough price for what he sold, or bought at the most favorable price available. But he and Charles were cut from different cloth when it came to deviousness.

William could not understand, nor did he want to, the intrigue and politicizing that went on in Taos and Santa Fe. It seemed as if Charles was in constant turmoil trying to make the business progress while fending off the machinations of men like Governor Manuel Armijo. William found he much preferred the openhanded dealings with the Cheyennes, or even the Comanches. The Comanches might be enemies, but at least one knew where he stood with those people. Unlike politicians and schemers like Armijo, and even Charles Bent.

William watched a little while longer, until the last of the wagons was out of sight. He turned, enjoying the newfound silence. Oh, the fort wasn't really silent, as anyone could tell, but after all the ruckus of preparing the caravan, this was pretty quiet.

Bent took advantage of the relative tranquility to spend time with Owl Woman and little Mary. Leaving the running of the fort to Ramsay MacGregor for a few days, Bent would take his wife and daughter down toward the river. They would picnic on foods prepared with Charlotte's wonderful touch. Or they would ride out to one of the Cheyenne villages nearby. Bent was inordinately fond of Mary and was always amused by the child's antics.

But the demands of business intruded—as they would all too often in his life—and he finally had to answer their call. He was expecting a big year for his traders since the Indians were no longer fighting each other. Besides, it was almost a year since the great peace meeting. The Indians had traded everything in at that time in order to buy gifts for their former enemies. They had not had a real chance to do much trading since, so they should be well-stocked with furs.

Within a week he had sent out twenty trading groups, three of them down into Comanche and Kiowa territory. Two of those were headed by Blackfoot John Smith and Mexican Sol Silver.

A third was being led by Emiliano Flores. The tall, quiet Mexican had gone from being a foreman when the fort was being built to a trader. In the fort's infancy, Flores had made himself invaluable to the company, so Bent had put him to work doing odd jobs. Flores never complained. A year or so later Flores accompanied one of the company's wagon trains to Taos. When he returned with another of the trains, he had a small, quietly pretty woman with him. They set up housekeeping in a tent outside the fort's walls, down toward the river. Bent gave him more and more responsible jobs, until about two years ago he had allowed Flores to go with one of the traders, partly as a helper, partly to be introduced to trading. When Flores heard Bent was planning to send traders down to the Comanches and Kiowas again, he asked to lead one group. Without hesitation Bent had agreed.

Just before leaving that time, Flores went to Bent's office and asked to speak with him. Puzzled, Bent said, "Sure, Yano, come on it." When both were seated, Bent said, "So tell me what's on your mind."

Flores hesitated a moment, then said softly, "I'm in your debt, *Jefe*, for all you've done for me. . . ."

"I hear a 'but' coming," Bent said.

"*Sí*. I just want to know, Señor Bent, that I'm progressing in the company, because of my talents and abilities and desire."

"Why else?" Bent asked, fairly certain he knew what was coming.

"Because of what I know." Flores looked directly at Bent.

"That's damn foolish, Yano," Bent said evenly. "You ain't ever tried to use that knowledge to further yourself. Besides, you ought to know after all this time that I wouldn't give you a job 'cause I thought you'd spill the beans on me. Hell, most likely no one'd believe you anyway."

Flores smiled widely. "That's what I wanted to hear, *Jefe*," he said in relief. He had thought all along that such worries on his part were foolish, but he had to hear it from Bent's lips to be sure. He left happy.

Bent sat a minute, smiling. He always felt good when he had uncovered a gem of an employee. Emiliano Flores certainly was that. Bent admitted to himself, though, that if Flores had revealed their secret, he could and very well might have had Flores killed. Bent was very glad it had not come to that.

Bent took out only a small trading party this year. Owl Woman was pregnant again, and so Bent had sent her out to visit her people a month or so back. Now he wanted her to return, so he figured he might as well do some trading on the journey. He could not stay out long, though. There were plenty of things to be done at the fort, and he didn't want to be gone too long in case Armijo decided to try something. He didn't think that likely, but one could never tell with Armijo. Besides, Charles would be back as soon as he could make it, and the traders would be coming in with their furs, and looking for more trade goods.

Instead of taking several men, as he usually did, he took only one—Solomon. He left the fort in the care of his brother George, Seth Walsh, and Ramsay MacGregor. Robert Bent was at the fort up on the South Platte, and Marcellin St. Vrain was trading out of that post.

When Bent and Solomon pulled into Sun Dog's village, the Cheyennes were preparing for their spring hunt. It was big medicine to these people, and they were edgy as the time to leave approached. After a cold, bitter winter, a successful hunt was sorely needed. And one could never tell just what might destroy their medicine.

Bent visited with Sun Dog, who had tamed his impetuous nature a little. He was, if not joyous at Bent's arrival, at least not unfriendly toward Little White Man. Bent picked up a fair amount of furs, and told the band that he would take the rest of their hides if they came to the fort. He had almost exhausted his meager supply of trade goods, truth to tell, because he had a mighty free hand with them, especially when it came to children, his little Mary not excepted.

Sun Dog distractedly promised to come to the fort after the big hunt was made. Bent was close enough to the Cheyennes that he did not want them angry with him for fouling their hunt. He stayed only a week in the camp before heading out. Behind him were Owl Woman, and three-year-old Mary tucked into a travois tied to one of the mules. Solomon came last, towing the other five mules.

Suddenly three Utes came barreling down on Bent's small party. Bent and Solomon stood their ground. The Indians charged up and stopped in a cloud of dust and horse sweat not far from the group.

With signs, Bent said he had many gifts for his friends, the Utes.

The Indians looked like they didn't believe him. Bent eased out of the saddle and went to one of the mules behind Solomon, who had a big horse pistol in each hand, not aimed at anything, but ready. His rifle lay across his saddle. He did not take his eyes off the Indians.

Bent pulled out a small bolt of blue cloth, one of red

cloth, and some tobacco. He walked to the Utes and held the goods out.

"That's not enough," one of the Utes said in Spanish.

Bent replied in kind. "It's all you're going to get."

"You must pay more for coming across the land of the Utes," the warrior said, still in Spanish. He was growing angry.

"Buffler shit," Bent said, returning to his own familiar brand of English. "This is Cheyenne land, and if they find you shitballs here, they're gonna have your nuts for breakfast. Nor will they be in good humors if you was to kill me, for I am a great friend of the Cheyennes."

The Utes looked unsure. They were only three, and it was true that they were in Cheyenne land.

Bent saw the uncertainty and said, "We just come from a Cheyenne camp over yonder there." He jerked his head back. "Them boys figure there's some trouble out here, they gonna come look."

After a few moments, as the tension built, the warriors nodded. "We will take your gifts."

Bent handed them to the warrior who had spoken, figuring he'd let the Utes argue over who got what. He backed away until he was at his horse. He mounted quickly, grateful for having Solomon with him.

Bent pulled out, moving almost within handshake distance of the three Utes. Solomon, bringing up the rear, turned in his saddle, still unwilling to take his eyes off the Utes. When he saw the Indians dismount and apparently begin to argue over their presents, Solomon faced forward. "I be thinkin' we bes' move on a mite fastah, Mistah Bent. They's occupied fer a spell, but maybe not so long."

Bent nodded, not bothering to look back. He touched his spurs to the roan's sides and picked up the pace.

Kit Carson and Bill Williams were at the fort, as was Tom Fitzpatrick. They were heading one way or another and stopped at the fort, not only because it was a safe place to stay a few days, but to see Bent. Enjoying Bent's company, the safety of the thick adobe walls, and Charlotte's cooking, the three former mountain men stayed awhile longer than they planned—long enough to see the Cheyennes start arriving, setting up their lodges in circles facing the east. The white men watched from the second floor of the fort. It still amazed them how quickly the women could raise the lodges. They soon wearied of watching. It was nothing new to them. They were in the dining room when a hue and cry was raised outside.

Bent charged out the door, Carson and Fitzpatrick right behind him. The much older Bill Williams took a little longer.

As he ran up the stairs toward the bastion, Bent bellowed, "What the hell's goin' on?"

"Look," one of the watchmen said, pointing.

The new arrivals looked out, down the river. Perhaps a hundred Cheyennes and Arapahos were charging toward the fort. The screeching of their war cries drifted to the men of the fort.

"What do we do, Cap'n?" Art Honnicker asked. He looked more than a little worried. He had been with Bent, St. Vrain & Company since the early thirties, just over ten years now. He still was basically a laborer, having shown little inclination or aptitude for trading. He had been a good trapper in his time, but now that the beaver trade had about died, he was once more relegated to helping around the fort however he could. He was not Bent's favorite man, but more than once Bent was happy to have him along when Indians were attacking.

Bent paused. It was unusual for the Cheyennes to do something like this, and he knew the tribe was not stu-

pid enough to attack the fort. Then he grinned.
"We're just gonna watch, Mr. Honnicker."

"Beggin' your pardon, Cap'n, but—"

"You know the way Injuns are, Art. Look at them—
their faces, the way they're dressed."

Carson howled. "Damn, there's gonna be a whoop-
de-do tonight."

Even Honnicker smiled. The Cheyennes and
Arapahos had painted their faces and they were
dressed in their most colorful, most fancified outfits.
They were celebrating their victory over some unfortunate tribe.

The warriors roared right up to the fort, but not
inside. Sun Dog, who was leading them, knew better
than that—someone might be nervous inside and start
shooting. So instead he and his warriors stopped with a
flourish, whooping and shouting. Many had fresh
scalps dangling from their lances, coup sticks, or
shields. Far behind, the women and children came at a
more sedate pace.

"Sun Dog," Bent roared over the wall as the Cheyenne noise began to ebb some. "C'mon on in, you and
your boys."

The warriors left their horses outside as they poured
into the *placita*. Soon the women joined them. A large
fire—the firewood donated by Bent—was started in the
center of the *placita*. A drum and eagle-bone whistles
were produced and the dancing and singing began.
Most of the warriors danced, with the women sitting in
a circle, their soprano trills weaving around the men's
deeper, huskier intonations.

Most all of the men in Bent's Fort had seen this
before, had heard the undulating chants. Many a one
had taken part in some tribe's victory dance. Sioux,
Crow, Cheyenne, Ute, Nez Perce, it didn't matter what
tribe. All were mostly the same when it came to the
enthralling chants and the captivating beat of the
drum. It made a man want to join in, feel his feet shuf-

fling and moving in time to the beat that was reminiscent of a heartbeat.

Many did join in, not getting the steps even close to correct, but making up for lack of talent with an overabundance of enthusiasm.

37

Bent, St. Vrain & Company did far better than they
had dared hope. Company traders returned to the fort,
left their peltries, and hurried out again. A friendly
rivalry built up between some of the men as they tried
to outdo the others in getting the most furs for the
fewest trade goods—within the company's framework
of rules. At the fort William had men working feverishly to bale the buffalo, wolf, beaver, fox, and mink
furs. The carpenter threw together two more fur
presses. Shirtless laborers toiled under the brutal sun
as summer inched along. They hauled and pressed,
then hauled and pressed some more.

Charles made the trip to Missouri and back in
record time. One of the men he had brought back with
him was Jim Hobbs.

"Well, how do, ol' hoss," William Bent greeted
Hobbs as he rode into the *placita* and dismounted.

"Better'n I would was I to be sufferin' some kind of
epizootic," Hobbs said with a smile. He tied off his
horse.

Bent grinned then sobered. "You saw Baptiste back
to his folks?"

"Sure did. Had enough cash to make the trip and
have a little stake of my own to go and visit my folks."
He laughed and leaned back against one of the
support poles. "Hell, I didn't pay for a drink in six
months. I just kept tellin' stories about the time I was

in that goddamn Comanche village. People kept a-buyin' me tanglefoot to keep me a-talkin'."

Bent laughed too. "Seems like you done well, boy."

"Middlin'," Hobbs said, and Bent noticed the tightness in Hobbs's face. "But I couldn't live on my laurels forever, so's I headed back to Independence and hired on again when I saw your brother in town."

"How was Baptiste?"

"Last I saw him was when I gave him over to some kin. He was as bad then as he was here. Hell, his brains is some addled, I tell ya."

Bent shook his head sadly. "Well, glad you're back with us, boy. Go'n set to a meal, 'less'n Charlie needs your help."

Bent hurried off, directing the wagons as they pulled in with their loads and pulled out again empty. They were stored alongside the fort, sometimes three and four deep.

Charles Bent was taken aback by the number of furs at the fort. It seemed like skins were stacked in every conceivable place. The blacksmiths and carpenters worked feverishly to keep the wagons in repair. Charles looked at the wagons he had brought and the ones in the fort. He sighed, and he and his brother headed to the dining room.

"Damn, Bill," Charles said at supper, "I got to get to Taos, pronto."

William grinned. "Can't wait to see your wife, eh?" he said glibly.

Charles looked up from his plate sharply. Then he laughed a little. "Hell, boy, leastways I know what to do with her once I get there. It's more'n I could say for the likes of you."

"Shit, Charlie, you're away from home so goddamn much, I'm surprised you still know how to hump. Or that Ignacia remembers you."

Charles nodded sadly. "That's more'n true." He paused. When he spoke again, his voice was soft, as if he were talking to himself. "I'd like to change that, I purely would. Maybe in a few years. Too much goin' on now to do it. Goddamn Armijo and Texians and Pawnees and every other pestiferent son of a bitch." He shoveled another spoonful of stew into his craw. It seemed to break the spell into which he had fallen.

"Anyways, as I was sayin' before," he commented, embarrassed at having shown some weakness, even if it was just to his brother, who had seen all his moods before, "I need to get to Taos."

"Why the rush?"

"Hell, I got to make two more trips out and back again, I figure, and I'd be a heap happier about it if'n I can do it before winter sets in."

"That ain't the only reason, Charlie. I can tell it in your face. You still worried about Armijo?"

"Nah, not really. We heard back in the States that he's kind of backed off the Americans down there. Seems he's so puffed up with himself for having bested the Texians that he's bein' benevolent to the rest of us. Besides, I ain't heard nothin' from Ceran, and neither have you, so things must be all right down there."

"Then what else is eatin' at you?"

"Business is too goddamn good," he muttered, then laughed a little. "Sounds plumb foolish, don't it?"

"Sure as hell does."

"Christ, I can't believe how many plews we got. I ain't got enough wagons to haul 'em all. And since you've been hearin' that a heap more'll be comin' in, I need more wagons to cart it all to the States."

William nodded. It was something, he thought, that business was so good it was causing troubles. It was another reason he didn't fancy himself a businessman.

It seemed something of a race against time as Charles rushed to Taos and back. Three more of William's traders returned and left again in that time. Blackfoot John Smith was one of them. He had a fair amount of peltry, but not nearly as good as anyone had hoped. Bent didn't much care since the company was doing quite well anyway. But he thought Smith looked a little angry or baffled.

"Somethin' stuck in your craw, Blackfoot?" Bent asked after Smith unloaded his furs. They were in the billiard-parlor-cum-saloon, leaning against the small, plain bar, knocking back cupfuls of Taos Lightning.

Smith took a long time before answering, as if debating whether he even should. Finally he nodded. "Somethin' ain't right with those fuckin' Comanches," he said evenly. "Trouble is, I can't puzzle it out."

"You think they got their faces painted black against you?"

"I don't goddamn know, goddammit," Smith growled, and drained his cup. He turned and filled it almost to the brim. With one huge swallow he poured half the cup into him.

"You don't have to go back out there, you don't want to. I can send you up to the Platte or somethin'."

"It'll be a goddamn cold day in the devil's outhouse before I let some fuckin' Comanches run me out."

Bent nodded. He drained his mug and set it on the bar. "You ever figure it out, you let me know." Then he left.

When Charles returned from Taos the second time, all the wagons at the fort were in good repair and loaded. Because of space limitations, the loaded wagons were stored outside during the day and hauled into the fort at night to prevent some adventurous Cheyenne or Arapaho from making off with some of the furs.

Charles brought a half-dozen big freight wagons from Taos. He nodded when he saw the wagons loaded already. "Figured you'd still be in a hurry," William explained with a shrug.

By the time the caravan returned to the fort, it was late August. The two brothers held a small council. "I got to get the rest of these furs back East, but I still got to go to Taos to take the supplies and trade goods," Charles said.

"Them furs ain't gonna go bad, we leave 'em here over the winter."

"Yeah," Charles said with a tired, crooked little smile. "But I ain't sure we'll get as good a price for 'em next year. If we make this fast enough, we might be able to beat the American Fur boys gettin' back to Missouri. Might help frazzle 'em some."

"That's a worthwhile endeavor," William said seriously.

"I'll consolidate what I need for Taos, and leave the rest of the wagons here. If you was to be so kind as to load 'em like you done last time, that'll save a few days. I've sent word to Ceran to have a heap of boys ready to unload." He grinned again, but there was little humor in it. William had never seen his brother looking so worn and tired.

"Reckon I'll have time for one night with Ignacia—if she'll let me in the house. Then I'll make a march up here, load up, and push on."

"You're gonna kill yourself someday, you damn fool," William said.

"Bah."

William was ready for him when Charles returned from Taos. All the wagons that had been left behind were loaded. As soon as Charles's feet hit the ground, William grabbed him and steered him to the dining room. "Eat," he ordered.

"But I've got to—"

"You've got to eat, goddammit, that's all you got to do right now. And when you're done eatin', you're gonna get a full night's rest."

"But—"

"Don't give me no shit, Charlie," William said harshly but with a solid footing of concern. "All your boys from the wagons're getting the same. I got my crew out there to load the wagons and do whatever else needs doin'. You and your boys are gonna get some sleep. By dawn the wagons'll be loaded and you can move on."

Charles nodded, feeling more tired than he could ever remember. He was grateful for his brother's care.

All of Charles's men looked a lot more spry when they pulled out of the fort in the morning. It was a clear, crisp morning in early October, the kind of day that made living a joy, where the cool air seemed to fill the lungs better, where the blood seemed to cry out for action. It was a joyous feeling, and Charles Bent was glad he could appreciate it.

In the entourage there were twenty-two heavily loaded freight wagons; a small wagon carrying food supplies, bedrolls, and such; twenty-five freighters; eight camp helpers; ten hunters, led by Robert Bent; and fifteen guards, including Hobbs.

"I thought you was stayin' out here now, Jim," William Bent said when he heard Hobbs was leaving.

"Don't think I'm quite ready for that, Cap'n. Maybe next time. Or the time after that." He shrugged, and Bent noticed that Hobbs was more tense than ever as he pulled himself onto his horse next to Robert Bent.

In many ways Robert Bent had never really felt like he belonged in and around the fort. He sometimes thought that he didn't even fit into the Bent family very well. While his brother George got the more responsible jobs, Robert often felt as if his older brothers did not trust him with responsible work. Because of that, he turned to his one talent, besides being able to attract women with his good looks—hunting. He felt needed and useful when he hunted for the freight wagons, and so he more often than not went along with Charles and the caravans.

Robert had also found a kindred spirit of a kind in Jim Hobbs, and the two stuck together fairly often. But where Hobbs had learned his lesson well, Robert had too strong a dose of the Bent rashness. Since Hobbs was a guard, not a hunter, he stayed with the wagons when Robert and the hunters went off to do their work. Often feeling melancholy, Robert was wont to go off on his own, despite Charles's admonishments. The more his brother nagged him, the more obstinate he got.

Two days out from the fort, Robert led the hunters afield, then drifted off by himself. Suddenly he stopped. Sitting still in the saddle, he looked around. Usually when he was off by himself, he kept the other hunters in sight. Now they had disappeared.

"Let's go, hoss," he said quietly as he touched his quirt lightly on the horse's rump. He moved on, eyes peeled for the rest of the hunters. He heard the telltale squeak of the poorly greased hunting wagon. A feeling of relief came over him and he picked up the pace a little.

Suddenly three Comanches popped up from a small ravine right in front of Bent. His horse reared, forelegs waving wildly. Bent fell off the animal, landing hard on his back.

Before he had time to more than grunt once with the impact of the fall, the Comanches were on him.

A hundred yards away half a dozen hunters swatted their horses. One of the Comanches saw them racing toward them. With a word to his companions, the three Comanches ran for their horses a few feet away where the coulee deepened. Brandishing Robert Bent's scalp, they galloped off.

Four days after leaving, Charles rode back into the fort, his face a mask of pain and hate. With him were Hobbs —and Robert Bent's body.

William felt an icy chill run up his spine. It was not caused by the cold day, but by the sight of the two men riding into the *placita*. Though Robert's body was wrapped in a blanket, William knew just by the look on his brother's face who it was. The fort came to a stand-still, the men afraid to move, afraid even to breathe.

With tears clouding his vision a little, William eased the body down. Steeling himself, he started to open the blankets.

"Don't," Charles said, voice broken.

"I got to, Charlie." William peeled the layers of blanket off and wanted to vomit when he saw Robert's head, with the blood-coated bone where his hair used to be. "Jesus goddamn Christ all-goddamn-son-of-a-bitchin'-goddamn-mighty," William roared.

They buried Robert Bent outside the fort, not far from the northwest corner. The funeral service was short, and the attendees were a mixed lot: the three remaining Bent brothers and a contingent of their friends—Charles never questioned how some of them who were out in the wilds knew—Frenchmen like Ceran St. Vrain and his brother Marcellin; Blacks like Solomon, Dick Green, and Charlotte; Scotsmen like Ramsay MacGregor; Owl Woman; Mexican laborers, and several Cheyennes and Arapahos.

Right after the hole was filled in and rocks stacked on the grave, Charles mounted his horse. "I got to go on, Bill," he said. "The others're waitin' on me."

William nodded. He was surprised when he heard Hobbs say, "I'm stayin' here, Mr. Bent."

The Bents looked at him. Hobbs shrugged. "I got a reason to stay now," he said harshly. "I aim to kill me some goddamn Comanches."

The Bents nodded. Charles rode off and William walked into the fort. The next time the Bents heard of Jim Hobbs was several years later. He had joined former mountain man Jim Kirker's band of scalp hunters.

❦{ 38 }❧

Out of the swirling snow and howling, frigid, unfettered wind appeared a small, capote-wrapped figure on horseback. Standing on the walkway, Gabe Foxworthy saw the figure suddenly appear perhaps fifty yards from the gate. Then the figure disappeared as the snow dropped its stinging curtain over the landscape again.

Foxworthy growled to himself, not liking any of this. He cursed William Bent, Walsh, the fort, and the weather. Most of all he cursed himself. He had gotten drunk three nights ago and picked a fight with Walsh. That was stupid under the best of circumstances; when one's coordination had been plundered by too much cheap whiskey, it was insane. Walsh proceeded to pound Foxworthy into a whimpering heap, then reported what had happened to Bent, who ruled his fort in a hard but fair way. Bent had come to have a small chat with Foxworthy and offered him an alternative. Three days on guard over the gate, where the north winds battered a body, or twenty lashes. Foxworthy could not face the lash. He had done so once and couldn't bear it again. So here he stood, in an arctic wind, face and body still mottled with bruises.

The lonely figure appeared again only twenty-five yards away. Foxworthy was about to raise the alarm, but just before opening his mouth, he stopped himself. The figure out there was alone, so it couldn't be an attack by Indians or bandits. Besides, Foxworthy thought there was something familiar about the person.

At ten yards he recognized the man. He spun and looked down into the *placita*. It usually was empty these days, as the winter kept a mighty grip on the fort. Foxworthy thought it fortunate that he saw someone. "Harker!" he bellowed, hoping his voice would carry over the wind. "Harker, goddammit!"

Jarrod Harker looked up, annoyed as snow landed on his face. It melted right off, but then refroze into miniature icicles on his beard and mustache. "Whaddaya want?"

"Get the cap'n. Now! Kit's comin' in."

Harker didn't bother to verbally acknowledge the order. He simply raced for the door to Bent's quarters. In moments Bent was outside, pulling on a long green capote. He belted the garment as he headed for the gate as fast as he could on the slippery snow. From outside he could hear a faint, "Rider comin' in. It's Kit Carson."

Bent and Harker yanked the gates open and Carson rode in, not stopping until he was at the railing in front of the dining room. As Carson started to dismount, Bent, walking swiftly toward his friend, thought Carson looked mighty awkward. He hoped Carson wasn't hurt.

Without waiting for Bent, Carson went into the dining room. Bent and Harker were only a few steps behind. As they entered the room, Bent's eyes widened in worry. Carson was unwrapping his four-year-old daughter Adaline from a thick blanket.

"Charlotte!" Bent roared. "Charlotte, get out here. Pronto."

She ambled out of the kitchen, wiping her hands on her apron. "Wha's wrong, Mistah Bent?" she said in an aggrieved voice. "I's jus'—" She spotted Adaline. "Gracious Lo'd almighty."

Her ponderous form moved more swiftly than anyone would have imagined, looking at her. She pulled the girl out of Carson's arms, almost smothering Adaline in her large embrace. "Lo'dy, Lo'dy," she muttered. Then she swept off toward the kitchen, where it was much warmer, and where there was many a thing to entice a child to eat.

Carson smiled, knowing his Adaline would be well taken care of. He pulled off his capote and dropped it on a table. Carson sat. Before he could say anything, Charlotte's husband, Dick Green, came out of the kitchen carrying a huge coffeepot in one hand and a tray on the other.

As Green set the things on the table, Bent turned to Harker, who had followed Bent and Carson into the dining room. "Please see to Mr. Carson's horse, Mr. Harker."

"Yessir." Harker turned and left.

When Bent sat moments later, Green had filled two cups with hot coffee and set out two big bowls of *caldo de cordero*. Carson gulped down coffee and spoonfuls of the lamb stew as if he might never get another meal. Bent smiled at Carson's actions, and ate at a more leisurely pace. He was not all that hungry, having eaten not long before. He mostly sipped coffee and picked at the stew.

Carson finished up his stew and the first cup of coffee. "You gonna eat that?" Carson asked, pointing a metal spoon at Bent's bowl. Bent shook his head and pushed the bowl toward Carson with a smile.

Finally Carson was done. Both men lit pipes. Green refilled their cups and took away the bowls. He left the coffeepot, honey, and sugar.

"Now, ol' friend, just what in hell brings you to my door in the midst of a goddamn storm like this?"

Carson smiled crookedly. "Makin' Out Road pitched my plunder out of the lodge."

"Nice of her to divorce you in such fine weather."

"She was a bitch right from the start," Carson said angrily. "Hell, she was the pick of the tribe. Had every goddamn Cheyenne buck in the world out for her. Between that and the spoilin' from her ol' man, she wasn't easy to please." He paused and shook his head. "Nah, that ain't true. She wasn't hard to please, she was goddamn impossible to please."

Bent nodded, understanding. "So, what're you gonna do now?"

Carson hesitated, covering his embarrassment behind his coffee cup. Finally he set the cup down. "I got a favor to ask of you, Bill." He didn't like doing such things.

Bent shrugged, seeing Carson's discomfit. He would've felt the same way had the situation been reversed. "You don't have to feel poorly about askin' an ol' friend for a favor."

Carson nodded, knowing it was true. It didn't lessen his guilt any, though. "I need to get down to Taos and see to some business. I was wonderin' if you can keep Adaline here whilst I'm gone?"

"That all you want to ask?" Bent said, surprised.

Carson nodded.

Bent grinned. "I suspect that if you was to try takin' Adaline out into this storm again, Charlotte'd knock you flat on your ass and then do a *fandango* on your head."

Carson grinned. "I'd wager she could do it too."

He pulled out the next morning, with Charlotte's assurances that Adaline would be well taken care of, and with a sack of stomach- and blood-filling pemmican. Life in the fort went pretty much back to normal, which, in the heart of winter, was slow. Most of the trappers and buffalo hunters who quartered there for the winter didn't go out unless they had good reason. The laborers were out and about more frequently, but they too tried to keep indoors as much as possible. Most times the only movement seen in the fort was that of the men patrolling the walls, and the only sounds were those of the blacksmith and carpentry shops.

When Carson returned, it was with Charles Bent and another friend, Lucien Maxwell. That evening they, William Bent, Seth Walsh, and Ramsay MacGregor sat at one long table in the dining room.

"How's things in Mexico, Charlie?" William asked.

Charles shrugged. "Better'n last year, but Armijo and that pissant padre of his are bein' royal pains in the ass."

"What's he done now?"

"The saintly fat bastard managed to convince ol' contrary Armijo that my name didn't belong on the papers for Lucien's land grant."

"Anything you can do about it?"

"I expect not. But maybe when I get back there things'll cool some. Hell, you know how the situation changes down there every other week." William nodded. Then Charles asked, "How's business up here?"

"Our take in furs since last fall was almost as good as last year's," MacGregor reported. "In some ways, though, we've done even better."

"How so?" Charles asked.

"We have a lot more horses this time," MacGregor said quietly.

Charles, who had been looking at MacGregor, turned his questioning gaze to his brother. William was grinning mischievously. "What the hell's goin' on, Bill?"

"Peg-Leg and some of his amigos have been visiting California, and you know what that means."

Charles laughed. He most assuredly did. It meant Peg-Leg Smith and whatever men he had with him had been stealing horses by the hundreds out there, and then driving them to the fort, where Bent, St. Vrain & Company would buy them, no questions asked.

Business out of the way, they talked about life in general. Maxwell, who had been married only days before leaving Taos for the fort, was the butt of a considerable amount of repartee concerning his attributes, or lack of them, and about his extremely short honey-moon.

Charles tired of it before long, considering that he and Carson had given Maxwell a hard time on the same topics on the ride out of the fort. So Charles turned his attentions elsewhere.

"Hey, Bill, did Kit tell you he's sweet on my sister-in-law?" Charles said rather innocently.

William was shocked. "Which one?"

"Little Maria Josefa," Charles said with a devilish smile.

"Little?" Maxwell snorted. "She's bigger'n Kit is already, and she ain't hardly more'n a sucklin' babe."

"Just how old is this lady?"

"Fourteen," Charles said with another grin.

"Jesus, Kit," William said, feigning shock, "fourteen? Damn, ain't there laws against that?" He wasn't nearly as shocked as he pretended. Maria Josefa Jaramillo was of marriageable age by anyone's standard these days, he knew, but it was still a good way to chide Carson.

The bandy little mountain man was beet-red from embarrassment. He was beginning to get angry too, not that any of his friends cared.

As the joking wound down, something tugged at William's mind, and it took a few minutes to figure it out. When it clicked, he nodded.

"Hey, Kit," he said, "ain't ol' man Jaramillo givin' you a hard time about you bein' sweet on his daughter?"

"He did," Carson mumbled amid new laughs and catcalls from his friends. Then Carson squared his shoulders. "I was baptized down there, and—" He stopped, since this was the part that bothered him most. "Well, hell, I need to do somethin' with Adaline. Charlie suggested I take her to a convent school back in the States."

"That what you're going to do?"

Carson nodded, his sadness stamped on his face. No one made light of him this time. They all knew to one degree or another what Carson was going through.

When Charles, Maxwell, and Carson pulled out a couple days later, little Adaline was sitting in one of the wagons. She waved her chubby little hand at Charlotte as the wagon rumbled out of the fort.

When Charles returned to the trading post in September, Carson was not with him. "Him and Lucien hooked on with some feller named Frémont, who wants to do a heap of explorin'." Charles shrugged. "Frémont was talkin' to any of the old mountaineers he could find. I had the honor to meet him, and told him about Kit and Lucien."

"You seem taken with him," William said.

"I suppose I am." Charles grinned. "Frémont's married to Senator Benton's daughter Jessie."

"Reckon he would be a nice feller to know," William commented. He rubbed a hand across his face. He felt as if he hadn't slept right in months, and he worried some about getting older. Shaking himself out of his doldrums a little, he said, "I got some news too, but it ain't good."

"Dammit all anyway." Charles managed to get control of himself. "Well, what is it?"

"A new post's been built up near the mouth of Fountain Creek not far from where we had our first little place."

"Who put it in?"

"Three fellers named Simpson, Doyle—and Barclay."

"Alex Barclay?" Charles asked, eyes narrowing in anger.

William nodded. "I don't mind so much that we hired him on here and gave him a heap of training," William said. "I don't even give a good goddamn if he built his own place. It does frost my ass, though, when he puts it in our territory as a direct competitor."

"Agreed. Anyone else we know of workin' out of there?"

William shrugged. "I imagine a few of the old boys are workin' for 'em. I can't hold them at fault. The only one I know of who's at least been there, even if he ain't workin' there, is Ol' Solitaire."

"He don't worry me. The ol' coot just goes his own way is all."

"What do you figure we ought to do about it, Charlie?"

The older brother shrugged. "I'll have to cogitate on it a spell."

⊰{39}⊱

Change was coming to the land where American, Mexican, and Indian forces collided. It did not come with a blast of cold wind charging across the prairies. Instead it came with a whisper of a breeze—not enough to sweep one up in its wake, but creeping with an insidious quiet that prevented one from realizing it was there until it was too late.

The principals of Bent, St. Vrain & Company knew there was something in the wind, but they were unsure of what it was. Their lives were wrapped up in keeping the company growing and prospering.

Charles Bent was almost frantic in his activity, seeming to race between Taos, the fort, and the States. When not traveling, he was writing letters and bending politicians' ears, trying to counter intrigues by Armijo and other old enemies who tried to shake the company's stranglehold on trade in the northern reaches of Mexico.

William, while not nearly as frantic, had much to do keeping the traders and Indians happy. It was getting harder and harder. Interlopers were trying to make inroads in their trade, bringing in whiskey by the barrelful to lure the Cheyennes and Arapahos away from Bent-St. Vrain. More men were using the Santa Fe Trail, hoping to fill their pockets with silver for paltry trade items the Mexican people could get nowhere else.

Perhaps worst of all, though, were the Comanches and the Kiowas, who seemed to have forgotten their desire to live in peace with Bent, St. Vrain & Company. They had taken to attacking virtually any caravan that crossed any part of the vast territory they claimed.

The Comanches' audacity rankled William Bent more than anything else. After the Comanches killed Robert, William had hardened his heart against the Indians. The continuing attacks on the company's caravans just sharpened Bent's anger toward them. As busy as he was, he never forgot his brother's death at the hands of the Comanches. He wanted vengeance, but he was not the type to just indiscriminately kill Comanches. Besides, he was too busy to go chasing Comanches.

It seemed to Bent that the world was beginning to revolve around his mud fort. It was not arrogance that made him feel that way, simply an observation. Just in the past couple of months, more traders than ever had come through the fort, Cheyennes and Arapahos were there in abundance, and visitors were becoming almost commonplace.

Little did Bent know that the seeds of war were sown that January. He did know, though, that the company was besieged on all sides. Charles's effort to do something about the fort on Fountain Creek had borne no fruit. In addition, he was required almost endlessly to fend off Mexican attempts to get rid of him. Lawsuits were filed against him, and he was threatened with jail numerous times. He had even been jailed once on trumped-up charges. Only Manuel Alvarez's efforts and duplicity got him out of what was a tight fix that time.

As winter drifted toward spring, the problems mounted. For one thing, Comanches and Kiowas were once again attacking trading caravans. In retaliation, William Bent pulled all his traders out of the territory claimed by those two tribes. All, that is, except Blackfoot John Smith and Mexican Sol Silver. Both were free traders who dealt almost exclusively with Bent, St. Vrain & Company. Still, as independents, they went where and when they wanted.

In addition, reports reached the fort that the Texians apparently were ready to launch forays into Mexican territory to the west. Governor Armijo had heard of the impending invasion and responded the only way he knew how—with force. He led an army of more than six hundred men toward the Crossing of the Arkansas, where the Cimarron Cutoff of the Santa Fe Trail crossed the Arkansas.

When Bent, St. Vrain & Company heard of that, the partners—including George Bent now—scheduled a council of war at the fort. The fort faced troubles from three countries, plus several Indian nations. The Texians were stirring up trouble; the Mexicans were trying to counter that; the United States was trying, from afar, to keep those sides apart while trying to protect its citizens on the wide, lonely frontier.

Nothing seemed to alleviate the growing problems in the region. Texians raided Mexican caravans, prompting escorts to and from the border. Armijo headed east with several hundred troops bent on stopping the depredations and sending the Texians scurrying home.

Worse, Governor Armijo had closed all the customs houses in Taos and Santa Fe. Americans could bring goods in, but they were banned from selling them retail. The tax was usurious. In addition, Comanches and Kiowas still attacked caravans, not caring whose they were.

Trade along the Santa Fe Trail ground mostly to a halt, as everyone waited to see what would happen. But just because they were waiting did not mean they were doing it in one place. Kit Carson had been through the fort several times in the spring and early summer.

On one of these trips, William Bent told Carson that the dispatches he was carrying were no longer needed.

"Damn, that's good news," Carson said in relief. He felt like he'd been running a foot race with a couple dozen Apaches who were taking turns in pacing him. "Looks like I got me a little time for a change to cut the dust in my throat. C'mon, ol' hoss," he added joyfully, clapping Bent on the shoulder, "I'll stand you a drink or two."

"You're on," Bent said. Despite his having been stuck in the fort, he also felt like he was constantly running. "What's your plans, Kit?" Bent asked after the two had appreciatively consumed a few drinks.

"Well, Frémont's supposed to be up at your other place. I'm about half froze to get up there and hitch on with him. Hell, we had us some shinin' times last time."

"You got a fast horse and no ropes to hold you here."

"My thinkin' too. I expect I'll leave at first light." He drained his mug. "And that means I've had enough of this shit." He set the cup down. "I best fill my meat bag good."

"Charlotte'll make sure you're filled, and that you got enough in your possibles bag to get you to the Platte."

Bent was up early enough to see his old friend off, and then he had to face the day's work, which was more than plentiful these days. Trading was still doing well, and Bent figured that maybe having the Mexicans close down the customs houses might not be all that bad a thing. It meant more business for the fort.

Bent was surprised when Carson rode in again a week later. He stood outside his office, the sleeves of his stained calico shirt rolled up past his elbows. A pipe was stuck between his teeth, a thin curl of smoke rising to the roof of the portico. "What the hell're you doin' here?" Bent asked. He was afraid there was bad news from the other fort, or about Marcellin St. Vrain, who was in charge there at that time.

"Hell, that pissant fort you critters built up on the Platte's about as useful as teats on your grandpa." He dismounted and slapped his shapeless felt hat against a buckskin-clad leg. Puffs of dust rose up with each whack. "Frémont needs supplies, Bill. You got enough to spare?"

Bent shrugged. "Don't see why not. You payin'? Or is he?"

"He asked me to ask you if you'll take his marker for now."

"You trust him, Kit?" Bent asked bluntly.

"I do," Carson said without reservation.

Bill nodded. "Go tell MacGregor what you need. You got mules to cart all that plunder?"

"Nope, need them too. You got any to spare?"

"Some. C'mon, let's go see what you need. Once we figure on that, we can see how many mules you'll need."

Carson rode out the next morning, ten loaded mules in his wake.

Not long after Blackfoot John Smith rode in with a load of robes. He stopped in front of the trade room and dismounted. Bent, who had been in one of the storage rooms across the *placita*, stepped outside and watched. "You there," Smith said, pointing to a Mexican youth, who suddenly looked scared to death. "Take care of my horse, boy."

"Si, señor," the boy said. He took the reins and towed the horse toward the corral out back.

Smith hitched up his pants, then bellowed, "Mac-Gregor! Get your goddamn skinflint ol' hide out here, you penny-pinchin' son of a bitch!"

MacGregor was as irascible as Smith, and not about to be beckoned in so crude a manner. He continued with his figuring in a tote book.

Smith stood out in the baking *placita*, looking aggrieved. He turned slowly, looking around. He spied Bent. "Bill Bent, you short-legged piece of buffler gristle, how's about you tell that fractious Scottish miser to get out here. We got business to tend to."

Bent shrugged. "You started this ruckus, not me. Hell, if I was over there and you pulled this shit on me, I wouldn't come out either."

A crafty look spread over Smith's face, though no one could see it since it was hidden in the shadow spread by his wide-brimmed hat. "I got some news you might want," he said slyly.

"Like what?" Bent asked disinterestedly.

Smith waited some moments before answering. He wanted the tension to build just a little. He spat some tobacco juice at a small, thin lizard. He looked up and over at Bent. "It concerns a few Comanches you might be interested in hearin' about."

Bent instantly headed across the *placita*. About halfway through the journey he roared for MacGregor. The chief trader could ignore a loudmouth like Smith; he could not ignore his boss. He stepped outside.

"Tote up these here hides, boy. I'll be back later for my pay," Smith said. He looked at Bent. "The noon meal's on you, Bent," he said roughly, enjoying the grip he had here. It didn't happen too often.

As the two headed toward the dining room, Bent said, "If you're pullin' my leg on this, Smith, I'll have your nuts in a jar and your hair hangin' from my lodgepole."

"Shit," Smith muttered quietly. As tough as he was, he knew Bent was just as tough. Besides, Bent had a bunch of men here who would be glad to carve someone up if the boss asked.

They entered the dining room and took seats opposite each other across a table. Bent was facing the door, which made Smith nervous.

Charlotte ambled up. "Can I he'p you, Mistah Bent?" she asked.

"Just some coffee for me, Charlotte," Bent replied, secretly enjoying Smith's annoyance at being ignored. "And I believe I'll have some of your *bizcochitos,* if you got some."

"Always got some o' dem fo' you, Mistah Bent." Charlotte finally turned toward Smith. "You want sompin?" Her tone was not kindly.

"Big plate of tamales. Some *posole,* corn bread, cheese, and a jug of any kind of 'corn' you got."

When Charlotte returned, she set a pot of coffee in the center of the table and cups in front of both men. Another trip and she placed a plate of cookies in front of Bent and a bowl of *posole* by Smith, who looked up at her, his face darkening with anger.

"Where's my damn tamales?" he demanded, getting to his feet. "And my whiskey?"

"Tha's all you gonna get from me tidday," Charlotte said, unimpressed with Smith.

"I'm of half a mind to—" He clamped his lips shut when Dick Green suddenly loomed up behind Charlotte. Green was a big man, and usually of mild temper. There were only a few things he'd get riled over. One of them was threats to his wife.

"You're of half a goddamn mind, all right," Bent said with a hoarse chuckle. "Now plop your ass down and tell me this great secret of yours. It's good enough, you'll get the tamales and some Lightnin'."

Smith glared from Bent to Green a moment, before his stomach gained the upper hand. He sat and tore into the hog and hominy.

Bent let Smith get about halfway through the bowl before saying, "I reckon it's about time you start talkin'."

Smith scowled but put down his spoon. "I know who kilt Bob."

Bent's eyes widened in surprise, then glared hotly. "Who?"

"Three Comanches—Wolf Tail, Bad Knee, and Bull

Nose." He watched for Bent's reaction when he said the last.

"That surly son of a bitchin' son of Old Wolf?"

"The very same." Smith felt like he had just shot a plump buffalo cow that was dressed and butchered when it hit the ground.

Bent could not see the gloating joy on Smith's face; he was busy thinking of how he could repay the three Comanches for all the pain they had caused. He finally came out of his trance when Charlotte asked him for the third time if she was to get Smith the things he demanded.

Bent nodded. "Yes, Charlotte, thank you." Then he fixed a harsh glare on Smith. "Here's what I want you to do, John. I—"

"Whoa now, ol' hoss," Smith said lightly. "I figure I've done about all I'm gonna in this matter."

"Now you listen to me, you sheep-humpin' peck-erwood," Bent growled in a voice made low by anger and annoyance. "You'll do what I tell you, when I tell you. . . ."

"What if I don't?"

Bent controlled his temper, then said, "You've knowed me long enough to know what I'd do in a matter of so much importance to me."

"Yes." The answer was surly. "What do you want from me?"

"Get those three bastards to come up here."

"How?"

"I don't much give a damn. But I figure you can tell 'em we've got some medals from our great chief in Washington to give 'em, just like we did with the Chey-ennes a while back."

"That might work." Smith didn't sound very inter-ested.

"If it don't, you tell 'em any goddamn thing you want to get 'em here. I don't give a flyin' shit if half the goddamn Comanche Nation shows up here, as long as those three are with 'em.''

"What're you fixin' to do to 'em?"

"That's none of your concern."

Smith shrugged. He figured to agree to anything, then as soon as he was out of sight of the fort, he would turn north, heading for Sioux land. "All right," he said flatly. It wouldn't do to be too friendly, lest Bent suspect he was lying.

Bent pulled his knife and sliced off a sliver of wood from the table. He used it to pick out a piece of cookie from between two teeth. Then he threw the splinter down. He rose as if leaving, then stopped with both palms flat on the tabletop. "Oh, and lest you think to try some deviltry, I'll be sendin' a few of the boys along." He strolled out.

As soon as he was outside, Bent went to the trade room. Emiliano Flores was there outfitting for another trade run. Bent pulled him aside and told Flores that he and his small regular crew would be going to Comanche country with Blackfoot John. Flores was almost overcome with pride, as he realized how much trust Bent was placing in him.

"I want you to make sure he does what I told him," Bent said. "He gives you any shit, you find he's been schemin' against me, you put him under. Then you tell them Comanches whatever you need to about him to make it all right. Then you talk 'em into comin' up here."

"*Sí*, Señor Bent." He was bursting with pride, but worried too. He had come a long way since he was first hired by Bent, St. Vrain & Company to make adobe bricks for this fort. He enjoyed being a trader, and found he was good at it. He also was good at directing men. He had encountered troubles since becoming a trader, and had been in a number of Indian fights. Still, he was not sure he had what it would take to kill a man with the ferocious reputation of Blackfoot John Smith.

Bent knew Flores was anxious. He gripped the man's shoulder and squeezed a little. "You'll be all right, Yano. You're a good man, and you have good men with you."

Flores nodded, not having the words to thank his *patrón*.

❦{40}❧

Day after day of rain pelting down sent the Arkansas River over its banks, reaching long liquid fingers toward the fort itself. The floods created problems for Bent, St. Vrain & Company, as its heavily laden wagons and mules had the devil's own time getting through to Independence. It was almost as bad on the way back, though it had not rained in a week. Charles Bent was a sour man when he finally arrived at the fort. George Bent was in a better frame of mind.

William hauled his two brothers into the council room, a whiskey jug gripped in one hand and three pewter mugs in the other. Inside, they sat around a small table. William filled the three cups.

When they had taken a sip, William said, "Glad you're back."

Charles shrugged; George nodded. George was grateful to be back after a trek hampered by mud, swollen rivers and creeks, cantankerous mules, and wagons that seemed to break down every other minute.

"I got good news, Charlie," William said.

"What's that?" Charles asked, a flicker of interest in his voice.

"Comanches ought to be here in a couple days, at most."

"So?" George asked, shrugging. He had been waiting for real news.

"So," William said with a harsh intensity in the

words, "Wolf Tail, Bad Knee, and Bull Nose'll be with 'em."

Charles looked up, a dark, humorless grin spreading across his lips. "You sure?" he asked, fingers tightening on the pewter mug.

"Yep." His nose flared, as if he were smelling hot blood after a fight. "Yano sent Chavez back with word almost a week ago."

"Yano have to kill Blackfoot?" Charles asked. He was not so much happy at the news as he was satisfied that some justice might be found.

"Nope. Surprised hell out of me." He would have laughed a little if he had had any humor left in him at the time. "Chavez said Blackfoot tried pullin' some shit once. Yano and his crew faced him down with rifles."

"Must've angered ol' Blackfoot no end," George said roughly.

"Must've," William agreed. "But that ain't our concern now. He wants to make somethin' of all this after it's over, we'll oblige him."

The three Bents left the dining room, where they had been waiting almost patiently since dawn, after Seth Walsh told them that a band of Comanches was spotted just across the river.

While Charles and George waited under the portico in front of the dining room, William walked out into the *placita*. He shaded his eyes as he looked up toward the bastion in the northeast corner. "How many are coming, Mr. Foxworthy?" he called to the man keeping watch.

"Looks to be a dozen, maybe fifteen. My ol' eyes ain't as good as they used to been. Looks to be all our boys with 'em too."

Bent nodded. "Everybody know what they're supposed to do?" He got a ragged chorus of affirmatives. Bent went to join his brothers.

"Riders comin' in!" Foxworthy announced, as the

guards always did when visitors approached. It sounded natural, and should not scare off the Comanches.

The Bents stood in the center of the *placita*, facing the gates.

Blackfoot John Smith was the first through the gate. He headed to his left and stopped in front of the trade room. By the time he had done that, fourteen Comanches had entered the *placita*. Finally Emiliano Flores and his small crew entered and turned to the right.

Four men sprang from inside rooms on each side of the "tunnel" and shoved the gates closed. Old Wolf, leading the Comanche band, glared at the Bents, while most of his warriors went for bows or guns.

"Don't!" William Bent shouted.

Old Wolf, still staring at him, waved his arm. His men settled back down. "What is this?" he demanded.

William walked a few steps closer to the Indians. "You remember how me and Kit Carson and ol' Blackfoot there showed you and some of your amigos around this fort?"

Old Wolf nodded, wondering what the trader was up to.

"It was then, when you made peace with the Cheyennes and the Arapahos, that you asked to make peace with me and my amigos here. You remember that too?"

Old Wolf nodded again, still baffled.

"Less'n a winter later, a few of your boys ambushed a hunter from one of our caravans. Killed him and tore his hair off so's his spirit'll wander forever with no peace."

"Our warriors have fought—and killed—many white-eyes," Old Wolf said with obvious pride.

"Well, I don't much give a damn about most of them."

"Then why this one?"

"He was our brother, you son of a bitch." His anger

was beginning to get the upper hand, and he fought to control it.

Old Wolf said nothing, but he was worried. His eyes circled the second floor. Several dozen hard-eyed and heavily armed men were there, rifles pointed loosely in the Comanches' direction.

"You like tradin' with Bent, St. Vrain and Company?" William asked.

"You have much we can use," Old Wolf acknowledged, wondering what Bent was getting at. "But we have lived without those things."

"You wonder why?"

"We thought the white-eyes were afraid of us," he said, sneering.

"Even an old fart like you can't be that damn stupid," William said.

The Comanche started as if slapped.

"We'll open trade with you, Old Wolf. There is a way."

"And what is that?" Old Wolf asked, interested despite himself.

"You give over the three bastards what killed our brother."

"Who are they?" He was doubtful and wanted to buy some time.

"Wolf Tail, Bad Knee, and . . ." Bent paused. "Bull Nose."

Old Wolf shook his head angrily, his silvery hair whipping.

"It'll be fair. Them three against us three."

Old Wolf looked at the men on the walls again. He was sure Bent was lying, but he knew his warriors had no chance here. His men might get a few whites, but all his people would die. "What if my men win?"

William shrugged. The thought had never occurred to him. "Then you and your men can leave."

Old Wolf was certain they were all going to be massacred. Still, the Bents had always been straight with the Comanches. He knew he had no choice, though. He would just have to trust the Bents. He nodded, showing great dignity. He turned on his horse and addressed his men.

Charles and George tossed off their jackets and dropped their pistols, then moved out to stand by William. "You do know, don't you, Bill, that I am way too old for such doin's," Charles said.

"Well, then, just go take your aging ol' ass down yonder and plunk it. Me'n George'll handle these bastards."

"Go to hell," Charles growled. While it was true that he was some older than his brothers and was showing a little paunch, he was still a hard man, and one not unused to struggle.

"Which one you gonna take on there, gramps?" William asked, looking innocently at his older brother.

"Just mind you don't get yourself put under," Charles snapped.

Wolf Tail, Bad Knee, and Bull Nose had dismounted and tossed aside their bows and quivers and strutted away from their horses, toward the center of the *placita*. Bad Knee limped some, favoring his right knee. All three warriors wore plain buckskin leggings and breechcloths. Bull Nose had a hair-pipe breastplate and two eagle feathers in his long, unfettered hair. Bad Knee wore a long, plain buckskin war shirt, and Wolf Tail had no cover on his torso.

The three Comanches and the three Bents gravitated toward each other, unconscious of how they selected their opponents. It just seemed natural that Charles, as the oldest, would face Bad Knee; Charles's age was a rough equivalent to Bad Knee's limp. George, as the youngest and hardiest of the Bents, would go against the biggest Comanche—Wolf Tail. That left Bull Nose, the most rancorous of the Comanches, for William Bent, who, though the smallest of the

Bents, probably was the toughest and meanest when it was called for.

Suddenly Bad Knee charged, head lowered like a bull. The attack set off a flurry of movement as the other men all reacted.

Charles braced himself, one foot behind the other, let Bad Knee crash into him, and grabbed him. The collision knocked most of Charles's air out, but he recovered quickly and head-butted the Comanche. Bad Knee grunted but seemed to show no other signs that he had just been hit. Bent began to worry a little, but he figured it couldn't be all bad if Bad Knee kept him wrapped up the way he was.

Charles suddenly jerked backward. He spun as he began falling, bringing Bad Knee with him. By the time they hit, Bent was on top. The impact broke Bad Knee's grip. Bent shoved up to his feet, panting already. He had a clear opening to attack Bad Knee, but he didn't think he had the energy.

Bad Knee charged. Bent tried to get out of the way but he could not. Bad Knee slammed a shoulder into Bent's chest, and Bent gasped, trying desperately to breathe. Fear radiated out from his sternum on the wings of pain. His mouth flapped as he began getting oxygen into his system. It seemed to be too late, though. Bent weakly punched Bad Knee as the Comanche grabbed him by the hair and yanked his head back.

A knife caught a sliver of sunlight as it rose above Bent's head. Sweating, Bent swung his left arm up, knocking the knife free.

Bad Knee's tenuous grip on Bent's hair slipped, and Bent fell heavily. Bad Knee moved in to stomp his throat, but Bent managed to roll out of the way and kick Bad Knee with both feet. He hit the warrior's namesake joint and Bad Knee listed to the side and then fell.

Bent rolled onto his stomach and began pushing himself up. Bad Knee rose and limped to his knife. He grabbed it and flung himself onto Bent's back. Instead of collapsing, though, Bent had enough fight left in him to shove his left hand—with the thumb extended —over his shoulder. His long, ragged fingernail sliced into Bad Knee's eye.

Bad Knee screeched in surprise and pain. He dropped the knife, to use his right hand to cover his injured eye.

Bent bucked, tossing Bad Knee off. He was still having trouble breathing, though, and so he was slow in getting back up. When he did, he turned just in time to have Bad Knee grab him in a bear hug.

Bent looked into Bad Knee's oozing eye only inches from his face, and knew that the Comanche was close to killing him. Bad Knee squeezed, grinning evilly as he exerted more pressure.

But Bent had proved to be a tougher opponent than Bad Knee had thought, and the Indian was not about to make that mistake again. He wanted to make sure he finished Bent off fast.

George Bent whirled like a bullfighter as Wolf Tail charged. He balled his hands together and swung the doubled fists at the back of Wolf Tail's head. He missed and fell down from the follow-through, managing to get his hands out to catch himself. He hung on hands and knees a moment.

Wolf Tail stopped, spun and took a few steps back toward George. He kicked him in the ribs. "Shit," Bent breathed as pain lanced into his side as he rolled from the kick. He came to a stop mostly on his back, his side hurting like hell fire.

Wolf Tail was on him in a flash, knife in hand. "Shit," Bent hissed as he managed to get an arm up and block the blade some. Still, it sliced across his arm and then glanced off his breastbone.

Wolf Tail drew back for another attempt to stab his foe. But Bent slammed the heel of his right hand on the underside of Wolf Tail's chin. It snapped the Indian's head back and threw off his aim. The knife grazed Bent's forehead, nicking out a small bit of flesh.

Before Wolf Tail recovered, Bent snapped his head back with another shot to the chin, followed by a punch to Wolf Tail's Adam's apple. Wolf Tail emitted a strangled grunt as he slumped off Bent.

Bent rose shakily. As soon as he got to his feet, Wolf Tail rammed into him, knocking him right back down. "Son of a bitch," Bent snarled. He jerked an elbow up and out. It mashed Wolf Tail's nose, knocking him onto his back.

Bent got up with a bit more speed and confidence. He kicked Wolf Tail in the face as hard as he could. It wasn't with his usual strength, but it was enough to break Wolf Tail's left cheekbone.

Bent reared back for another kick, but Wolf Tail got him first, kicking him on the side of the right knee. "Shit," Bent muttered as his shoulder hit the hard-packed earth.

Wolf Tail grabbed his knife and dove at Bent, who warded off the weapon with his left forearm, suffering another cut in the process. Bent's right hand flew to his own knife. As Wolf Tail drew his blade back for another strike, Bent shoved his knife into Wolf Tail's chest. It hurt like hell to push the dying Indian off him and stand, but he did it.

William Bent charged at the first movement, slamming a forearm into Bull Nose's face like a runaway freight wagon. The Comanche grunted and snarled something in his own language. William was not paying any heed to the warrior's words. He simply reared back and let fly a fist.

Bull Nose was quicker than Bent had thought he'd be. The power of the blow hitting only air carried Bent forward and sideways. He realized with self-anger that his back was wide open to Bull Nose.

The Comanche whirled like a cat and pounced on him, trying to get a sweaty, greasy forearm around Bent's throat. He missed the throat and got the arm across the lower part of Bent's face. Bent clamped his teeth on the arm and bit for all he was worth.

Bull Nose did not vocally acknowledge the pain, but he did try to jerk the arm away. In so doing, his body moved back a little.

Bent snapped an elbow back. It cracked into Bull Nose's side, breaking a rib. Bent did it again, still not taking his teeth out of Bull Nose's arm. The second blow broke another rib, and Bent felt Bull Nose getting slack as he tried to compensate for the cracked bones.

Bent finally freed Bull Nose's arm from his teeth, but quickly grabbed the forearm in his left hand and twisted it. At the same time, he spun and shoved the arm away from him. That created an opening, and Bent slammed three quick punches into Bull Nose's broken ribs.

Bull Nose showed nothing, though Bent knew he had to be in considerable pain. Bent spit out the foul taste of Bull Nose's arm.

Bent moved swiftly, figuring to finish Bull Nose off quickly. But it seemed as if the Comanche was uninjured. Bull Nose grabbed his left forearm and yanked it forward. At the same time, he jerked a leg up. Bull Nose's knee caught Bent between the belly button and pubic area.

Bull Nose swung around behind him, jerking Bent's arm up and back. Bent hissed as ligaments stretched. He was a moment from having his arm broken. He snapped his head back, hitting Bull Nose in the face with the back of his head, then repeated it. He thought he could feel teeth loosen this time.

Once more, and Bull Nose lost his grip on Bent's arm. Bent jerked free, whirled and hit Bull Nose twice with a forearm—once in the forehead and once in the mangled mouth.

Bull Nose gasped once, then clasped his lips closed. He would show no fear, no pain, to this puny white man. Then Bent's knife darted out. There was nothing Bull Nose could do. One moment he was standing there staring at Bent, and the next, Bent's knife was buried hilt-deep in his guts. Bull Nose felt his knees grow weak, and he tried to keep himself upright. It was hard though.

Bent jerked the blade free and spun, crouching, in case one of his brothers needed his help. George appeared to be doing all right, but Charles was in trouble.

After the frozen moment of time staring at each other from inches away, Charles could feel the life slowly being squeezed out of him. He used what little leverage he could get and kicked Bad Knee in the shin three times. It did little good that Charles could tell.

Suddenly a fist appeared, smashing into Bad Knee's ear. Charles felt the Indian's grasp slacken. Then the fist came again.

Charles, using what little strength he had left, broke Bad Knee's grip. He shoved the Comanche away and then kicked him on his bad knee. The Indian's lame leg buckled and he started to fall. Charles helped, shoving the Comanche down and away.

The warrior bounced in the dirt, but immediately tried to get back up. Charles was not about to give him that chance. He swooped in, butcher knife raised. In moments Bad Knee was dead.

Charles Bent stood with his hands on his knees, gasping for all he was worth. "Thanks, little brother," he wheezed, looking at William.

The younger Bent had thrown the two punches. He too was having trouble breathing. "I figured you was gonna raise that bastard's hair sooner or later, but I was of no mind to see you take a week at it."

"Ten days'd be more like it," Charles said, failing to chuckle.

"Maybe a month," George added. He was the freshest of the three.

Owl Woman hurried up and shyly slipped an arm around William's waist. William smiled at her.

The three Bents turned to face the Comanches. "This can be the end of it, Old Wolf," William said, still panting.

The chief nodded. His face betrayed none of the pain he felt inside at the loss of his son, Bull Nose.

"You gonna leave our caravans alone?"

Once again the old man nodded.

"Take your men and bury them as you wish," William said quietly. "They fought bravely and died like men."

⟨41⟩

Summer lay heavy over Bent's Fort, like a soggy wool coat. Mosquitoes bred prolifically in the stagnant nooks and crannies of the Arkansas and plagued the area. Horseflies added their annoying presence, and gnats swept on waves of heated wind got in mouths and noses. The heat slapped the people in the fort with brutal malignancy.

Into this slice of hell walked the First Dragoons. The first arrivals were led by Tom Fitzpatrick, but within the week the other troops arrived, as did the commander —Colonel Steven Watts Kearny. War with Mexico was on now, and there would be no turning back from it.

For William Bent, the soldiers brought nothing but problems. The troops, having just survived a grueling march across the harsh plains, thought they were the cocks of the walk. They swaggered into the fort, casting lecherous glances at the Indian women who lived with fort employees. Lower-ranking officers demanded Bent's time to discuss, as all put it, the best place to camp for their men. After all, each unit had the best troops, who should have the most favorable camping sight, the commanders hinted not so subtly.

Bent tried insulating himself from these insidious whiners, but to no avail. Finally he went to Kearny, at the colonel's large tent set up among the shady trees along the river.

Kearny received Bent warmly, though with an imperial tone to his voice. They sat at a small table inside the tent. "Now, sir," Kearny said briskly, "what brings you to the tent of an old soldier?"

Bent was not deceived by Kearny's sincere tones. "I've had about enough of your goddamn company commanders pesterin' me every goddamn five minutes lookin' for the best goddamn place to camp," Bent said, managing to contain only a portion of the anger he felt.

"My apologies, Mr. Bent," Kearny said unctuously. "I'll see to it that they leave you alone."

Bent did not believe him for a minute. But there was little he could do. He might throw the annoying soldiers out of the fort, but that would only bring down Kearny's wrath. With a couple thousand soldiers at his command, the colonel could take over the fort lock, stock, and barrel. Bent sighed, nodded, stood, and walked out.

Increasing problems were encountered with the foot soldiers. The men, hardened by their trek to Bent's Fort, continued to strut and swagger around the fort, trying to impress the mountain men—and the women —with their toughness. They were quite unhappy at the prices MacGregor charged for tobacco, whiskey, food, and more, all of which was sold rapidly with the thousands of soldiers around.

A Missouri volunteer, Private Lem Richardson, who was almost out of tobacco, took exception when Mac-Gregor told him that the cost of tobacco was eight dollars a pound.

"Tha's goddamn rob'ry," Richardson said, voice thick and slurred from the rum he had consumed.

MacGregor shrugged, unconcerned.

"Son of a bitch," Richardson cursed, and started to haul out his pistol—one of the still-newfangled, .36 caliber five-shot cap-and-ball pistols.

MacGregor grabbed up the ax handle he always kept

within reach in the trade room. He whapped the soldier a good shot on the forehead.

Richardson grunted and his eyes rolled as he staggered backward out the door. MacGregor vaulted the counter and went after him. The trooper had fallen in the dust, but he again tried to get his pistol out. He managed it this time, but before he could cock it, MacGregor swatted him on the gun arm. The pistol dropped in the dirt.

"I dunna let anyone pull a gun on me, laddie," MacGregor said harshly. He began whacking the soldier with the ax handle, not hard enough to break bones, but hard enough to bring up welts all over.

"Hey, you son of a bitch," someone yelled. "Leave him alone." The soldier, a friend of Richardson's, charged MacGregor.

MacGregor was just about finished beating Richardson anyway, and he turned just in time to swat Private Dan Dalton in the left temple with the ax handle. Dalton went down, legs tangled together. Five more soldiers, most of them drunk, bellowed and headed toward MacGregor.

Suddenly a shot rang out. Everyone stopped, looking for the source. Bent was walking toward the combatants, a smoking pistol in his hand. Many of Bent's men lined the second floor walkway, weapons pointed at the dozen or so soldiers in the *placita*. More troopers, however, were pouring into the fort, all armed and looking grim.

Bent boldly walked to stand between the growing number of soldiers—most of them Missouri volunteers —and MacGregor, who stood waiting, apparently unconcerned. Richardson was all but unconscious. Dalton lay and moaned, holding his head in his hands.

"You boys best get the hell out of this fort," Bent said grimly.

"Like hell," a corporal said harshly. "I ain't about to

let you go 'round thumpin' the bejesus out of one of my men.''

Bent shrugged. ''If Ramsay's beatin' on him, he's got a goddamn good reason for it.''

''Horseshit.''

''Well, then you boys come on and commence this fight,'' Bent said harshly. ''We'll make dead beaver out of the lot of you festerin' pukes.'' Bent finally found an outlet for his anger and frustration. He was hellbent for going against some soldiers.

Soldiers were cocking pistols and rifles, spreading out, some aiming at Bent and MacGregor; most of them, though, were looking up, sighting on men on the second floor.

''Well?'' Bent asked. ''You boys gonna shit or get off the pot?''

Suddenly there was a hoarse bellow: ''Attention!''

The soldiers reacted slowly, but they were finally standing at attention, their rifles held by the muzzles, butts on the ground.

Bent watched as Alexander Doniphan, a colonel for the Missouri volunteers among the army force, strode up to stand beside him. He dwarfed the diminutive Bent. Doniphan was not only tall, but broad, with a thick, fleshy face and bristling black eyebrows.

''What's going on here, Corporal Marshall?'' Doniphan demanded.

''That crazy goddamn trader there was beatin' poor Richardson to death with that ax handle. When Private Dalton went to help him, that crazy son of a bitch started in on him.'' He looked smug. He and his men had elected Doniphan their colonel. He wouldn't let his own men down.

''Mr. Bent?'' Doniphan said. ''Is that truthful?''

Bent shrugged. ''You'll have to ask Mr. MacGregor.''

Doniphan did not turn, but spoke over his shoulder to MacGregor, ''Is that the way it happened, Mr. MacGregor?''

"Nae, Colonel." He explained it.

Doniphan watched Marshall, and could see in the corporal's face that MacGregor was telling the truth. When MacGregor finished his short narration, Doniphan said, "When Privates Richardson and Dalton have come to, you will bring them to me, Corporal. You understand?"

Marshall was still not concerned. He figured Doniphan would congratulate the men under the guise of punishment. He nodded.

"You, and those two, will carry sacks of sand between the fort and our camp, two hours on, two hours off, for three days. You, Corporal, will begin immediately. Privates Richardson and Dalton will begin when they are sufficiently recovered from their injuries."

Marshall's face was pale. "Beggin' your leave, Colonel," he stuttered, worried, "Mr. MacGregor's as much to blame as—"

Doniphan's face hardened. With the beetling brows and his size, he was imposing. "We are Missouri volunteers in the service of our country," he roared. "We are not back-street brawlers in the waterfront dives of St. Louis. As such, I expect the utmost obedience and courtesy to those who are helping us in our duties. Is that understood, Corporal?"

It was said in such a way that Marshall knew that with another rebellious word, he would no longer be a corporal. "Yes, sir," he said.

"The rest of you under my command are forbidden to enter this fort for three days. Corporal, assign a few men to drag that riffraff back to our camp. Dismissed!"

"My apologies, Mr. Bent," Doniphan said, when they were alone. He held out his hand. "I hope there're no hard feelings."

Bent shrugged, but he shook hands. Doniphan was one of the higher-ranking officers whom Bent and his brother George had had to entertain so frequently since their arrival. Bent had not known what to think of the man before, but he was impressed now.

"A favor, Mr. Bent, if I might impose even more on your hospitality?" Doniphan asked. Bent nodded, and Doniphan said, "A number of the men are ill." A look of distaste flitted across his broad features. "Dysentery is afflicting a couple dozen, and scurvy a few more. Lieutenant Abert has a raging fever for which we find no source. They'd be considerably more comfortable here than in the camps."

"That's a tough favor for me to fulfill, Colonel," Bent said as he stuck his pistol into his belt. "Your quartermasters keep lookin' for more storage space, which, as you can see, is rather limited. Your suppliers keep askin' for more supplies, supplies we no longer have. To accommodate the ailin' is almost impossible."

Doniphan sighed, but nodded. "Well, I'm obliged, Mr. Bent, for at least listening. And I'm obliged that you intervened in that little fracas before. It seems a miracle that no one was killed."

Bent nodded, more impressed with Doniphan. "We might not be able to put 'em up inside here," he said, "but why not set 'em up in tents right outside? The doctor could be stationed nearby, and any other injuries or illness could be placed there."

Doniphan nodded. "An excellent suggestion, Mr. Bent, considering the alternatives. Then, with your leave, sir, I'll go see to that. And again, thank you for your help."

Bent shook his head wearily as he watched Doniphan stride away. There seemed to be no end of troubles brought by the army. Adding to the woes were the Indians. The Cheyennes and Arapahos had had a poor summer of hunting, and many of them had come down to the fort to see what supplies they could get there to tide them over.

Bent had met with Sun Dog and other chiefs in the council room just after the Indians began arriving. Sun

Dog was in awe of the soldiers, because of their numbers. He had ridden out right after arriving, to find the end of the whites. But there seemed almost no end. From the fort he had ridden miles in each direction, and yet the whites continued. Between the poor hunting and the many whites he had seen, Sun Dog was thoroughly disheartened.

Bent told the Indian leaders that he was powerless to make the army go away—since both he and the Cheyennes figured it was the army's movement that had caused the poor hunting. Nor did he have the power to fill his larders with trade goods and supplies. What goods hadn't been bought by the army were of little use to the Indians.

Bent felt sorry for his friends, though, and gave them a couple dozen of the poorer mules and horses. The Cheyennes and Arapahos were not fond of eating horse meat or mule meat, but they had done it before. They would make do now, especially since Little White Man promised to help more once the army had gone on its way. There was nothing else they could do anyway. Still worried for their families, the chiefs headed forlornly back to their camps north of the fort.

Troubles remained at the fort, as the tension between the fort's employees and the army escalated. Still, in some ways there were fewer problems, since the fort had run out of almost all supplies, and the soldiers had about run out of cash. With little liquor left in the fort, and little cash left in soldiers' pockets, trouble was trimmed considerably.

With all the activity around the fort these days, it was hard to keep track of newcomers. Fort laborers would see many men they did not know, but they were afraid to tell Bent, lest they be mistaken and the visitors were friends of the *bourgeois*.

Longtime employees and old friends, however, had no such compunction. If they spotted someone they thought suspicious, they would report it to Bent right away. Most often they were mistaken in suspecting the men of some wrongdoing, but it did bear fruit one day.

Three Mexicans strolled into the fort one afternoon, looking for all the world like they belonged there. Emiliano Flores watched the three. He was on the second floor, leaning against a wall, enjoying a cigarillo and speaking with one of the men in his trading crew. He narrowed his eyes when he saw the three men. Flores dropped the burning corn-husk-wrapped cigarette and stepped on it. "Come," he said to his companion.

There was no question that the man would. Flores had Ortega's job in his hand. One word from Flores, and Ortega would be a beggar in the streets of San Miguel. Flores strode up to the three newcomers, with Ortega right behind him. The two stopped in front of the three. "What do you want here?" Flores asked in Spanish.

The three took in Flores's colorful shirt under the short Taos-style jacket; the slightly flared pants with *conchos* down each side; the blanket *botas* on his lower legs; the fine sombrero. Most of all, they took in the two big double-shot pistols in the red sash around Flores's waist.

"We're looking for work," one answered in Spanish.

Flores did not believe for a moment that they were seeking employment. There were no settlements around here, and three men would not ride all the way up here to the fort on the possibility of finding work. "What are your names?" he asked.

"Estevan Rodriguez," the one who had spoken before said. He pointed to his right, "Roberto Sena," and he indicated the man on his left, "Miguel Naranjo."

"Where have you come from?" Flores's voice got a little harder.

"A trading post in the San Luis Valley."

"You're full of shit," Flores snapped.

"I won't take that from any man," Rodriguez said. He produced a dagger from under his serape.

Flores ripped out one of his pistols and clubbed Rodriguez atop the head with it. Rodriguez went down, dropping the dagger. Naranjo and Sena said nothing, but looked quite scared.

"You two," Flores said to Naranjo and Sena, "pick up your *compadre* there and then march." Flores pointed to Bent's office.

Sena and Naranjo picked up Rodriguez and started walking toward Bent's office. Ortega knocked on the door. When Bent called, "Enter," Ortega stepped inside, followed by the three visitors and then Flores.

"What's this about, Yano?" Bent eyed the newcomers suspiciously.

"I found these hombres wandering around the *placita*, *Jefe*. I've never seen them before, and I don't think they're here for any good."

"Oh?" Bent cocked his eyebrows at Flores.

"They say they've come from one of the trading posts out in the San Luis Valley, and that they're looking for work."

"That doesn't seem right, now does it?"

"No, *Jefe*."

"Search 'em," Bent ordered. "See if they have any papers on 'em."

Within moments Flores handed Bent a piece of paper. "Colonel Kearny's name's on it."

Bent took the paper, still staring at the three men, and opened it.

"What's there, *Jefe*?" Flores asked.

"Not a goddamn thing." He rose and stood in front of the three. "I'd say you boys are spies. That right?"

Sena pulled himself up as straight as he could, then launched into a blistering tirade of Spanish. He stopped when Flores clouted him on the back of the head with his pistol. "Speak English to Capitán Bent."

The man had sagged from the blow but had not fallen. "We are spies for Governor Armijo," he said proudly. His accent was not very evident. "We were to use that paper to get past the sentries."

Bent sat again, tapping the paper against a thumb as he thought. Then he nodded. "You want to see what the army's got, then by Christ, you'll get to see." He looked at Flores. "They have any weapons?"

Flores shrugged, then told Ortega to search the men. All he came up with was two knives. He tossed them on Bent's desk.

Bent nodded. "Mr. Ortega, please go saddle horses for Yano and me, and mules for these three hombres." When Ortega left, Bent said, "Yano, bind them." He pointed to Rodriguez, Sena, and Naranjo.

Three hours later the Mexican spies were heading out of the fort. They had no weapons, but Bent saw that they had a little food and the mules. They had been taken through some of the army camps, and then were brought before Kearny, who explained the futility of resistance.

Rodriguez and his two companions believed Kearny. They had seen the number of soldiers, plus the munitions, cannon, twenty thousand or so horses, huge wagonloads of supplies. They were convinced that Mexico did not have a chance against these invaders.

"Think they'll change Armijo's mind?" Kearny asked as he, Bent, and Flores watched the three spies riding off.

Bent shrugged. "Even if they don't convince Armijo, it'll still give him somethin' to cogitate on."

{42}

"I'd like you to form a small company of scouts, Mr. Bent," Colonel Kearny said. It sounded like an order. He had asked for a meeting with Bent, who opened the fort's council room for it. "I want you to lead it. We'll need you to scout Raton Pass and beyond, all the way to Santa Fe, to make sure General Armijo has not set a trap for us."

"Reckon I could do that," Bent said, his voice reflecting his disinterest. All he really wanted was for the damn army to be gone.

"Good. I'm prepared to offer a hundred dollars for your services."

Bent was livid. "That's a goddamn insult," he snapped, barely containing his anger. "You've taken over my fort for weeks, stripped me of all my supplies, overtaxed my repair shops and my workers. You've abused the Indians and my freighters. And a heap more, dammit. You either pay me what this's worth or you can kiss my ass, Colonel." He stomped out, leaving a shocked Kearny sitting there flabbergasted.

Kearny sent Colonel Alexander Doniphan to the fort the next day to mend fences between Bent and himself.

"Nobody knows more about these lands than you, Bill," Doniphan said. "Besides, you're the only man who'll command enough respect."

"How much is he willin' to pay?" Bent demanded.

He found it hard to be angry at Doniphan, who had become a friend.

"He told me to dicker with you," Doniphan said with a sly grin.

"What's the top?" Bent asked, a smile tugging at his lips.

"Five hundred," Doniphan laughed.

"Each?"

Doniphan nodded. "Up to eight."

"Sold," Bent said. "When's he want us to leave?"

"Tomorrow."

Bent nodded. "We'll be gone come first light."

The next morning, Bent, Walsh, Flores, Solomon, Honnicker, Ramsay MacGregor, and Red Water rode out. It was still two hours before dawn, but Bent wanted to get well away from the fort and the awakening army. George Bent was being left behind at the fort. He had objected to that, but then William told him in no uncertain terms that that was the way it was going to be, and if Georgie didn't like it, he could wrassle the whole scouting party for the chance to go along. George quickly decided that staying behind was the better part of valor.

They pushed hard awhile and then slowed, not wanting to overtax their horses. They were traveling light, and knew the trail well, so they foresaw no trouble with the trail. Armijo's army would be an entirely different matter.

They moved slowly down the Purgatoire, and eventually away from it, heading into the rocky defiles of Raton Pass. They stopped early that night, since they had left so early. Bent also didn't want to get too far ahead of the army, in case they had to face Mexican soldiers.

The next day was the same—riding a steep, rock-cluttered trail that all the men had been on more times than they could count. It was hotter than blazes, with no clouds to cut the sun's viciousness.

The men took turns riding out ahead of the group,

checking the trail; the rest of the time they were bored. Once again they called an early halt. They were just past the crest of Raton Pass, and pulled into a copse of pines and junipers along Raton Creek.

The men had been together so long that there was no need for them to sit and jabber around the fire. None needed or wanted to tell tall tales. If anyone did talk, it was usually what the man thought he and the others would face down here in Mexico.

They found their answer the next morning. Red Water had gone out to reconnoiter while the others broke camp, such as it was. He galloped in twenty minutes after he had ridden out.

"Damn Mexicans," Red Water said as he jumped out of the saddle.

"How many?" Bent asked.

Red Water shrugged. "More'n us."

"Goddammit, Red Water," Walsh snapped, "can't you ever answer a goddamn question straight?"

Red Water laughed, his barrel-shaped body shaking with humor. "I can't say. There's more'n us, less'n the whole goddamn Mexican army."

"Hey, Cap'n," Walsh called, "you mind if'n I take my 'hawk to this stump-humpin' Delaware?"

Bent shook his head. "Probably wouldn't learn nothin' that way, and you'd have a stove-up 'hawk besides."

Red Water laughed a little more. "I say they have maybe fifty, maybe sixty of 'em."

"Damn, *Jefe*," Flores said, "we could be in big troubles here."

"I expect that's so. But I figure we'll find out just what kind of men Armijo's got working for him."

The men moved up a half mile and then split into two groups, one on each side of the trail. Due south, the pass trail stretched out straight for a quarter of a mile or so. There was really no protection for the Mexicans on the sides of the trail, since each side was virtually nothing but cliff. Only a few boulders shaken down to the trail in a bygone age would allow some safety. It was the most advantageous position Bent's small force could get.

"Think one of us ought to ride for help, Cap'n?" Honnicker asked.

"Hell, them army fellers ain't gonna get here in no time to help," Bent replied. "Nope. I reckon we'll just have to show these boys what goin' against some old mountaineers means."

"You did hear about that trouble down there in San Antonio, didn't you, Cap'n?" Walsh asked calmly.

"That where Santa Ana's men overran that old mission?"

"Yep," Walsh said, spitting some tobacco juice. "I hear tell there was nigh onto six thousand of them greaser soldiers, and less'n two hundred Americans. Kind of reminds me of our position right here. Them Mexicans get it in their minds to overrun this place, there ain't gonna be shit we can do to stop it."

Bent shrugged. "We all got to cross the divide some day," he said evenly. "If I can take a couple soldiers with me, I won't be too melancholy about it."

"Well me neither, goddammit," Walsh said with a laugh.

Half an hour later the first soldiers came into view as they turned a curve and started up the straight stretch.

Bent glanced across the trail, which was about fifty yards wide at this point. He received a reassuring nod from MacGregor across the way.

Both forces were buried deep amid boulders scaling up the side of the pass. It would be very difficult, at best, for the soldiers to pick anyone off; not impossible, but difficult. The horses were tethered to some small trees as far back from the trail as the men could get them.

Seth Walsh was a better rifle shot than Bent, and to him would go the "honor" of firing the first round.

When the first soldiers were less than a hundred yards away, Bent said, "Let's commence this *fandango.*"

Walsh fired, and a soldier in the front rank fell. The sound of the shot slapped off the mountain wall and then back.

The mountain men opened up. Firing evenly spaced volleys, they decimated the first several ranks of foot soldiers. The arrival of mounted troops forcing their way forward did little to stem the destruction. Finally an officer reared his horse and shouted at his men. The soldiers turned and fled, leaving more than a dozen dead men and several dead horses behind.

"That'll show you sons a bitches!" Walsh bellowed.

Then the men waited. Almost an hour passed before the troops came at them again. This time a dozen riders roared around the curve and jammed their horses to a stop, pulling them down as they did. Each man had a pistol in hand, and as their horses fell, they shot the animals. Then they hunkered down behind the still-quivering wall of horseflesh.

Moments later foot soldiers raced around the curve and flung themselves behind the flesh barrier.

Walsh chuckled. "They got enough horses, they could climb right up here into our laps," he said.

"I sure as hell hope they ain't got that many horses," Bent said. Like Walsh, he did not seem too concerned.

The two groups sniped at each other through most of the day, not hitting much but not allowing the other side to do much but sit behind whatever protection they had.

Sometime about an hour or so before darkness was expected to fall, the Mexican side got very quiet. "Them boys're plannin' something, sure as shit," Walsh said.

Bent nodded. The statement did not need a comment. But he looked across the trail and shouted for MacGregor. When he heard the crusty Scot's "Aye?" Bent said, "Best be prepared."

"We are, laddie."

Moments later the whole force of soldiers, screaming at the top of their lungs, raced around the curve on foot.

"Sweet Jesus," Honnicker breathed.

"Amen," Walsh added as he fired.

Only their well-protected positions saved Bent and his men. Close to fifty soldiers had come around the curve at the same time. In a less defensible spot, Bent's men would have been overrun easily. As it was, they had more than their share of trouble.

Five soldiers went down in the first volley; seven in the second. As Bent's men fired a third, the first wave of running soldiers scrambled over the rocks shielding Bent's men on both sides of the trail.

Bent's men got off two more volleys with their pistols before the tide began to sweep over them. The soldiers had trouble climbing through the rocks, and because of it they could not manage to make a concerted effort; there simply was not enough room.

Bent's men fought desperately, wildly. They used tomahawks, war clubs, knives, even rocks. They wielded their rifles like clubs, and fought by hand when it came to that.

Then the soldiers were gone, running down off the rocks faster than they had run up them. Several mounted officers screeched orders, but in the din of the fading battle, Bent's men could not tell if the officers were ordering a retreat or another assault.

Calm finally settled in. Bent's men warily stood and looked around, a little dazed by what had happened. "Ramsay!" Bent shouted, his voice breaking. He had not realized until now that he had added his voice to the many others yelling in the heat of battle. He cleared his throat and shouted again. His voice was closer to normal this time.

"Aye, Bill?"

"You lose any men?"

"Aye. Red Water was killed in the last rush." Mac-Gregor had never cared much for the Delaware, but he had been glad to have the Indian on his side during this battle. "Ye?"

Bent nodded, then shouted: "Art Honnicker. He gave a good account of himself, though."

Bent sent Flores to scout out the trail ahead. It was clear, Flores soon reported. He could see the dust of the Mexican soldiers fading away. He also had found a soldier—an officer—who was wounded but alive. He brought the man to Bent.

"Ask him how many more soldiers are 'tween us'n Taos," Bent said.

Flores asked the question in Spanish, got the answer, and translated it. "He says none. He says that Armijo has taken nearly all his forces east toward Texas."

"Do you believe him?" Bent asked.

"Maybe not fully, but enough. I think the way is clear."

"Then we'd best find out."

43

The scouting mission was quite a success. Bent and his men had ridden all the way to Taos unmolested. Somewhere deep in Raton Pass they had buried Honnicker and Red Water. Then they moved on, encountering no one other than peons all the way to Taos.

Finally they headed back toward Raton Pass. Just on the southern side of it, they met Kearny and his army.

"You saw action?" Kearny—who had received his promotion to general along the route—asked.

"Some," Bent answered. "Lost two men, but, by Christ, we cleared the way for you down to Taos. You won't have no worries about it now."

Later Bent learned that Kearny had marched all the way into Santa Fe without a shot being fired.

Figuring the army was out of his hair, Bent and his men turned and headed back to the fort. But Bent found out that he was still plagued by the army. Supplies for the soldiers were still arriving at the fort, the rendezvous point for the force, much faster than they were leaving to chase after Kearny. Army goods were piled up. Men and wagons to move them were difficult to come by, and tempers were short again.

One of the things that helped keep Bent's temper in check was some news. A courier had raced into the sweltering *placita* three weeks after Bent had returned to the fort. Bent read the dispatch and let out a whoop.

George charged out of the trade room, expecting

trouble. Anyone else within hearing distance looked down at Bent as if he had suddenly lost his mind. "What the hell's got you so worked up, Bill?" George asked as he ran up to his brother.

"Listen to this, boys," William shouted, wanting everyone to hear the good news. "Charlie's been named governor of northern Mexico! Them's shinin' doin's for certain."

With the help of his men, Bent appropriated some of the army's supplies and broke out the small hidden stash of fort whiskey. That night the *placita* reveled in the news. Tin whistles, fiddles, and guitars provided music as fort employees danced with Mexican women. With the whiskey flowing, the Bents kept the Cheyennes and Arapahos out, barring the oak doors as soon as darkness came. The only Indians inside then were the Indian wives of some of the men, including Owl Woman.

The next day was a slow one, with nearly all the men suffering hangovers. Men grumbled as the remaining army traders and troops loaded wagons and sent them on their way.

Eventually, though, the last supplies were moved out and something resembling normalcy returned to the fort. The relative quiet was almost exquisite.

There was plenty of work to be done yet, though. With Charles now the governor of Nueva Mexico, George was given the responsibility of leading the wagon trains between the fort and Independence, and between the stores in New Mexico and the settlements.

The Bents got the fall wagons out shortly after the army left. It was tough waiting for the caravan to return, since the fort was low on just about everything.

George returned three days after a blizzard had swept across the plains with a biting wind driving thick, wet snow ahead of it in roaring gusts. In the fort, William and his employees waited it out, knowing that in less than a week they would be facing starving times.

The sun broke through two days later, but its warmth was almost nonexistent. When the wagons did roll in the next afternoon, a loud cheer went up from everyone.

The trains discharged much of their cargo and then pulled out for Taos and Santa Fe. They were blessed by the weather this time, as Indian summer replaced the wintry storms.

When winter did return, however, it did so with a vengeance. The fort hunkered down to wait it out, for the most part. With a welcome respite from the storms, William left the fort in the hands of his brother George and Marcellin. He took Owl Woman and their children to Big Timbers, east of the fort. Bent had a small cabin there, and he had agreed to meet some of the Cheyennes for a little trading, storytelling, and visiting.

He was so employed when a rider raced into the camp. Half frozen, his beard and mustache coated with ice, Louis Simonds tumbled off his blowing horse and stumbled into Bent's cabin. "Where's Bill?" he asked, breathing harshly and erratically.

"Jesus, Lou," Walsh said, alarmed. "You look more'n half done in."

"I am, by God. But I got to talk to Bill. Get him here. Pronto!"

Walsh nodded. "Yano, get Lou some grub and coffee. I'll be back quick." He ran outside and leaped on the first horse he found. Bareback, he galloped off to where Bent was visiting Black Feather's lodge.

Without bothering with amenities, Walsh charged into the tipi. He knew the others would be reaching for weapons, but he didn't care. Worry stabbed at his insides. "Bill, you're needed back at your lodge."

Bent looked at Walsh. He had never seen his big, fearless, longtime friend looking so distraught. "What is it, Seth?" he asked.

"I ain't sure. All I know is that Lou Simonds charged in a couple minutes ago. He looks half dead, and he's real agitated. I figure somethin's gone wrong some-where.''

Bent nodded and jumped up. He and Walsh raced outside and galloped hard for Bent's wood lodge.

Simonds was still wolfing down bolts of pemmican and gulps of hot coffee when Bent and Walsh ran into the room. Simonds looked up, eyes bleary from hunger, cold, and sickness of heart. He set down the piece of bread he was holding.

"Jesus, Bill, this's harder'n any goddamn thing this chil's ary done," Simonds said.

Bent nodded and took the seat across the table from Simonds. "Just tell it, Lou. It's best done quick if it's bad."

"The worst, Bill, the abso-goddamn-lute goddamn worst." He seemed on the verge of tears. "Jesus." He sucked in a breath and let it ease out. "Charlie's dead, Bill."

"Dead?" The word cut through Bent's heart like a knife. Trouble was, he heard it, but he could not believe it. "How?"

"All Taos is up in arms. The goddamn greasers and son of a bitchin' Taoseños have gone loco. They're rampagin' through the city, killin' every American they find."

Bent wanted to cry or scream or hit something. But none of that would change the facts. He kept himself in tight control, forcing the sickness in his belly to stay there. He would grieve later—after he killed the sons of bitches who'd committed such an atrocity. "What happened to him?" Bent asked, lips tight.

"Shot him through several times," Simonds said, voice hardly a whisper. "Then they . . . they . . . Jesus, Mary, and Joseph . . ." He choked out the words only with difficulty. "They scalped him." His chest was tight with anguish, knowing how Bent felt. "They fuckin' raised his hair."

"Ignacia and the kids—they all right?" Bent asked,

his voice cold as the day outside and as hard as a piece of petrified wood.

"Ain't sure. I think they got out."

Bent nodded. "Leave me alone, boys," he said quietly.

The others went outside into the biting cold wind. Somebody saw Simonds shaking from the cold and threw a blanket around him.

Emiliano Flores was more frightened than he had ever been before, but not for himself. He was afraid for his *patrón*. Had it not been for Bill Bent, Flores knew he'd still be living a peon's existence in Taos. Now he wanted to do something, anything, to help ease Bent's pain, to help in some way to make things right again. He didn't know what, though.

Then it dawned on him. Like Bent, Flores had taken a Cheyenne wife. Her people would help. He momentarily considered explaining his plan to Walsh, but decided there was no time. He slipped away from the others and jumped on a horse. Minutes later he was babbling his tale to Winter Hawk, his brother-in-law, and many other warriors.

Bent stepped out of the cabin and stared at the twenty-five Cheyenne warriors who were mounted on their ponies. The Cheyennes were painted, and they carried their shields, lances, guns, and bows. In front of the Cheyennes, Bent's American companions stood, armed.

"We're ready to go, Cap'n," Walsh said quietly.

Bent nodded. "What're you doin' here, Sun Dog?" he asked.

"We will go with you to fight the white-eyes who have done this wrong," Sun Dog said quietly, dignity in every word. "You and White Hat and Black Beard have helped the People many times. Now we will help you." All the other Cheyennes solemnly nodded their agreement.

Bent sighed. He would like the help, but knew it would only cause trouble. "Thank you, Sun Dog," he said in Cheyenne. "It fills my heart with good to hear of your willingness to sacrifice for us. But this is a white man's fight, and it'll be decided by white men."

"But—"

Bent shook his head. "You must stay here, with your wives, your children," he said in Cheyenne. "Keep them safe. If the Mexicans attack here, you'll be needed. Watch over your own families, and if you want to help me, you must watch over Owl Woman and my children."

"They'll be as safe as if they were in your stone lodge."

Bent nodded and went to get his horse as the Cheyennes rode back to their camp. In moments Bent and his friends headed back to the fort.

George Bent's eyes were bright with rage and a desire for vengeance. "When're we leavin', Bill?" he asked harshly.

"Soon's we can round up the boys and pack up a few supplies."

An army captain at the fort was dead set against lending even a small escort to the traders. Bent nodded. He had neither the time nor the inclination to argue. He gathered all twenty-three of his men. "I want volunteers to head to Taos and repay them bastards. Who's with me?"

Twenty-three men's hands went up. "*Bueno*. Let's make ready. Powder, ball, and other necessary possibles are on the company. Ramsay'll hand it out over at the trade room."

"Where're we gonna get horses, Cap'n?" he asked.

The army had grabbed up most of the horses in the area, leaving barely enough for a few of the men in the fort. There were none to spare here. He wished he had taken some from the Cheyennes. It was too late for that now, though.

"Those who got animals can ride. Those that ain't can double up. Head for the ranches along the Purgatoire. We've got horses there."

As Bent and his men were preparing to leave, one of the company traders arrived with a supply train from the company's ranches. As soon as he heard Bent's plan, he, George Bent, Seth Walsh, and Lieutenant Jackson went to see William Bent.

"I ain't of a kind to tell you what to do, Bill," Frank De Lisle said. "But I suspect a goddamn Mexican army is on the way here. It's the most logical thing for them to do. Once they overtake Taos, which seems a done fact, they'll be certain to come after this place."

"Much as I hate to admit it, Bill," his brother said, "Frank's right."

"So?" William said.

"You ought to stay here, Bill," George said.

"No." Bent shook his head. "Me'n Charlie was the closest. You know that, Georgie. I aim to be there to pay those bastards back."

"If them goddamned Mexicans attack the fort, somebody who knows what's what should be here, Bill," George said.

Bent's brow knotted. His heart told him to ride for Taos as fast as possible and extract a full measure of revenge. His head, however, told him his brother was right—to some extent. "Leave me'n George alone a few minutes, boys." When the others had left, William said harshly, "You stay here, Georgie. I'll leave a few of the boys with you."

"No!" George shouted. "You left me out last time."

"You'll stay here or I'll throw you in irons." William was enraged.

"Dammit, Bill—"

"Shut up. We ain't got time for such bullshit. If the rebellion moves up here, it'll likely mean we've all been put under. That means there should be someone can be trusted—somebody in the family—here."

"Bill," George said coldly, "Charlie was my brother too."

"I know, Georgie," William said, clapping a hand on his brother's shoulder. "But you ain't as used to these doin's as the rest of us. It don't make you no less of a man." He paused. "In some ways, Georgie, holdin' this fort against the Mexicans is more important than vengeance."

George looked at his brother. The younger man's eyes were misty. Then he nodded sadly. "All right," he sighed. "But there's one more thing—Dick Green says he wants to go along."

William shrugged. "It ain't my decision."

"Yes it is, Bill. He's yours now that Charlie's rubbed out." He still had trouble believing that. "Him and Charlotte both."

William nodded once more. "I got no problem with him goin', if you and the others don't mind."

"Ain't any one of our boys gonna say no to Dick comin' along," George said flatly.

{ 44 }

The ride was frigid, made even more so by the depth of despair the men felt. All of them—Seth Walsh, Solomon, Emiliano Flores, Dick Green, Luis Saltillo, Ramsay MacGregor, and the fourteen others who went along—thought of Charles Bent as a friend; in many cases, more. His loss was almost as great for them as it was for his two brothers.

The rage they felt, though, helped keep them warm on the long, bitter ride. Most of the men rode double. A small wagon brought up the rear. It was pulled by two mules and was loaded with the men's tack.

Half a day of hard riding against the slick, crusted snow and ice brought them to William Bent's ranch along the Purgatoire River. Their stop there was short, lasting just long enough for the men to down a hot, fast meal and a couple cups of coffee. Then they saddled horses and pulled out. Two of Bent's workers at the ranch—Gabe Foxworthy and Jarrod Harker—asked to come along. Bent nodded.

Then someone mentioned that by allowing the two men to come along, the ranch would have no one left to care for the animals.

Bent nodded again. "Gabe, Jarrod, one of you has to stay."

"Somebody got some cards?" Foxworthy asked. Someone held out a worn deck of playing cards. "Pick one, Jarrod. High card goes with Cap'n Bent. Other'n stays here."

Harker nodded and pulled out a card. "Ten of spades," he said.

Foxworthy took a deep breath, let it out and picked a card. He held it out, face up, showing the king of diamonds.

"Lucky bastard," Harker said in regret.

"Let's go, dammit," Bent snapped.

The men rode out, leaving the wagon behind, but bringing a few extra horses. They stopped that night only because they had to. The horses were worn from being pressed so hard on the slick ice and clinging snow. The bitter cold temperatures didn't help man nor beast.

It was well past dark when they stopped—in a spot half a mile from where Bent's small force had stood off part of Armijo's army. Supper was hasty and ill-prepared. It was enough just to get some hot coffee and a few chunks of half-raw meat into their bellies.

The men were breaking camp when Walsh called, "Rider comin'."

The men grabbed pistols and rifles and turned. Then, "Well, I'll be damned," Walsh said quietly. Louder, he said, "It's Blackfoot John."

Smith stopped and dismounted. He had icicles on his mustache and beard, and his face was blue from the cold.

"What'n hell're you doin' here?" Bent asked.

"I heard," Smith said quietly, with none of his usual arrogance.

"So?" Bent's voice was cold.

"Me'n you—and your brothers—have had us our differences, Bill," Smith said evenly. "That don't mean I didn't respect Charlie. Or you either. I come to pay my respects to Charlie," he added, voice harder. "The only way I know how." He patted the pistols in the belt, holding his blanket coat closed.

Bent nodded solemnly. He turned. "One of you boys get him coffee, and there should be some meat left. Another of you take his tack and saddle one of the horses from our cavvy for him."

Smith nodded when Solomon handed him a tin cup of coffee.

Twenty minutes later they were on the trail again.

The squalid mud houses, covered with enough powdery snow to give them almost a friendly look, finally came into view. Even from a quarter mile out they could see the surging throngs of men whooping it up and firing weapons.

"It appears they've slacked off their riotous behavior," Lou Simonds said. Having seen the beginnings of it, he was in a good position to judge. "Still, there seems to be enough of 'em causin' their deviltry."

Bent nodded and pulled his rifle from the blanket case. He checked the lock to make sure it had not frozen. He did the same with his two belt pistols and the two horse pistols. The others followed suit.

Bent suddenly put spurs to his horse, bolting down the ice-coated track leading toward the plaza. Twenty-two men followed, silent and deadly, relentless.

One of the rioters glanced north and saw two dozen or so fearsome figures thundering toward him. He turned to flee, but ran into a wall of flesh. He screamed and shouted, trying to get some attention, to warn his friends of the ghostly, ghastly army flying toward them.

But his feeble voice was no match for the concerted screaming of a hundred men. He suddenly felt a punch in his back, and he thought someone had hit him. He tried to turn, to see who would do such a thing. But he could not turn. He felt himself slipping toward a permanent darkness.

The sound of one shot, of two dozen shots, did not alert the mob. Gunshots had been going off almost constantly for more than a week now. Even men falling bloody to the ground could not elicit a response from the rebels.

Bent and his men slammed into the crowd. Men screamed and bellowed, guns fired, horses whinnied and reared. So packed was the mob that a score or more went down under the steel hooves of nervous horses. Gunfire lay waste to more of the mob.

The mob broke up as the men began scattering, trying to get away from this maniacal force. As they encountered more of their friends, the stories about the attackers grew more and more. By the time Bent and his men had hacked, slashed, and shot their way to the plaza, stories were circulating through Taos of men ten feet tall riding monstrous horses and wielding the scythe of the Grim Reaper himself. More than one man dropped to his knees, besieging his patron saint, begging for succor from the devilish intruders.

Bent and his men made it to the plaza. They stopped and reloaded, not quite sure what they should be doing. Their blood was still boiling, urging them to kill some more. But there was no one left to kill now. They stood alone in the plaza.

The wind swirled and blew in frigid gusts over the low roofs of the adobe houses. A shutter clacked somewhere, and the wind made a church bell toll softly and irregularly. Hooves crunched on the icy ground, and freezing saddle leather creaked.

"What now, Cap'n?" Walsh asked.

Bent shrugged. He was no more sure of this than his men were. His ears perked up, though, when he heard what seemed to be another mob, off to the southwest a little. "Let's go," he said grimly.

Three blocks from the plaza, they found a mob of several hundred. The men were armed with a few guns, some bows and lances, and anything else they could use for weapons—scythes, machetes, pitchforks. The leaders of the mob saw Bent's force and knew instantly that this was the group that had driven their *compadres* out of the plaza. They turned and charged.

Bent's fury was awesome, but it was matched by that of his men. Big Seth Walsh fought with a wild abandon, battering men with a war club and the old trade musket he carried as a spare. One of Bent's men—Ramón Avilla—went down, lost amid the swirl of flesh and bone.

Bent smashed a rebel in the face with the butt of his rifle, and cast around with wild eyes. A man grabbed his leg and tried to pull him from his horse. Bent clubbed the man on top of the head with his rifle. As the man's grip loosened, Bent kicked him in the face. The man disappeared, trampled under the feet of men and the hooves of horses.

There was no sense, no reason to any of this, Bent thought in a moment of lucidity. One simply swung what one had in hand at whatever moved. One thing that was clear about all this, though, was that Bent's small force was horribly outnumbered. Worse, more and more rebels were pouring into the small, crooked street.

"Ride!" Bent screamed with as much voice as he had. "Ride!" He spurred his horse, forcing the animal to part the mob swirling around him. The horse—the reddish roan that once belonged to Bull Hump—did not like this crush of bodies around him. But the pony, used to dealing with irascible buffalo, answered Bent's call.

Little by little Bent worked though the mob. It came at great cost to the rebels, though, as Bent smashed and hacked his way inch by inch. Suddenly he was free of the mob. He spun his horse, and ice clutched at his heart. Some of his men looked to be hopelessly surrounded.

He and Seth Walsh barged back into the melee. Two more of Bent's fighters were down, and Bent had to give them up for lost. There was no way anyone could survive being at the bottom of this deadly fracas.

He and Walsh made progress, and at last the two got to where most of the others were. Forming a tight, vicious circle of men, they once more worked their way toward the fringes of the mob. Bent was sure they were all going to die soon. He didn't mind that so much, but he was determined to take as many of these murderous rebels as he could with him when he went under. And he didn't think that time had come yet.

After what seemed an eternity, Bent and his remaining men managed to get away from the mob by working through a narrow adobe archway into a courtyard. The mob could only get two or three men at a time through the entryway, and as soon as they did, they were battered down. Within minutes the mob began smashing down the adobe wall.

"We're in deep shit, Cap'n," Walsh said calmly.

"I hadn't noticed, Mr. Walsh," Bent said dryly. "But we best get our asses out of here and pronto." He paused. "Go on and see if you can find us a way out of here, Seth."

The big man nodded and moved off on his horse. He returned in minutes. The wall was coming down at a much quicker pace now that some holes had been made. "We can make it out there, Cap'n," Walsh reported. "There ain't nobody there now, so we'd best get a move on."

Bent nodded. "Let's go, boys," he roared. Letting Walsh take the lead, they raced around the side of the house and out another gate that had been broken open.

They entered another small street and swung west, not knowing for sure where they were going—or even where they wanted to go. A surging mob popped up down another street to their left. They swung up a third street, only to find a mob there too.

"This ain't goin' so well, Cap'n," Walsh said.

"It's goin' just fine for them assholes," Bent said bitterly. It was clear now that the mob was herding Bent's small force toward the plaza. Once there, Bent's men would be at their mercy, with no place to run.

Bent knew that was what was happening, but he was powerless to change it. "You know what they're doin', don't you, Seth?" he asked.

The big man nodded.

"I figure we're gonna go under here. And soon."

"Yep."

"So I figure to go out like a Cheyenne."

Walsh nodded again. He knew Bent planned to stake himself out and try to kill as many rebels as he could, never leaving his spot. Though he didn't have a sash to peg down, he felt the same in spirit.

"You get a chance, you and the boys haul ass."

"Shit, Cap'n," Walsh snorted. "I been with you since the beginnin'. Goddamn, back to 'thirty. We weren't more'n a couple of young snots lookin' to take on the world."

Bent laughed tightly. "Just like now."

"Yep." He paused. "I ain't goin' nowhere, Cap'n," he said firmly. "And I don't reckon none of the other boys'll do so neither."

Bent nodded. They had been talking while on the move, being shuttled from one street to another, kept just far enough from the mobs so that they couldn't do much but let themselves be herded.

Now they found themselves back in the plaza again, surrounded by Mexicans and Taos Indians screaming for their blood. The noose began tightening. Bent loaded his two pistols. *"Adios, amigo,"* he said.

"Vaya con Dios, Cap'n," Walsh responded.

Everything seemed to stop all at once. Bent could see the first line or two of rebels in utmost clarity. It was a startling thing to him. The mob, now numbering more than five hundred, Bent estimated, had stopped, giving his men a few moments to ponder their impending doom. Then one man in the mob stepped forward. He held a pistol in one hand and a sword in the other. Bent shot him. The mob seemed to take a collective deep breath, preparing to charge.

Then there was a wild screech. Bent shook his head, trying to clear his ears. He could have sworn the sound did not come from the mob.

Nearly a hundred Cheyenne and Arapaho warriors —led by Winter Hawk, Black Feather, and Sun Dog— charged around the corner and into the plaza. The painted Indians thundered into the mob, tomahawks and lances doing their bloody work.

"Hot damn, Cap'n!" Walsh bellowed. "Lookee there." He kicked his horse and followed the Cheyennes into the fray. Bent and the rest of his men were right behind him.

Nearby, Flores grinned slyly. It wasn't for naught that he had taken a few more minutes than the others before leaving the cabin in Big Timbers. Now he had another secret—one that his *jefe*, William Bent, did not know. He was happy to have been able to help in such a way.

Slowly the combined force drove the mob back. Numerous bodies lay on the frozen ground, tracking the mob's desperate passage. All of a sudden the mob seemed to stop, bunched up.

Bent wondered what had stopped the mob's progress. Then there came a muffled roar as if from a cannon, and several bodies at the back of the mob were suddenly thrown into the air.

A few minutes later Ceran St. Vrain with another two dozen or so mountain men, and Colonel Doniphan with a couple hundred soldiers, had worked through the mob and had the rebels penned in. As his troops arrested the rioters, Doniphan stopped in front of Bent. "You have my deepest sympathies on your loss, Mr. Bent."

Bent nodded.

⊰❰45❱⊱

By spring the fort had mostly gotten back to normal.
The mountain men who rode south from Bent's Fort,
and others who had ridden north from Santa Fe with
St. Vrain, had helped the army put down the rebellion
in short order. Then a jury, on which St. Vrain, Lucien
Maxwell, and ten other friends of the Bents sat, con-
demned the rebel leaders to death, a sentence that was
carried out forthwith.

William stayed in Taos for the trial. With St. Vrain
and other good friends in the jury, justice was not long
in being dispensed. The day after the hanging, Bent
and St. Vrain rode back to the fort.

St. Vrain left the next day, accompanied by some of
the men. William brooded around the fort before finally shaking off the gloom a little. He had lost friends
and family before, but none had struck him so hard.
He figured part of that was because he and Charles
had been so close. Still, he could not understand the
depths of his pain.

As he often did when he was melancholy, Bent
turned to Owl Woman. They had been together ten
years now. She had given him three children, and was
pregnant again. He loved her more now than ever.

Owl Woman let Bent talk. He jabbered on and on,
hating himself for babbling, yet feeling a sense of relief
at airing it.

Owl Woman did not know what to do for Bent when

he was like this. Listening helped, she knew, and she tried to tell him things she thought might soothe him. Making love generally seemed to help him too, and Owl Woman was pleased to see that it worked this time, though perhaps not as much as she might have wanted.

When Bent left Owl Feather, he was feeling a little better. Charles was dead and buried, and William knew there was life yet to live for himself. He asked George to bring Dick and Charlotte Green to his office.

When the two blacks and Bent's brother arrived, William had them all sit. He held up a piece of paper. "I know you can't read, Dick, neither you nor Charlotte, but this is paper of manumission."

Two blank, black faces stared back at him.

William smiled a little. "It means you two ain't slaves no more."

The Greens were stunned. Charlotte blubbered and cried; Dick was speechless, looking like he had just been kicked in the head by a mule. "But I's don' wants to be free, Mistah Bent," Charlotte sobbed, finally making some sense. "We's happy heah."

"Ain't nobody said you got to leave here. I'd be put out if you was to go someplace else. All this means is that you ain't slaves no more. You stay workin' for me, I'll have to pay you now."

"Why now, Mistah Bent?" Green asked.

"Couple reasons, Dick. For one, Charlie wanted you freed if he was to go under after me. It was in his will. If I was still livin', which I am, I was to get you. It's also in my will that if I die, you'd be freed. I decided to do it now 'cause of the service you did in fightin' to avenge Charlie."

Charlotte took the paper from Bent almost reverently. She folded it ever so carefully and put it into a leather pouch she wore under her dress, pressed between her formidable breasts. It was where she kept the few treasures she had.

As summer began to creep in, Bent packed up Owl

Woman and took her to Sun Dog's village. A month or so later Owl Woman gave birth to her and William's fourth child, a son that Bent named Charles.

His joy was short-lived. Minutes after learning he was a father again, Yellow Woman came out of Owl Woman's lodge and in a cracking voice told Bent that Owl Woman had died in giving birth.

Bent stood there, in the midst of the Cheyenne village, feeling his gut ache with his grief. He could not cry, but he felt this loss even more deeply than he had Charles's. He didn't know what to do with himself while waiting for Yellow Woman to prepare her sister's body.

Numbed, Bent finally realized he should build a travois. With Winter Hawk's silent, caring help, it got done. The job had offered, however little, a chance to push the grief aside for a few moments.

Finally Yellow Woman got him and took him inside the lodge. Owl Woman was dressed in her finest buckskin dress and wrapped in a thick buffalo robe. Hardening his heart, Bent lifted his wife's corpse, carried it outside, and set it gently on the travois.

With a leaden lump where his heart used to be, Bent rode out of the village, towing the horse with Owl Woman's body. Black Feather, Winter Hawk, and Yellow Woman rode with him.

Half a mile away, near the confluence of Horse Creek and the Arkansas River, Bent found a suitable spot. With Winter Hawk's help, he placed the body—and some small personal effects—into a hastily made scaffold in a tree. Bent then said a prayer for her. Still numb, he left Winter Hawk to escort Yellow Woman back to the village. Bent rode back to the fort, and after telling George and a few other close friends what had happened, he locked himself away for almost a week.

As he had with Charles's death, he soon concluded that he had to go on living. Reconciled to Owl

Woman's death, though certainly not forgetting it, he rode back to Sun Dog's village. Without any formality beyond giving Yellow Woman's brother, Smoke Wind, two horses, Bent married Yellow Woman. Such a thing was common among the Cheyennes, and Bent saw nothing wrong with it. He did not love Owl Woman any less for it, but he needed a wife, someone he could turn to. And he needed a mother for his four children, one less than a fortnight old. What better mother than Owl Woman's sister? he figured.

As summer began to wane—much sooner than usual, William thought—George took sick. William tended his younger brother, dosing him with every kind of medicine he could think of. That did not work, nor did the physician brought up from Taos at William's urgent appeal. He even called on Buffalo Horn, the medicine man in Sun Dog's village.

William reached the depths of despair in late October of that year, as George lost his fight with the galloping consumption that had afflicted him. He was buried next to Robert outside the fort.

William began to spend more and more time at the ranches down on the Purgatoire, not even wanting to be at the fort. Of a time, Kit Carson, or Seth Walsh, or Emiliano Flores, or Ramsay MacGregor, all old and treasured friends, would visit.

Eventually William got tired of hiding out from life, and he returned to the fort in time for the spring. He was still despondent, but trying to overcome it. As summer rolled in, business was good, and Bent was slowly coming back to being his old self. It helped when old friend Tom Fitzpatrick rode in. Fitzpatrick had been named Indian agent for the southern tribes, and he planned to use Bent's Fort as his headquarters. The thought pleased Bent, but Fitzpatrick spent precious little time at the fort. He most often was traveling among the tribes.

Later in the year, the army returned to Bent's Fort.

Bent could care less, even though St. Vrain had traveled from St. Louis with the soldiers for protection. Bent greeted the commander, Alexander Doniphan, without enthusiasm. He showed no more interest in St. Vrain.

Doniphan and St. Vrain managed somewhat to break down the wall that Bent had built around himself. The three drank some cheap whiskey, sitting in St. Vrain's apartment.

"I'm gonna need some supplies, Bill," Doniphan said, forcing some joviality. "I'd like for you to be my supplier."

Bent shrugged.

"There's good money in it, Bill."

"I agree, Bill," St. Vrain added. He had already promised Doniphan that Bent, St. Vrain & Company would do the supplying. Now all he had to do was to get Bent behind the deal.

"You remember what happened the last time we had a contract to supply the goddamn army, don't you, Ceran?" Bent said. "We got stuffed good that time. I swear, it'll happen again."

"Not with me it won't," Doniphan commented.

Bent shrugged again and drained the whiskey from his mug.

William managed to find some modicum of his old self after a few months. The winter had been harsh again, keeping things slow at the fort. But as spring appeared, Bent felt renewed. He was still rankled by St. Vrain's move the year before promising the army, that Bent, St. Vrain & Company would supply it. Finally he sent a courier to Taos asking St. Vrain to come to the fort to discuss business.

When a curious St. Vrain arrived, Bent did not even take the time for pleasantries. He simply brought a jug of whiskey, his pipe, and tobacco to St. Vrain's apartment.

"But I need to refresh myself," St. Vrain protested.

He was a little worried. Bent had been so morose of late that St. Vrain feared his partner would try something rash.

"You'll have time for such crap later."

They entered and sat. Bent got two tin mugs from the table and filled them. "I heard you tried sellin' this place to the goddamn army last year when you were in St. Louis," Bent said.

"*Oui,*" St. Vrain said warily.

"Without askin' me?"

"Zere was not time."

"Buffler shit. My brother wasn't even cold in the ground and you were tryin' to sell the fort out from under me. Presumptuous bastard."

St. Vrain was quite worried now.

Bent took a deep breath and eased it out. After a swallow of whiskey, he said, "I think we should go our own ways."

St. Vrain did not have to think about it. He had been feeling too confined by the rigorous bonds of the company. He wanted to take some leisure for himself before he was too old to enjoy it. He nodded.

"I figure to make this easy." When St. Vrain nodded, Bent said flatly, "You get the stores, I get the fort."

St. Vrain had no reason to question that. Bent had spent most of the past sixteen years in or near this fort. St. Vrain had spent the same time mostly in Taos and Santa Fe. "Agreed."

They drank on it, and while Bent smoked a pipe, St. Vrain wrote the words dissolving the company.

St. Vrain left two days later. After the Frenchman had gone, Bent strolled through the fort, trying to find some excitement in knowing that it was now his alone. He should be happy, but he was not. His three brothers had died, two violently. His first wife, with whom he had spent a decade, was dead. And, despite being married to Yellow Woman, having four children and no lack of good friends, he felt alone.

A few days later he took Yellow Woman out to her village. He felt a little easier after visiting there, and with renewed spirits he returned to the fort, leaving Yellow Woman behind for some more visiting.

He was a little surprised when not too many Cheyennes and Arapahos came to the fort, and he began to wonder about it. Some of his traders returned, saying that finding Indians was plumb hard. A few even hinted that something was wrong.

"I seen signs of cholera," one said.

Bent began to worry. If cholera was spreading across the southern plains, Yellow Woman, his children, and all the Cheyennes were in danger. He was just ready to leave for the villages to see for himself when Yellow Woman staggered into the fort.

Walsh saw her first and rushed over. She was exhausted, and collapsed in Walsh's arms. Bent was there immediately afterward.

"Yellow Woman?" he yelled, stroking her cheek. "Yellow Woman, what's wrong?" Fear clutched his heart.

"Gone. So many gone," she stammered in Cheyenne. "The 'big cramps' have taken so many."

"Jesus goddamn Christ," Bent muttered. "Seth, send some boys out. Now! Tell 'em to find Injuns. Any kind. See what they can find out."

A few weeks later Bent—who had nursed Yellow Woman back to health—called Walsh and MacGregor into the council room. "From what Yellow Woman said, and from the reports comin' in from the traders, I figure that half the Southern Cheyennes have died," Bent said.

"Jesus," an awed Walsh breathed.

"Seems the Arapahos were hit almost as hard," Bent said. "The others . . ." He shrugged. "I don't know. Blackfoot John said the Kiowas were hit pretty hard, but it's tough telling with the Comanches. Some of them bastards live so far from anything, they might've been spared."

"What're we gonna do, Cap'n?"

Bent shook his head. "Ain't much we can do."

The Comanches, Kiowas, and Pawnees soon learned of the ravaging the Cheyennes and Arapahos had taken from the cholera. They knew that with so many Cheyennes dead, Bent had lost a lot of his protection. Feeling that they had been cheated by the Bent traders, and in retaliation for the warriors that company workers had killed, enemy tribes began taunting Bent workers, both near the fort and out on the trails. Medicine Bear, whose brother Bull Nose had been killed by the Bents, even threatened to attack the fort.

Bent knew it was a hollow boast since the fort could withstand any attack. He angrily told the warrior to try it. Then he fired the small cannon from the bastions. Afraid and angry, the Comanches fled.

They did find some measure of retaliation in attacking not only Bent and St. Vrain caravans, but any others they came on.

All the troubles that escalated as the summer wore on were frazzling Bent's nerves. He was tired of it all. He brooded about it for weeks before finally making his decision. Once he had, he felt much better. He stepped outside into the blazing sun and hellish heat.

"Mornin', Cap'n," Walsh said as he headed for his shop.

"Mornin', Mr. Walsh," Bent said. "Stop a moment, please."

"Sure." Walsh had been worried for some time about his old friend. But Bent seemed to be more cheerful than he had been in a while. Lord knew, Bent had had enough to keep him in a dispirited state.

"There ain't no need for your forge today, Seth," Bent said.

"Cap'n?" Walsh asked, thinking Bent had gone loco.

"Round up the men and start loading everything in the fort onto wagons."

"You all right, Cap'n?"

"Yes, I am, Mr. Walsh. Better than I've been in a time." He looked around at the fort coming to life. "This place has outlived its usefulness. It's time for us to move on."

Walsh smiled. "Right, Cap'n." He rushed off, shouting orders.

It took two days, but finally everything was packed in freight wagons. Bent, sitting on the big roan that had been stolen from the Comanches so many years ago, led them out of the fort. Five miles away he pulled to a stop. "This's far enough for one day," he said. "Tomorrow we'll ride on down to Big Timbers." He spoke quietly a few moments with Yellow Woman. Then, "I'll be back directly, Seth."

"Goin' back?" Walsh asked, worried about Bent again.

Bent nodded.

Walsh saw something in Bent's eyes. "Mind if I ride with you?"

Bent was on the verge of saying no, but then stopped himself. Walsh had been with him almost twenty years, had stood by the Bents and Bent, St. Vrain & Company all along. He nodded.

They rode into the eerily deserted *placita*. Bent stopped in front of his office, dismounted and walked inside. Walsh followed him. "Grab a couple," Bent said, pointing to some kegs of powder.

"I'm beginning to like this," Walsh said as he picked up two kegs.

The two men placed the powder in several locations around the fort. Each had a fuse that was lit. The two men rode out of the fort and stood a hundred yards away. Moments later the powder blew and parts of the fort went flying. Other parts simply fell in with nothing left to support them.

"Let the ghosts of my family rest in peace here," Bent said quietly.

"Amen," Walsh added. The two turned and rode off.

Author's Note

War at Bent's Fort is a work of fiction. It is, however, based on fact, and is true to its time and place in history.

Many of the characters in *War at Bent's Fort* are real. The most obvious, of course, are the Bents and the St. Vrains. Also real are Kit Carson, Old Bill Williams, Dick and Charlotte Green, Gray Thunder, Owl Woman, and others. Since not much is known about some of the minor true characters—such as Jim Hobbs and John Baptiste—I have given them a partially fictional history. Other characters—chiefly Seth Walsh, Ramsay MacGregor, and Solomon—are fictional.

Much of *War at Bent's Fort* is true, in one way or another, though I have taken some liberties with the settings of some incidents. Other depicted events are entirely fictitious, though I hope that they are realistic enough to possibly have occurred in this time period and at this place.

William Bent did hide two Cheyennes from a Comanche war party, though not in so dramatic a way as the fictional event. It did, however, lead to the establishment of Bent's Fort. The fight with the Shoshonis did take place, but it was at a small log stockade near present-day Pueblo, Colorado. Bent won the real, much smaller battle. Smallpox did strike the men just as construction on Bent's Fort began. There was, however, little drama to it. William Bent did ransom Jim Hobbs and John Baptiste from Old Wolf, whom Bent had gotten drunk inside the fort. Hobbs soon after did become a scalp hunter with James Kirker. What happened to Baptiste is unclear.

The war with Mexico was, of course, real, and Kearny did ask Bent to put together a small group of scouts. They found nothing, and Kearny's army marched all the way into Santa Fe without firing a shot.

Perhaps the biggest departure from reality is in the scenes of the January 1847 revolt in Taos. Governor Charles Bent was killed by a group of rebels and was mutilated. His family escaped through a hole they had dug in an adobe wall of the house. A force rode down from Bent's Fort, but were a bit too late to help in the "reconquest" of Taos. Also, William had decided to stay at the fort, since in the heat of the times, he was fairly certain the fort would become a target of the insurrectionists. Soldiers, accompanied by a group of former mountain men led by Ceran St. Vrain, did come up from Santa Fe. The army took care of subduing the rebels.

The main resource used was *Bent's Fort,* by David Lavender.

Sitting on the Arkansas River about six hundred miles from the Missouri border, Bent's Fort was the first sign of civilization seen on the Mountain Branch of the Santa Fe Trail. The Mountain Branch of the trail was rarely used for the first decade and a half of the trail's existence, so Bent's Fort's first years were mainly as a supply point for mountain men and for the many Indians who roamed the area—this was the homeland of the Southern Cheyennes, and not far off were their allies, the Arapaho. Across the river roamed the fierce Comanches and Kiowas, who were allies and, until 1840, enemies of the Cheyennes.

In 1840 William Bent—whose Cheyenne wife bore him four children—helped arrange a peace conference between the enemy tribes. They forged a peace treaty, and from then on the tribes often were on the same side in battle, though fighting between them did not entirely stop. Still, the peace did give Bent, St.

Vrain & Company an opportunity to open trading posts in Comanche and Kiowa country.

By 1846 Bent, St. Vrain & Company controlled a vast trading empire, directed from Taos and Bent's Fort. The partners of the concern were well-known and well-respected.

In 1849 cholera decimated the Southern Cheyennes, killing about half of them. In addition, of the four Bent brothers, only William remained. George had died not long before the epidemic of (probably) consumption, and Robert had been killed by Comanches in 1841. Both had been buried just outside the fort's walls. Later their remains were taken to St. Louis and reinterred. Also, early in 1849, William Bent and Ceran St. Vrain dissolved their partnership.

Because of all of this, Bent decided to abandon the fort. He could have sold it to the army, probably for a substantial sum. But it is believed by some that he did not want anyone else using the place. So he and his workers packed up and left.

What happened next is subject to conjecture. The most frequently believed story is that after he had his workers make camp five miles away, Bent went back to the fort, placed kegs of gunpowder at several points around it, and then fired the place. Another theory holds that the fort was burned by nature.

Whatever happened, it appears that the fort was not too damaged, since in 1859 it was being used as a stage station by the Barlow & Sanderson Company. It apparently was still in operation as such ten years later when Bent came by for the last time.

After leaving Bent's Fort, Bent built a small log trading post some miles away from the original. He spent about four years trading there and in villages from the Canadian River to the Platte. In 1853 he chose a site overlooking Big Timbers, only a few miles from the Old Fort, and built a new stone trading post, called, of course, Bent's New Fort. He ran it for several years before selling it to the government. But before Bent got paid, the government decided to build a new military post nearby—at present-day Las Animas, Colorado. Bent had to fight for his money.

In the summer of 1865 his second wife, Yellow Woman, was killed and scalped by Pawnees under the command of General P. E. Connor.

An ailing Bent made his final journey on the familiar Santa Fe Trail in 1869. He got as far as the Purgatory ranch, down past Raton Pass. He died there of pneumonia on May 19, 1869, with his first child (daughter Mary) at his side.

Bent's Old Fort has been reconstructed and is administered by the National Park Service. It is about eight miles from LaJunta, Colorado, on Colorado 194.

HERE IS AN EXCERPT FROM *TREATY AT FORT LARAMIE* BY JOHN LEGG—BOOK TWO IN THE FORTS OF FREEDOM SERIES FROM ST. MARTIN'S PAPERBACKS:

Summer 1848

Henri LaPointe scrunched down among the thorny bushes as much as he could, hoping that none of the Crows rampaging through his small camp had seen him. One minute he, his wife, their two children, and one of his wife's brothers had been sitting at their fire, eating some freshly killed buffalo and talking idly. The next, ten Crows had swarmed in over them all.

LaPointe fired his flintlock rifle and then his single-shot flintlock pistol, before caching in the brush near the mouth of the Rawhide River. He turned and hunkered down just as his wife's twelve-year-old brother Wolfskin went down, his attempts to battle back futile under the power of the Crows.

As he sweated in the intense heat, LaPointe watched the massacre of his wife and children with dark, hate-filled eyes. His only touch of satisfaction was in noting that one of the Crows was down and it did not appear that he would get up again. It was a small thing under the weight of the horrors still going on.

LaPointe and Yellow Quiver had been together more than ten years now, and both were pleased with the other. LaPointe was not sure if what he and Yellow Quiver felt for each other was love, but he had to bite his rifle stock until his teeth felt as if they would break to prevent himself from crying out as he watched the horrifying scenes before him. Tears leaked from his eyes.

LaPointe remained in the midst of the thicket—unmoving though several sticks and thorns were jabbing into him—throughout the long, hot evening, his hate-filled eyes drinking in the Crows' savagery. He wanted more than anything in the world to charge out there and start laying waste the bloodthirsty Crow warriors. But that would be futile—and fatal—he knew. He might get one or two of them, but then he would go under. He didn't mind that all that much, but it would mean the Crow butchers would go unpunished. And that was something he did mind.

The same fate would result if he just sat here and tried to pick off several of the Crows. With only a single-shot rifle and a single-shot pistol, he would be able to do little damage before he, too, was dead and mutilated. So he stayed put.

After their butchery, the Crows enjoyed a small feast made with the foods of the recently deceased, eating while sitting within feet of the victims. Finally the Crows fell asleep, sated by blood, food and victory.

LaPointe gave it some time before he risked leaving. But finally he moved, going ever so slowly in an attempt to rustle the thorny, entwined brush as little as possible.

After what seemed like hours of movements with the rapidity of frosted molasses, LaPointe was out of the thicket. Breathing shallowly, so as not to disturb either the animals or the men, LaPointe moved toward his own horse. The beast was ungainly in looks and odd of coloration, but the gelding was a good match for the stocky Frenchman.

LaPointe patted the horse's neck softly and murmured a few words into the animal's ear. Man and beast had been together a long time, and the horse settled down as soon as it heard the familiar voice. La-Pointe bent and undid the simple, rawhide rope hobble. Then he leapt onto the horse's back. Leaning over the animal's neck, LaPointe whispered to the horse, *"Allons au-devant. Mais lentement, mon ami. Lentement.* Let's go. But slowly, my friend. Slowly."

The horse stepped off, slow and easy. LaPointe remained lying along the horse's neck. If any of the Indians awoke, LaPointe hoped they would simply think that one of the animals was moving around in search of forage.

Some of the other animals shuffled a little nervously at LaPointe's movement, but then settled. Finally, when he was more than a hundred yards from his camp, LaPointe let the horse have its head. He thundered across the prairie throughout the night and into the next day. . . .

TREATY AT FORT LARAMIE—
BOOK TWO IN THE FORTS OF
FREEDOM SERIES BY JOHN LEGG
—COMING IN JULY!

TERRY C. JOHNSTON
THE PLAINSMEN

THE BOLD WESTERN SERIES FROM
ST. MARTIN'S PAPERBACKS

COLLECT THE ENTIRE SERIES!